With tertiary qualifications in education and psychology, Jillian's work over the last 25+ years has focused on complex ERP and CRM Projects, Business Management, Business Intelligence, Change & Talent Management, Sales Effectiveness, Executive Mentoring, Organisational Restructuring and Management Consulting. Jillian has applied her skills to roles requiring business, government, manufacturing and/or supply chain knowledge, interpersonal skills, problem-solving skills and communication skills in work which demands a comprehensive and integrated approach to business, and which has as its catalyst best practice and often IT related business change and improvement. Jillian has also served on and advised several boards. Today Jillian's work focus is fostering resilience within others.

Dedicated to my inspiring daughters and the memory of my son, my greatest teacher.

Jillian Ginn

PLAN *2B* REAL

A TRUE STORY OF CONVERTING PAIN, FAILED PLANS AND TRAUMA INTO ACCEPTANCE AND LOVE

AUSTIN MACAULEY PUBLISHERS™

LONDON · CAMBRIDGE · NEW YORK · SHARJAH

A CIP catalogue record for this title is available from the British Library.

ISBN 9781528942317 (Paperback)
ISBN 9781528946001 (Hardback)
ISBN 9781528971096 (ePub e-book)

www.austinmacauley.com

First Published (2019)
Austin Macauley Publishers Ltd
25 Canada Square
Canary Wharf
London
E14 5LQ

I thank my mother and daughters for their support and the team at Austin Macauley for their professionalism, backing and dedication.

Table of Contents

"Our greatest weakness lies in giving up. The most certain way to succeed is always to try just one more time."

Thomas Edison

Foreword

Most of us face times when we feel like an outcast, different to others, traumatised or in my terminology, *one of them*. Many life experiences foster resilience. Perhaps we are presented with certain situations to teach us, please us, break us or grow us. Perhaps we are required to invent our own meaning. Do things happen for a reason or do we find reasons for things that happen in our lives? What matters is that we find reason. Throughout this memoir, I provide examples of how I have used the Plan2bReal framework for navigating difficulties I've faced as I have journeyed through life. Plan2bReal has guided me in how to aim to respond to unwelcome circumstances. I reveal many choices and actions which have contributed to consequences beguiling sporadic success, joy, sadness and failure. Experiences, thoughts and memories become foundational cornerstones, influencing how we navigate life and the degree to which we feel like we are one of *us* or one of *them*. We have control over little. We do have control over how we think, respond and react.

My son, Edison Hellmuth (2003–2015), was an inspiration. Edison came into this world without, I presume, existential angst. I doubt he understood the value of each minute of his time from the perspective of others. Regardless, he touched the lives of many. He was my greatest teacher, and throughout this book, I share many of the lessons my son graciously and most likely, inadvertently taught me. My son's disability endeared him with the ability to be pure, honest and deeply loving. I will be forever grateful for the gift bestowed upon me in being Edison's mother. I hope that for Ed, his passing was peaceful. I cannot know. My son's death was not peaceful for those who loved him. Media fervour followed the dramatic events surrounding Edison's death, providing a spotlight on the way Eddie chose to live. His manner of existing and interacting, whilst he was alive, taught many how to live in acceptance of what life serves us.

Not long after losing almost all our family belongings in a house fire, I came across A.B. Facey's book, *A Fortunate Life*. The book had landed on a donated bookshelf. A.B. Facey lived a most challenging life by anyone's standards. His humble, honest writing awakens the reader into an appreciation of the slightest graces. I perceived the gifted autobiography as a ghost-like article. My original copy was a much loved and dog-eared version. The replacement book was a gift from a brave person. Who would have the gall to donate such a book as this to me, at this time? I'd recently buried my son and didn't yet own anything which I had purchased personally, post the devastation of our home. My grief regarding loss at the time permeated my every breath. Why was A.B Facey on my bookshelf? Eventually, I discovered that it was my mother who gave me this book; a lady who also experienced a fortunate life.

My mother's life saw her as the carer of her husband, my father, since he was forced to retire from his successful civil engineering career at the age of 47 due to ill health. My father died in 2016, one week short of my parents' 50th wedding anniversary and 6 months after the loss of their grandson, Edison. I've watched my mother struggle with migraines resulting from her broken neck which caused her to endure two life-threatening surgeries, many months of traction and the eventual trapping of body plaster which ran from her hips to her scalp. My mother managed these hurdles whilst raising a tribe of four, all the while contributing to society to the point of receiving an Order of Australia Medal (O.A.M). Yes, indeed, we are fortunate to have challenges to grow us in Australia, this most peaceful and beautiful country.

I prefer to thrive rather than to survive. I remember attending my first autism conference and being confronted by numerous stories of survival. In attendance were hundreds of people gathered together to learn how to deal with autism in their lives. Many of those whom I met were not a particularly happy mob. Following the conference, I decided to plan to be real and plan to thrive rather than simply survive. I'm still working on that… Over time, I developed a method of turning my life's challenges into life's rewards; what I refer to as Plan2bReal. I have learned that I do not need to accomplish every aspect of Plan2bReal to achieve a better outcome that might result if I were to simply follow my natural inclinations. My method inspires me to play out my life, submitting to personal responsibility rather than habitual tendencies developed within my comfort zone, which in the past included hoping to be perceived as *one of us*. A key aspect of Plan2bReal in addressing challenges and trauma, is the **b**. To *be* is a verb. I am great at planning; I am still learning to **b**.

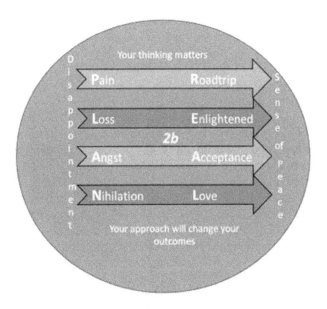

I share lessons I have learned via Plan2bReal throughout this book, illustrating where I have refined, failed in, and succeeded with my method.

Generally, when we experience trauma or stress, the stressor wasn't part of our **PLAN**. Thus, we experience emotional and/or physical **Pain.** We feel something is **Lost**; something that was rightfully ours. In **Angst,** we question the meaning of the traumatic event and our role in it. Some people are more prone to anxiety than others. Understandably, those people often find themselves falling prey to **A**nxiety. For others, a plan gone wrong may give rise to feeling **A**ngry. Ultimately, when our

PLAN fails, we can feel less worthy and as though our value has been reduced closer to Nothing – to **Nihilation**. My natural trajectory when my plan goes horribly wrong is the **Pain, Loss, Angst, Nihilation** trajectory. I never planned to be *one of them.*

The mechanism I have adopted to counter my habitual response to stressors, is to *be* **REAL**. By being **REAL**, I allow myself to adjust my plan and find myself living. **REAL** acknowledges that I am not in control and that life is more of a **Road-trip** than a string of planned experiences and outcomes. **REAL** encourages **Enlightenment**, **E**ducation and **E**ndurance. **REAL** forces me into **Acceptance**. **REAL** supports me to come from a place where acting with **Love** provides motivation, satisfaction and a source of strength. I'm not a great lover of myself but I am learning. I know that my life is richer as a result of many of the challenges I have faced. I also know that I feel of value when I am giving to others from a place of Love.

Once a planner, always a planner; I do not stop planning my life. I always pick backup with a modified plan. The modified plan rarely plays out in reality, as I imagine it should. Hence, I attempt to eliminate *should*, from my vocabulary.

This memoir illustrates how I have applied Plan*2b*Real in my life. I outline a little of my journey to encourage and foster hope and productive, authentic living in the face of adversity. This is a storybook, and by no means do I pretend to be an accomplished writer. I have compiled a collection of select stories as I recall them, many of which I would not have experienced without the privilege of loving my son, Edison. Some readers may find my approach of Plan*2b*Real, of no use whatsoever. I accept and respect this. I trust that readers will, at a minimum, finish reading this book a little richer, having shared some of my experiences of loss, enveloped in the memories of the joy of growing with Edison. This is not a self-help textbook, yet if readers have experienced times when they feel excluded from the in-group and find encouragement joining my *one of them group*, that is a good thing.

I am blessed and I have worked hard. I have applied my talents and challenged my weaknesses. No blessing would have me experience life as I do today, without effort and application. My son, Edison, fought for every life-skill he mastered. Little of what society expects of children, came to Edison naturally, nor easily. With fortitude, dedication, effort, and love, Edison taught me that by living a **REAL** life, one can experience a fortunate life. Plan*2b*Real encourages me to live with hope, even when I feel like an outsider, *one of them* wrapped in the camouflage of bourgeoning resilience.

Chapter 1
Train Spotting

Tuesday the 1st of September, 2009

8:00 am

"Hi, Mum. Can I talk to the kids, please?"

"Oh, Jillian, sorry we can't talk right now. We've lost Eddie. Dad's on the other mobile phone and we have to leave the landline free for the police, we'll call you back. The girls are fine. We are on top of this. Love you. Talk soon." Click.

I didn't think twice as to the brevity of the phone call. My mother's fast-paced and worried tone wasn't a catalyst for anxiety nor concern. My mum met most distressing circumstances throughout her life with grace, dignity and composure. Mum and Dad were well aware of how often I lost my son, Edison. That morning, I was a couple of hundred kilometres away from where Eddie's most recent drama was unfolding. I reluctantly heeded and accepted my complete lack of control over their situation. I reminded myself, *'I am one of them.'* My life was far from normal, as I perceived normal. I flopped back onto my fluffy Sofitel pillows, wondering, *'What's gone wrong this time in Eddie's world?'* I had been away from home for only 16 hours. I closed my eyes a while and imagined playing as *one of us*; as inconspicuous and drama free, during the next four days of a work conference.

Pondering the situation evolving back at home, I assumed Edison had again, gone walkabout. At the ripe age of 6 years and 2 days, Edison was notorious for wandering off. I imagined that the police and my parents were on top of Edison's latest adventure. As the minutes elapsed, it occurred to me that it was time to move into damage control (school management) mode. We didn't need the school stressing about another minor drama. I didn't consider Ed a school flight-risk, yet school staff hovered over him constantly. Harshly, I contemplated whether my son's autism somehow justified their disrespect for his independence and personal space. I called Mum again, and respecting her predicament, I didn't mess with details. I didn't ask questions, knowing that she would provide answers. Quickly, I learned during this second phone call, that Eddie remained missing. I asked Mum to take the girls to school, 'business as usual', no explanations before telephoning the school to let them know that Edison was delayed.

The first day of spring 2009 unfolded with a minor crisis when I was primed to experience four nights at the Gold Coast, participating in a Microsoft conference. It was no surprise that my first week of being a single mum was marked with drama. In high school, I was always the top performer in speech and drama. As a teen, I created drama. I gave my parents more than their fair share of rebellion. Potentially, Karma dictated that for several decades, drama came to me. My parents were determined that my work life would not be hindered by my marital break, announced just three days earlier. Mum and Dad were due to visit our home in Brisbane for the four conference nights to watch over the kids, whether my husband had been around or not. To support my parents in my absence, I had engaged a live-in Au Pair and a month earlier, I had also organised an on-call babysitter. This was my first time away from all three children overnight, and I was confident that the replacement 'Jillian team' of four adults could do the job. They did well, they did a great job.

As I gradually readied myself for the day, I wondered what might have occurred that morning to provoke Eddie's sojourn. I continued to foster hope that I could function under the radar, free of unwanted attention during the conference week. These events had become a little more balanced than they used to be. A decade ago, it was let's play 'spot the other female in IT'. Today, IT senior management is more balanced. Readying myself, that morning, I caught myself considering that it was refreshing to not think of how I should dress 'as a woman'. It's interesting how change that creeps up can be unnoticed or readily taken for granted. I recognised and accepted that I was *one of them*, as a woman in IT, a newly single mum and the mother of a special needs child. I was not living in my comfort zone. My life wasn't going according to my plan and it was strangely unfamiliar to me. Regardless of my circumstances, when I could pull it off, I enjoyed the façade of fitting in.

With a busy mind, I continued to prepare for day one of the conference. Respite is what support-workers would call this professional junket… I, on the other hand, saw the junket as a role that was simply required as part of my work. Earning a living was fundamental. I didn't expect anyone else to pay my family's expenses. That morning, half of my brain was dressing up – pretending to be innocuous. Meanwhile, the dominant voice in my mind was tracking my boy and his runaway morning adventure. The girls would have been at school by the time of my musings. During those early parenting years, the children would leave for school each morning at precisely 8:15 so that Edison could be met by a teacher's aide at 8:20. The bell would ring at 8:50. I wondered whether there would be enough time to find Edison and have him at school on time.

8:30 am

My mobile phone rang. My mother's relieved tone was palatable. *"The police have just left. They found him in the Queen Street mall. Everything is fine."* I learnt that during the morning, Mum had risen from bed at around 6:30 and had first checked on Eddie. He was not in his bedroom. Four-year-old, Freya-Grace was playing on her Nintendo DSi in the sunroom. Mum asked Freya-Grace where her brother was. Confidently, Freya-Grace replied, *"Oh, he left about 5 minutes ago,"* her head remained buried in her game. Mum woke Dad, she checked the bottom of the swimming pool, the trampoline, the cubby, the chook pen, cupboards... Mum then began frantically searching the streets. During her pursuit, she ran into our back neighbour who was a senior detective sergeant. She relayed the Edison disappearance story, and immediately he alerted his police colleagues.

Fortunately, Edison wore a stainless steel, identifier man-band. When Edison was 2 years old, I purchased this wristband, had it engraved with my phone number and his first name before permanently securing it on his wrist. As soon as Ed found his legs, he was easy to lose. The band had come in handy on many occasions. Living close to a train station with a son fixated on trains, I had spent many a weekend teaching Edison train safety. He knew which station to wait at to go to the city and which platform was the right one to wait at for a trip to the beach. He knew to stand behind the yellow line. I had written many a 'social story' with photos as support on how to ride trains safely. He also had learned that he was not allowed to catch a train without an adult. My passed-on genes interfered with my teaching, as Ed embarked on what he considered a higher priority to stupid rules – an adventure.

On this first day of spring, the police put out an alert and arrived at my Wooloowin home. Mum and Dad gave the police a couple of photos of Edison and confirmed that the train station, which had already been contacted, was his most likely destination (Ed had done a runner for the train station before). The local police station's wall was adorned with several copies of a one-page A4 laminated 'All About Edison' information sheet (which I had prepared earlier). 'All About Edison' was updated a few times a year and re-distributed to classrooms, police, the local train station, trusted shop-keepers and the like. I had eyes on most local corners. The laminated A4, 'All About Edison', listed Ed's likes and dislikes, how to approach him, where he might wander to, contact information and it displayed a recent photo of him.

Via eyewitness accounts and various re-runs of CCTV (closed circuit TV) footage, we pieced together Edison's morning adventure. As per Freya-Grace's report, Edison left home around 6:30 am. He was aware that I wasn't home. Although his speaking skills were seriously lacking, his receptive aural skills were pretty good. Before I left, he had understood that Mummy was going away for a few days and

Granny and Papa would be staying with the family while I was gone. A perfect opportunity to experience an adventure. *Carpe Diem!* Edison had left our home bare-foot, wearing his pyjamas. He exited via the front gate and walked (more likely ran) to the end of the street. To reach the train station, he had to cross a busy, wide road. He must have managed to navigate this difficult and dangerous crossing effectively. Edison was a well-behaved runaway. The CCTV footage showed that Edison was very careful to stay behind the yellow line, awaiting the next city-bound train. Edison boarded the train and disembarked at Central Station in Brisbane's CBD before heading for McDonald's.

Up until the age of 8, Edison wouldn't eat hash browns and so I had taught him that before 10:30 in the morning, McDonald's could serve him a big chip instead of fries (a big chip = a hash brown). Edison must have asked the McDonald's attendant for a big chip. CCTV footage showed Ed's frustration as he was told that McDonald's doesn't serve chips until after 10:30 in the morning. Edison can be seen looking annoyed as he watched other people walk away with big chips. With no luck at Central Station, Edison moved onto the next McDonald's, which he knew was in the Queen Street mall (the central Brisbane city shopping district). He needed to cross at least two busy inner-city intersections to make it to the Queen Street mall. Police were on the lookout everywhere, searching for Edison. One unit was placed in the centre of the mall in a marked car. Remarkably, not one member of the public reported a lone six-year-old pyjama-clad, barefoot child. Thankfully, successful Ed-hunting police spotted Edison entering his next McDonald's and encouraged him into their car. Fortunately, I had taught Ed to identify uniformed police and trust them. The police reported to my parents that Edison was terribly disappointed on missing out on a big chip. All the way home, he sat in the back of the car, tearing up, repeating, *"big chip please."* The police officers very nearly bought him a hash brown to repair his broken heart. Ed needed calming before his day of school began and so my parents coaxed a session on the trampoline to calm him. There were a few other tips and tricks Granny and Papa used to try to settle him. Sometimes, Edison was fed salami, allowed to rock back and forth a little and find his internal peace and compass. Soon, he was ready for school. During our various phone calls that crisp spring morning, I reminded my parents not to tell the school the events of the morning. I was pleased that he had never run away from school and I did not want to unnecessarily cause alarm and encourage a host of over-reactive protocols designed to prevent, in my mind, unlikely drama. Ed went off to school having recovered from missing out on McDonald's; I was informed he was sent off elated, as a result of his escapade. I finished preparing myself for the day, eager to appear inconspicuous. Whilst readying myself, the phone rang again. This time it was a leading TV news station asking for an interview about Eddie's happy ending that morning. Clearly, given my circumstances included being recently single and having never abandoned my children overnight before, I refused. I turned up at the conference trying to be discreet and fit in, hiding the fact that I had become *one of them.*

Chapter 2
Seeds of One of Them Acceptance

It takes something shock worthy for my alarm bells to ring. Life with Edison was an adrenaline rush. Trite conversations which would have typical caring mothers' adrenalin racing, required qualification before action was justified in my life with Ed. For example:

"Mum, Ed's on the roof again and he's going to jump into the pool!"
"Deep end or shallow end?"
"Deep."
"Ok, I'll be out in 5, stay with him."

The qualifier is 'the deep end' and my judgement call is 'acceptable risk'. I was working from home at the time. I had to earn a living and I couldn't stop work for every little drama...
...another

"If you are going to come to this church again, can you please not bring your son or make sure you attend Sunday school with him?"
"But I checked! We've been going to play group for months and they said it would be OK."
"Well, I'm afraid it's not. We can't manage him."

Seething acceptance... I was not a regular churchgoer, yet that day was Mother's Day and I had convinced my husband to take the family to church with me. *'Happy Mother's Day'*, I whimpered to myself silently. Places we are not welcome... add the local church to the list.
...another

"I think your son just bit my son's face."

"Oh crap, I'm so sorry! I'll grab him. Edisoonnn! This is soooo not OK. So, sorry."

"Ahhh, that's ok, what goes around comes around." The other mother was so accepting. In hindsight, I recognise that her tolerance shocked me out of out of high-alert mode. My demeanour became somewhat relaxed in the context of an improbable run-in with a well-intended playground companion. The moderator in this example is how I reacted to the magnanimity of the other mother's reaction. She was super accepting and so I calmed down. I had never met a mother like this before. We became best friends for the next decade.

Edison gave his 100% to everything. He lived a full life. He packed more into nearly 12 years of life than many people pack into 82 years. His love for life and his investment in life was unrelenting. He was satisfied by good things. Milo, marshmallows, a happy mother, a rainbow, swimming, popcorn, rain, people, sisters' hair to pull and music were all good things for Edison – he relished in these. When I dropped Edison off at his second primary school in the morning, he would stand by the lollipop lady, eagerly perched on his haunches, waiting for the whistle to blow. At the shrill sound of the whistle, Ed would launch into gear and run full speed across the pedestrian crossing. He'd run up the stairs to the school office entrance and catch his balance. He'd swagger from left to right, right to left, his legs positioned around 70 centimetres apart and he would wave and scream, *"I love you, Mummy!"* He knew the names of all the school office staff and upon entering the office, predictably he would greet them one by one and by name, before perching on the padded form, waiting eagerly for Mr McKinnon to collect him. Arriving at school was a good thing. School was something to run towards with glee. Ed opened and closed doors I would never have imagined existing.

Making friends was tough and keeping friends was tougher. Edison would generally upset my friends' kids unintentionally. The experience of raising a child with autism caused me to redefine friendships. I guess this can be viewed as a good thing. I certainly treasure those whom I consider solid friends. The lady in the park whose son sported Ed's bite on his cheek presented a rare reaction to Ed's indecipherable behaviour and it was quite unexpected that we bonded after the inexplicable incident. In the park, as we settled into me scolding and she comforting, we chatted about our respective days' events. I explained to this quirky, likeable Canadian stranger that I had just attended my 3-week obstetric check-up for which was a little overdue. *"I am busy,"* was my understated remark. As I chatted and observed my three children, Francesca, Edison and Freya-Grace, I shared with her the story of my afternoon…

During the obstetrician visit, I lay on my back on the doctor's table with eight-week-old Freya-Grace settled on my chest and Edison wreaking chaos, switching lights on and off whilst also moving items and furniture in the consultation room. Amongst this scene, Francesca stood at the obstetric business end, intently observing the doctor's actions. With my knees high and apart, and Freya-Grace beginning to cry, Edison climbed the step intended for the patient and levered my knee that was closest to him and rocked it back and forth somewhat thwarting the obstetrician's consultative process. As the doctor performed his inspection, Francesca asked why someone other than Daddy was touching me *'there'*? I assured the doctor, right knee being swayed back and forth with a crying infant on my chest, that Francesca has never seen her daddy look at me nor touch me like this. I felt indignant for a nanosecond in my attempt at composure before I realised the futility of hoping for some dignity amidst the chaos ensuing all around. Oh my, I had thought that childbirth taught humility… I guess lessons in humility never end. As I shared my afternoon's events to my new park companion, whose son displayed Edison's teeth-marks deep and now purple on his cheek, I was surprised at how quickly a mortifying experience became relatable. Somehow, maybe just through sheer honesty and by sharing my recent humiliating experience, we became friends then and there. She counselled me, advising that I might need some time off and she encouraged me to send Francesca to kindergarten… which I did. That afternoon in the park, a lady I had never met before caused me to feel somewhat *one of us*. I felt accepted. I felt a little typical.

It is hard to imagine the Jillian I would be today had Edison not entered my life. I have no doubt I would be shallower and less appreciative of the little things that add up to meaning and love in life. Maybe I'd be happier, having not lost a son. What a

capacity Edison had to transform the lives of those around him…
He embraced this gift and he shared it generously whether
invited or not. Edison was my first solid bridge from *us* to *them*.
I have learned by experience that *us* and *them* are relative, and
fluid terms. There are lots of things that happen in life to *them*.

For me, *them* is those people who experience the life they
did not plan. *Them* are people who are not like *us*. Growing up,
from my perspective, *us* meant being raised by two parents who
were happily married, enjoying several siblings, a stay-at-home
mum, a professional dad, a house in the suburbs, a pet and
weekly attendance at church. We didn't know criminals. We
didn't know really poor people nor really rich people. We didn't
know any special needs people – but we saw *them* going home
from school on yellow buses. In my teens, drama was Jillian
staying out too late and drinking too much, embarrassing her
father who always kindly came to pick her up late at night from
a party. I was ignorant of the danger I repeatedly exposed myself
to and my parents predictably provided a safe landing point when
I fell.

What happened to people on the news happened to *them*.
Fame, fortune, disability, trauma did not belong in my limited *us*
mentality. I was sheltered and rebellious. Not a safe nor wise
combination. Over many challenging and arduous years, I
longed to go back to being *one of us*. It turned out that being *one
of them* was my destiny. Being *one of them*, one of those people
whom I had considered during my youth as outliers, eventually
had me succumb to experiences far more colourful than my plan
for living had me anticipate. I craved finding my way back to the
comfort of my idea of normal – a concept which I now
understand as malleable. It turned out that my life road trip took
me further along a path of relative challenge, which I never felt
destined for. In some circumstances, my choices became
crippling as I fought acceptance of my reality. Eventually, the
chasm between my expectations and the certainty that I was
morphing into *one of them* was impossible to ignore. Today, I,
now, embrace my *themness* and I know all people have some
themness in their lives.

Chapter 3
Before Children

My first home was purchased by my dog (Max) and I, when I was in my 20s, three years before I married in 1999. When my husband-to-be entered the scene, there were few investments on his side and there was talk of much property he shared with his father. I later learnt this property was not made of bricks and mortar and toted no RPD (Real Property Description). He did possess a bed, sent straight to the spare room, and a Toyota Camry valued at the same price as his car loan. My car and furniture were paid for and I was managing my modest mortgage responsibly. I didn't marry for money. Home was important to me and by the time I met my future husband, I was well and truly nested. Fortunately, I married a man who also valued nesting, and we worked best together when creating, renovating or improving our homes. We were both somewhat handy and whilst he didn't thwart my creativity, I didn't get in the way of his muscle work.

I married a guy who wasn't mean to me during the early years, who wasn't uneducated, who wasn't an alcoholic, who wasn't addicted to pornography and who seemed to love me. In addition, he wasn't a chef, so he might be home for dinner. He didn't wear white gym shoes with jeans and with my encouragement, he wouldn't wear singlet shirts as outing apparel. He'd un-ticked my 'no' boxes. He also had some good genes to pass on to offspring. He had better hair than I did, he was tall and possessed long eyelashes... At the time, I overlooked a complete lack of relationship with his sisters and his mother. I overlooked a lot. Most of us excuse unappealing traits of our partner-to-be early in our relationships. I am sure my fiancé fell into the trap of overlooking some of my less desirable traits also. For over a decade prior to marriage, I had been abused, used and raped by men. I believed with certainty, that a tick-box list was foolish work when selecting a fiancé. For me back then, a no-box list was realistic. Clearly, when it came to men, I lacked self-confidence and I showed little common sense in this regard during my youth. In retrospect, I see that I was also a slow learner and I was impatient – not an excellent union. I passively accepted my fiancé selecting me, rather than actively choosing a life partner myself. His proposal, 12 weeks into our relationship, came as a huge surprise. I had only, just that morning, shared with a friend that I thought I could maybe grow to love this guy.

My fiancé was lovely in the months leading up to our wedding. He was attentive to domestic duties to the point of once making a pie for me that read in pastry on the top, 'I love you, Jill'. No one but my parents were allowed to call me Jill, and only then on the odd occasion. 'Jillian' was a little long to write on a pie and so the baker was forgiven. He followed the recipe of courtship to the letter 'T'. I did grow to love him and he could be quite sweet. He was also academically intelligent and he sported a wicked sense of humour. On the other hand, he lacked empathy and he was emotionally deficient. I considered him emotionally shallow, but a man who did his best whilst motivating himself by following role models of men who exhibited acceptable behaviour. I imagine that Tony Attwood, a global thought leader and expert in Asperger's would have a hey-day with my courtship story. I honestly can't say whether I was in love with my partner. At the age of 27, I didn't consider being in love as necessary criteria for a long-term, successful marriage. I have learnt since that it's likely a good start. By observing my own parents, I knew marriage was hard work and that true love wasn't the result of 'falling' it was the result of mutual respect, tolerance, patience, caring and putting the other first... This model was great, but it didn't work in my marriage. The emotional connectedness I had with myself was extremely lacking. I had stopped believing my generation could produce men like my wonderful father – so I settled for a nice guy I could love. I now know that my expectations regarding men of my generation were foolish and inaccurate. There are many, many wonderful men of my generation. Today, most of my closest friends are happily married men who are around about my age.

Back in 1998 though, my maternal clock was ticking, and this guy ticked all my no-boxes. I was sure we could make things work.

When I first met my husband, I started spending less time with my dog, Max. I couldn't manage my emotions regarding Max's loneliness (which of course I humanised). Max had been with me for several years. We shared a bed, a TV, shopping at the markets – all manner of things. Neighbours told me she (Max) would cry when I was absent from our home. To appease my guilt, Sam, a beautifully natured Fox Terrier, was purchased as a companion for Max. My husband and I had different views of a dog's place in the home, with his views being far more practical. Eventually, I moved closer to his way of thinking in managing pets with one win on my side; the pets were allowed inside and out. My husband went on to build many a doggy door for our various homes. Our furry kids were played with, walked and taken on trips to dog parks. Reminiscing, I bark back to the early years when I thought our beloved pets were training for parenthood. I needed more training than that. I liked that we both enjoyed having pets. Later I learned that being part of a family with pets is healthy for children. Pets can be challenging and rewarding. Max died at 15 years of age in my arms. As she struggled to hold onto life, I eventually told her it was time to go and she died in my arms. That was a deeply spiritual experience. There are ups and downs involved in growing a family. Marriage, work, parenting, health challenges, fluctuating friendships, pets – so many circumstances contribute to re-fabricate our norm and what we think we are made of.

In the early years of marriage, I learnt that my husband was the boy with the 'curl in the middle of his forehead'– when he was good he was very, very good but when he was bad, he was horrid. I guess we can all be like that at times… The mental maps we each had formed to guide us towards a loving marriage were quite dissimilar. Whilst I was navigating Sweden, he was navigating Japan – or something like that. He had an uncanny ability to eventually forgive me for sins I did not perceive I had committed. Often the forgiveness came after several days of 'the silent treatment'. Mostly, I could overlook his lack of ability to explain why I had been relegated to the doghouse. I eventually learned to accept that no apologies would be forthcoming and I'd just have to suck up his hurtful misdemeanours. In a vacuum of ignorance to his ways, I witnessed that he bounced back, eventually. Whilst he could bury our relationship difficulties under the carpet, I was prone to ruminating and then challenging. I, of course, had my own faults and was always pleased when those were overlooked. We did have some good times and we both shared interests in IT, business, politics and home making.

My husband chose a winter wedding in June and we were married in my parents' Toowoomba exquisite acreage garden. It was a fairly low-key wedding with around 80 guests. I am still amazed at how many of our guests we never saw again after the wedding. My betrothed had given me a few bridal instructions. I wasn't to wear a long dress nor a stick out at the bottom (inverted melting ice cream) dress. I wasn't allowed to wear a veil and he would choose his own suit. Alarm bells! Nope, I didn't hear them. He did a great job of organising an adrenaline filled New Zealand based honeymoon. I would never have chosen such a holiday, but I am pleased that the honeymoon planning was left to him. My dream honeymoon destination would have been somewhere like Vanuatu; a wee exotic, safe yet a new-to-me culture boasting warm weather to be enjoyed with cocktails on a remote beach. Instead, we headed for the beautiful, bitterly cold South Island of New Zealand on an action-packed travelling adventure.

My first (and last) experience skiing was during our honeymoon. I was brave to attempt skiing with the grown-ups. My new husband persistently persuaded me to face my fear and attempt skiing on an 'adult' slope. After my first couple of days enjoying lessons with the children of the resort, I capitulated to my husband's pleading on the condition that if I fell, he would help me and not leave me stranded. He promised. Of course, I fell. Inevitably, I also had great difficulty getting back up. I then endured the humiliation of having my lover sail by, literally laughing out loud whilst I struggled in the snow, with experienced skiers swearing at me as they passed me stuck on my behind, in the cold snow. Mulled wine and a good book became my companion for the rest of the skiing chapter of our honeymoon.

I have some happy memories of our honeymoon. One cold night, snow falling all around, after being lost and driving on black ice in the dark for hours, we arrived in Nelson on the north of the South Island. It was a State of Origin night. The State of Origin is a football competition which occurs every year between my home state of Queensland, and our neighbours in New South Wales. Although I have no interest in football, I am a loyal Queenslander and I enjoy the three matches of the annual competition. Upon arriving in Nelson, we drove around a dark, quiet town seeking a motel with a satellite dish and a vacancy sign. We found a cosy little motel settled in the heart of the town. While checking in, we greeted a large man who was watching over the quiet reception. We asked whether we could watch the State of Origin from one of his rooms. I couldn't pick his accent…

"Where yer from?" we were asked.

"Queensland."

"Well, that's lucky."

"Why?"

"Yer see, buddy, yer can't watch the Origin in yer room – yer need the atmosphere. The Queensland pub is just across the road. If yer were supporting the Blues, yer'd have to walk another 150 metres."

We decided to experience a little of the New Zealand culture in the pub across the road. I was pleasantly surprised to be greeted by a sea of maroon wearing football fans who made it clear to us that our welcome was 100% conditional on our support of the Queensland side. We enjoyed a raucous night, and of course the Blues (New South Wales) lost.

The scenery of the South Island of New Zealand was breathtaking and there was something magical about experiencing a honeymoon with snow falling all around. My husband carried all my luggage during the honeymoon. In this regard, he was a true gentleman. In other matters, I was genuinely shocked at his new post marital-vow priorities. I took a second seat to a host of activities, including football viewing and couch TV-surfing. I made my first snowman alone, watching my partner watch football, refusing to join me in my fun. I then decided to create my own fun, providing my snowman creation with breasts and dead foliage for hair – it became a snowwoman. I told myself that *'all marriages take some adjusting'*. In the main, we had a great two weeks.

Chapter 4
Creating Home

I am a believer in renting cheap and buying potential. My first purchased home was a little three bedroom, weatherboard cottage in Brisbane's inner north. If I stood on the top northeast corner of my block, I could glimpse the city. Hardly city views, but I was as happy as a pig in mud nesting in my own place whilst enjoying the freedoms that came with being single. They say that one attracts others when we are happy in ourselves. I had ripped up the carpet, polished the floorboards, replaced curtains with blinds and made a few other renovations. Mostly, I enjoyed gardening. I created a courtyard garden and populated the existing garden with natives having no real understanding of how large some of the plants I selected would grow. I would often garden late into the night and would celebrate Sunday nights with take-out pizza, sometimes after church. My silky terrier, Max kept me company. Those were good years.

Home routines naturally changed post marriage. We muddled along finding our own rhythm including who was responsible for what and which domains we each prevailed over. Much of this fell naturally and there was little conflict over how to dwell together. There was one incident, which in retrospect, I probably overreacted to. I had been working in Sydney for a few days whilst my newlywed partner worked on some surprises for me around the house. My sense of self was confronted when I arrived home from an exhausting business trip to find just about every piece of furniture and all our pictures and nick-knacks rearranged. Having taken enormous pleasure in nostalgic, harmonious and aesthetically pleasing home decoration, I was appalled to see my home transformed into a completely (to my mind) disordered mess. The lounge room had been changed around so that every chair or couch could readily worship the television. The cosy kitchen nook table had been moved to resemble a cheap, formal dining room at the end of our now cluttered lounge. From our bed, I could no longer look out upon treetops and hills. I was mortified. Within a few days, all was rectified and we had a home again. Living as a newlywed was fun so long as I could remain the in-home queen bee. We enjoyed many projects together and my husband took over the role of overseeing all outdoor renovation projects. He built driveway gates, laid pavers in the courtyard and even, against my will, tamed my old bathtub fishpond at the bottom of the garden – upon which I am sure, the fairies fled.

In the spring of 2000, we moved from the first home I had purchased to another, which my husband and I purchased together. This was our first shared ownership home and it was healthy to be equally empowered in nesting. We renovated our second home and made a little money. It was a suitable home for a couple, but it was not the sort of place I wanted to raise a family in. We eventually sold this second home and purchased 12 ½ acres of land to build our forever home in Brookfield. I had visions of healthy city kids living country style. We enjoyed the months in which our dream house was being built. We carted plants and water out to the property most afternoons, dreaming, planting and nurturing one another and our land. During this planning and hope chapter, I became pregnant with our first child and this made the dream-making even more exciting. Eventually, we built a home that kept growing in concept. The end result was a magnificent home. It was thirty-three metres long with more rooms than a modest family could justify. I loved that home. My soul was at peace. *'Take me out in a box!'*

'Garden, create, breastfeed, work, walk, comfort, cook, breathe in the views.' The place had its own rhythm. I felt fully alive.

My husband and I designed the Brookfield home together, mostly over hope and dream dinner conversations. I caringly sketched out on the back of napkins, drawings of homes which would accommodate how we planned to live. The design process began before I knew that I was pregnant. Life was simple. Two dogs, two jobs, two in a marriage and friends whom we had time to see. We were naïve and happy. We didn't always agree, which was not a problem. Disagreement was a minor challenge. My solution was that there must be a better way to think. During the home design process, I contemplated, *'I'm pretty smart, he's pretty smart... so our points of view must have some credibility, even if they oppose one another.'* I asked my husband to agree to not compromise. My concept was based on lateral thinking. Instead of doing things either my way or his; with a respect for one another, and some creative thinking, we could come up with a better third alternative. He liked this challenge and via this method, we mud-mapped our ideas, plans and the final design of our family home. Eventually, I drew the to-scale draft work which was the next step in turning our dreams into reality.

I wanted a smaller house to begin with; one we could add to as we moved forward (hopefully) financially in our careers. I lost that battle and we ended up with a property which made us look far wealthier than we actually were. Designing a home is one thing, project managing the build and creating tamed gardens from Australian bushland is quite another. Gardening is a creative endeavour which my parents taught me to love. Gardening gives back. It was exciting to design and plant an acreage garden from scratch. I soon learnt though, that gardening on acreage required adding another zero. If it was $300 to mulch a suburban garden, it was $3000 to mulch acreage. We became creative in addressing some of these financial challenges, but the demands of living the country dream did not abate. I had agreed to the larger scale home on the condition that my husband would become the primary income earner. We had similar qualifications, and I determined that our capacity to earn was relatively equal. He agreed, and a mini-mansion was born.

The top of the mountain we'd purchased was flattened and a builder was finally selected. Pregnant with Francesca, our eldest, I learnt that when desperate, tears were my best weapon to rouse activity from tradies. Our builder was a hopeless project manager and although I worked full-time up until the week before I became a first-time mother, our builder's deficits became my problem alone. To see my home completed before my first child arrived, I pleaded, hoping to inspire in our builder, a sense of decency... all fell on deaf ears. My growing womb and genuine tears ended up achieving the desired effect. This was not a ploy but I soon came to realise that it was the only thing that worked to rouse the tradies' motivation. Eventually, the home was finished just four months behind schedule. To save money, my husband worked at night, tiling and painting; completing most of the jobs a qualified tradesperson was not required to perform. With my womb swelling, I also contributed what I could.

In this, our third home, which I felt was my resting place, I lived on views and relished in motherhood. The realisation of my dream home habitually fed my soul. Disappointingly, however, in the main, living in our completed home was not as I had expected it to be. Outside of my love for family and people, I was not particularly happy. For starters, I had not anticipated the enormity of the impact that one tiny human can have. I was now responsible for a whole human being and everything else had to take a back seat. When I first learned that I was with-child, my mind-set and behaviour changed. I was living for two. It was somewhat easy when Francesca was in the womb and therefore quiet and contained. Ceasing smoking and drinking only occasionally, following my obstetrician's advice was easy. While pregnant, I didn't need to do much but work, love, live responsibly and carry an unborn baby around. I was loving this new mother stuff. My unborn child was very easy to manage. Early lessons in motherhood of a born child did not equate to my idealistic expectations.

As promised, my husband did step up to a higher earning job, which he lost. Amongst all this change, I began to feel isolated with the closest shop a 10-minute drive away and no family support nearby. In addition, I became for a while, the only income earner whilst breastfeeding. Being the money ticket in a man's world would bite me many times over, both in my personal life and professional career. I learnt that attempting to be one of the boys in the workplace wasn't for me. Being true to myself in a male dominated industry became my modus operandi. Learning how best to function in my work caused a few hiccups, yet somehow I managed to muddle along fairly successfully. This was professional training-wheel stuff, nevertheless I still found many aspects of my early work-life and motherhood rather daunting.

Acreage afforded privacy in squabbles. Once, I became so angry, lost and broken as a result of the abuse I was experiencing that I kicked a hole in the wall. There is no excuse for violence, even towards walls designed on the back of love napkins. Family life was becoming increasingly unstable and unsafe. My husband, no longer the centre of my attention, was often unkind, aggressive and unsupportive. The insults he would conjure suggested a different background to the stable, loving Christian environment in which I was raised. There must have been more to it than that though as both of his sisters are wonderful, kind people in stable long-term loving relationships.

There were positive aspects of this chapter of our life. My husband was very loyal to the whipper-snipper. He was strong and worked hard on taming our 12 ½ acres. Perhaps he had a better chance with taming Australian scrub than taming his wife. I wouldn't succumb to the abuse, and attempts to defend myself or alternatively avoid conflict, became a way of living. To this day, I am still quite useless at self-advocacy. The life we were living was unsustainable within the parameters which we had inaccurately predicted. My reality was certainly at odds with former dreams of a happy housewife.

Chapter 5
A Son! A Family Growing

30 August 2003, I gave birth to a downy, blonde-haired, fair skinned, perfectly healthy, blue-eyed son. Edison immediately sought comfort, cosying up and suckling from my breast. I was in awe that a boy came out of my body; it seemed crazy, odd, unnatural – a wonder. Brisbane's River Fire festival fire-works occurred on the day Ed was born and as I watched the impressive display from my Mater hospital window, I felt my city was welcoming my boy. Secretly, I had wanted a boy as my first child. Instead, I became the mother of a beautiful baby girl, Francesca Hope. Being a mother to a daughter came easily. As a female, I potentially, and perhaps mistakenly felt confident in raising girls. I may not have been competent, but I brazenly thought that I understood girls. Us females are infinitely complicated in our simplicity. With Edison's arrival, my parental confidence was a little shaken. I spent many a breast-feeding nighttime, pondering *'this boy is perfect – I don't know how to raise a boy – I hope I don't break him'.*

After Eddie entered our lives, I purchased Steve Biddulph's book, *'Raising Boys'*. Over the years, I have followed much of the advice Steve offers in his book. I found that the advice was not always exclusive to raising boys. Much of the content is useful, generic parenting guidance. I took very seriously the recommendation to place positive male role models in my children's lives. Notably, Brain Stenzel and Rob Cheesman have followed through, accepting my formal request and they remain active role models for my children to this day. There are other men I never formally asked to play this role who stepped up of their own accord. These men include Nat Cooper, my brother, Bruce, and of course Papa (my Dad). Each of the men who invested and continue to invest in the lives of my children have made our lives just that little bit richer. I pat myself on the back for fostering and encouraging these men to be involved in my children's lives. I could have left this important part of growing up to happenstance. There's so much we do as parents and there's so much we do not…

My beautiful boy was aptly named after Thomas Edison, the inventor of the light bulb (and many other world-changing firsts). His full name is Edison Maxwell Hellmuth. My father, Alan's middle name is Maxwell, his father's first name is Maxwell. I wanted to incorporate Frank Hellmuth, my son's paternal great grandfather into Edison's name. Edison's father did not support this notion. As Edison developed, light and how it played upon him, became a notable aspect of his life and drew my mind back to the inspiration for his Christian name. Although Edison developed late onset autism, I maintain that he was my perfect boy. There is nothing imperfect about embracing autism with joy and happiness. My children's father had a shock of wavy dark hair and almost black irises. I am blonde with green eyes. Edison was pale with electric blue eyes. Immediately, I drew comparisons between my boy and his massive, strong, blue-eyed and fair paternal grandfather, Bill, whom I loved. Edison's paternal grandfather was a kind-hearted man and he was enormous in stature. He always offered a large, genuine hug, which complimented the twinkle in his North Queensland sea blue eyes. At one point, much to my eternal disappointment, my husband had us evacuate, mid-holiday from his father's Cairns home in the middle of the night. I have not seen Bill since. As Edison grew, I was often reminded of Thomas Edison, Alan Maxwell Ginn and Bill, by my boy's demeanour, behaviour and physical appearance. It's interesting what one pays attention to.

Edison was a relatively easy baby. So long as he was moving, in my arms, or on my breast, he was content. He was happiest outdoors and was definitely not happy to be separated from me. His first 12 months of developmental milestones were on target or a little advanced. His paternal grandmother, Jan Guthrie (Ma), who always made an effort when it came to family relations, was at our Brookfield home for Edison's first birthday. For Jan and I, this was a special time, celebrating 12 months of life with this wonderfully typically developing Edison. Jan lived around 2000 kilometres away from where we lived. As such, time with Edison's Ma was infrequent and always special. Although my husband very rarely spoke with his mother, he was proud to show her his growing family and grand home.

One of Edison's favourite cheeky-monkey zones was the poolroom. He was able to climb right up onto the billiard table by 15 months of age without the need of anything to aid him to step up. The 360-degree views overlooking Brisbane city lights, the Moreton Bay islands and the beginning of the Great Dividing Range were visible from most rooms, but best from the poolroom. I came to love watching the weather perched atop our 12 ½ acres. The outlook fed my soul whilst I ran about ensuring the safety of my children and all matter of other day-to-day tasks. Edison and Francesca would play with the free-range chickens and our dogs on the front lawn. I have happy memories of this time, including the discovery of a doorframe jumper brace for Edison. Francesca, at around two years of age was dealing with early toilet training and objections to daytime sleeps. The doorframe jumper proved not only an energy dispenser for Edison but also a bonding vehicle for my children. Francesca would sing and read to Ed as he bounced, providing me precious minutes to go to the toilet or perhaps even shower. Pure luxury. Over the next decade, the chuckles of Francesca, Edison and eventually Freya-Grace planted many special memories. Today, they are immortalised together in a three in-a-row picture nest on my living room wall. I digress… During the Brookfield era there were snippets which looked like the dream life – almost like *one of us*.

Sadly, my Brookfield days came to represent my first great broken dream. It was where I began to realise that many of my hopes were an unattainable fantasy. My dream of being happily married with typically developing kids whilst enjoying being emotionally and financially supported as a mother, worker and wife were slowly shattered. My vision had merely become empty childish imaginings. Regardless, I really liked my plan and I knew I had to somehow incorporate into my planning, the road-trip that life was throwing at me. There was always another way, a third option. I determined that I had no practical, responsible choice other than to become real about what life was presenting to me. I acknowledged that I needed to foster acceptance and I needed to adopt new ideals. Maybe I could learn something through this undesired living picture…

There were some good times as a typically developing family and there were also many aspects of parenting that magazines like Woman's Day and Huggies TV commercials hadn't prepared me for. Somehow, my own mother had impressed on me the joys of parenthood. I did not remember her struggles. I now know she suffered, yet even today, she does not complain of her time as a young mother raising four children born within a five-year age range. Without complaint, my mother parented and actively helped in her local community, caring for a chronically ill and loving husband. She managed this whilst nursing migraines, which was one of the consequences of being born with a broken neck… Mum's list goes on. My mother certainly faced more than her fair share of burdens, yet she played out the early mothering chapter of her life so graciously that I honestly expected my own experience of motherhood would be bliss.

I can't say I took family life easily – in my stride… Parenting can be over-rated. Parenting can offer extreme rewards and it can also expose us to depths of suffering not previously imagined. I am deeply grateful for the lessons that my children have taught me. I love my children and I have done my best, as my offspring continue to teach me on a fly-by-the-seat-of-your-pants basis. When the children were very dependent and young, I found that they were more easily managed when I organised daily outings. Our early childhood out-of-home adventures were often lonely for me, yet they were essential for my sanity. McDonald's was an easy target to fill an hour or two and give Francesca and Edison an energy outlet. The play equipment was well designed, and the food was affordable. Twenty-four hours before breaking to my husband, the news of our further growing family, I had peed on a stick in a McDonald's toilet with two kids, aged 10 months and 19 months in tow. I had recently changed their nappies and their tummies were full. Time to check the pregnancy test… Two red stripes appeared. Two red stripes! Another whole human being was growing inside me. I was anxious about imparting this exciting news to my husband. My third pregnancy was unexpected as I was on the mini-pill, still breastfeeding and only having sexual relations to support the silk thread holding my marriage together.

My husband also found it difficult to adjust to family life with children. When I told him that we were expecting child number three, his dramatic reaction confirmed his angst. The day following my two red stripes encounter, I set our two children for breakfast and ensured they were busy and hopefully, as such would cause their father little or no stress. I made my hubby a cup of tea and placed a note under the cup and on top of the saucer which read, *'I love you and I'm having your love child'.* I believe saucers are like workforce unions which often create their own purpose. No one spills tea without a saucer – with a saucer present, a spill is guaranteed. That day, I found a real purpose for a saucer.

The marriage was already stressed. I waited and waited upon serving the cup of tea wondering, *'who wants to drink cold tea'*? Mums are forced to drink tea cold whilst others who have less distractions can experience the luxury of a steamy cuppa. A sip… My ears were penetrated by a groan one would only heave on acreage property. *"Noooooooooo!"* Baby number three, Freya-Grace, wasn't part of the plan but what a beautiful child she turned out to be. She is intelligent, resilient, responsible, funny, musically talented and a high achiever in every field she pursues. More importantly, she is kind, self-motivated and content. The road-trip of three kids born so close together was far more rewarding than my original plan. Exhale…

Early years of parenting were exhausting; they are for us all. I remained the main income earner and at times, the only income earner. I didn't attempt to express milk as a day-to-day ritual. All three children refused a bottle in any case. I know where they got this stubbornness from. I can be determined. Wisely, before becoming a mother, I had forged a career which allowed for time and location flexibility in my work. I knew that being a mother would be my most important role and so I had spent the first 10 years after graduating from my second degree, ensuring that I had an income which would allow for work-life balance. Plenty of people who plan to be parents don't have the opportunity to fulfil parenting related dreams. There are also many people who hope to be parents where their life unfolds to prove that their plan to parent is impossible. I have a heart for those people who wished to be parents but never had the opportunity. Some of these people may judge those who declare statements such as 'parenting is over-rated' as selfish and narrow-minded. I can only share my own experience and thankfully, becoming a parent was an aspect of my plan that worked out. Financially, my parenting plans were on track; I could feed, educate and house my children well. I wasn't a 'career mum', yet I didn't expect other people to pay for my children. I soon worked out that such a thing as work-life balance did not exist with three children born three years and one week apart. I did my best to support a husband who was overly challenged by emotional turmoil, while at the same time, likely not proud of the fact that he was not a reliable provider. I had work and I had life, but there was no balance.

Chapter 6
Learning to Juggle

Today, I can't recognise the Jillian of the early 2000s who sat in boardrooms breast-feeding. Most often, I was the only woman in the room. Who was that gutsy, naïve woman – surely not me? I do recognise the lady in a partitioned workspace (of sorts) in Gladstone expressing milk (the only time I remember successfully doing so). I needed to express to ensure that during the business meeting, I would return to convene, I would sport a dry blouse. Gladstone is a short plane flight from Brisbane, which amounted to a full ten hours abstinence from breast-feeding. A breast-feeding mother produces milk regardless of whether her infant is in another city. Feeling my breasts swelling and leaking, I called for a break, and unfortunately the room I was ushered to for my fake phone call 'break' was on the other side of a divider (not a wall). The separation from my male colleagues might as well have been fabricated from cardboard. I acted out my imaginary call all the while pumping my breasts to alleviate the pressure and pain building with unspent milk. I hoped my fake conversation would drown out the sound of the manual pump. Who knows whether it worked? Francesca, at the time was old enough to sustain ten hours without me, yet it was difficult for me to sustain such a long period of time far from my children. Most of the men in the meeting were likely fathers and after hearing the 'swish swash' of the breast pump, went home that evening with an amusing story to share with their wife. Early years of parenting as a working and breast-feeding mother were not only trying, in many instances, they were embarrassing.

A significant and positive aspect during the early years of being a mother was the support of my 'Mums' Group'. Today, it would likely be more politically correct to call the group a 'Parents' Group'. Our group consisted of only mums and their children. We were mums from all different walks of life. I had met one of the ladies, Roz, at a Queensland Health nursing clinic and together we began a list, left on the nurse's counter for others wishing to meet inexperienced parents and share their contact details. Roz was a great organiser, and soon we had a group of around 12 women who met at a different mother's home each week. Some mums were tertiary educated, some were content housewives and homemakers, some had mastered a trade, some were incredibly wealthy, most were middle class. We were different colours, sizes, and the array of personalities was extremely diverse. With all these differences, we came together through our one commonality – motherhood. We cared for one another sincerely, and at times with gusto. The group was authentic and thankfully honesty abounded. No one pretended their experience of early motherhood was easy. We shared joys, milestones, setbacks – the good, bad and indifferent. We encouraged one another with stories regarding our family relationships, and most importantly, we provided one another morale and a determination to do our best. Today, I am only in seldom contact with two of these wonderful women, one of them being Roz. At the time, the weekly meet-ups were a lifeline. I encourage all new parents to find a peer group of some kind and to be generous of spirit in providing support to others. Relationships developed in such an environment will surely be a leveller and will contribute to sanity.

All three of my children suffered from colic. Echoes of the resultant incessant crying still haunts me today. Like many girls, as a child, I had dreamt of being a mother. As a youngster, I developed a completely delusional view of parenthood. My goal to be the perfect housewife and mother proved unattainable. I never expected that by obtaining a tertiary education that my existence would be one of sleeplessness, unrelenting motherhood, a strained marriage and being the main income earner. Early on in my primary school years, my mother was called in by one of my teachers to discuss that my childish dream of becoming a housewife and a mother (*one of us*) was not appropriate for a child of my talents. What did that teacher know? The dream to be *one of us* was difficult to give up. During early adulthood, my ambitions were slowly replaced by reality, fabricated one day at a time as I gradually accepted and then embraced my life. I have lived a rewarding and full life thus far, and wouldn't change my circumstances should someone give me a magic wand. Who came up with that stupid question anyway? *'Would you have ABC be XYZ if you had a magic wand?'* That's the beginning of a road to self-indulgence and fantasy, which can sadly lead to depression. Hope is one thing – self-pity is altogether different.

I am deeply grateful for the rights men and women have fought for and won, for female equality. Equality, to my mind, meant equal opportunity. I hadn't considered that certain choices I made such as motherhood would erase for me, many opportunities afforded to men. My body supplied life and food for my babies whilst my mind and energy supplied the money required for housing, education and clothing. The stresses of holding a marriage together by silk threads over five years of being pregnant or breastfeeding and working, directly led to limited work opportunities. For example, when my third pregnancy was not publicly known, I was offered a promotion to a national managerial role. Upon learning that I was to have a third child, my employer withdrew their offer and I eventually was forced to succumb to a less skilful, bullying and chauvinistic, male boss. He didn't last long, yet reporting to him was extremely difficult to endure; to the point that I quit my job... Another story... Having earned a couple of degrees, forging a successful early career and entering marriage and motherhood, I found myself in a difficult predicament in which I was traversing an unfamiliar road-map with no role model.

Before Freya-Grace arrived, when Edison was around 10 months old and crawling, he became very ill with high temperatures and frothy green poo. I whisked Eddie off to the doctor and asked that she send a sample of his faeces to pathology. I was extremely worried. Edison was limp, he wasn't his usual cheeky-monkey self. He was seriously unwell. The doctor refused to touch nor even look at the nappy and chastised me for my request. She stated she would not deal with nor look at poo (ever) and gave me a prescription for antibiotics. Feeling stupid, I filled the prescription and took Ed home, refusing to leave his side. It was a tough night. I felt what was going on with Ed wasn't bacterial so I had little faith in the antibiotic prescribed.

The following morning, the sun broke, providing the promise of a fresh, hopeful day. My vision, however, was of a dying boy. Soon, I was at the emergency department of a hospital. Not long after, Edison was transferred to the ICU (Intensive Care Unit) whilst I stroked my growing baby bump and waited with my 20-month-old daughter, Francesca, for news. I focused on occupying Francesca and said a few prayers. I could only deal with my present moment and had to accept Edison's fate was not in my hands. Again, I asked myself, why acceptance was so difficult for me to practice? Edison had acquired, I learnt, Streptococcus poisoning. He only fed on breast milk but as a crawler, perhaps he'd picked up bacteria from our pond or, I considered perhaps, from gecko poo? Berating myself, I asked, *'Could I have done anything to avoid this poisoning?'* Perhaps my laisse fair doctor had bought us time with her prescription. Streptococcus poisoning is rare and scary enough that we were put on a Queensland Health watch list. Ed was eventually discharged from hospital and I was telephoned regularly by Queensland Health to track his progress. Edison was monitored, and after a difficult and stressful few weeks, he was well on his way to recovery. Life continued as usual – with morning sickness, work and motherhood.

When I was 21 and ready to leave my parents' home, my father bought me a book entitled *'The Road Less Travelled: A new Psychology of Love'* by Dr M Scott Peck. Of course, I no longer have this book. It burnt along with everything else in 2015. If my memory serves me correctly, Dad's inscription on the inside cover read something like this: *'My dearest Jillian, relationships are important – they need to be tended to, like a beautiful garden. If left untended, they become a mess. This book teaches some of the how's and why's for tendering love and relationships. Love, Dad.'* The introduction of the book reads: *'Life is difficult. This is a great truth, one of the greatest truths. It is a great truth because once we truly see this truth, we transcend it. Once we truly know that life is difficult – once we truly understand and accept it – then life is no longer difficult. Because once it is accepted, the fact that life is difficult no longer matters.'* A decade or so after first reading this, I struggled with the acceptance concept. I accepted that my life was difficult (in relative terms), but that didn't stop me constantly trying to fix it.

As with many failing marriages, whist I set about fixing my husband, he similarly set about trying to fix me. How lacking, in insight, we were. I had a plan for change because my reality certainly wasn't as I had imagined it would be. As part of my fix-it plan, I began to consider selling our home to reduce financial pressure. I conceded that something needed to give, with a third child entering our lives. The notion of living without my soul-feeding views was devastating, yet something really had to change.

Chapter 7
Chasing a Diagnosis

My second great broken dream began to reveal itself within a week of Edison having his triple antigen injection, when he was approximately 14 months of age. During a short period of time following this immunisation, my perfect boy began to exhibit violent behaviour. Ed's behaviour became so challenging that I could not take him the 30 metre or so walk to his change table to place a clean nappy on him, without him bighting, kicking and fighting me all the way. He lost his words. He would turn in circles and cry. He was lost. He became animal-like. His father witnessed this and I assume that he concluded his son was becoming an increasingly naughty boy. Likely, he was distressed by Ed's diminishing abilities. Perhaps he was processing stress about Ed's new behaviour internally. Externally, whatever he was experiencing emotionally presented as aggression. I begged parents, friends and doctors to acknowledge the changes in Ed. I was assured by those I beseeched that I was accustomed to girls and Eddie was just a boy – and boys take longer to mature. As a two-time mother, I was silenced but not comforted. My boy was changing.

Now, in Australia, it is not politically correct to couple Edison's declining abilities with the timing of the triple antigen vaccination. Politically correct or not, Edison was a typically developing boy who became a boy typically developing autism post immunisation. My psychology degree had taught me about validity, ethics and other requirements of psychological and medical studies. I have not yet worked out how, whilst competing with pharmaceutical companies and remaining ethical, one could scientifically link autism to immunisation. The link can neither be proven nor disproven whilst ensuring a control group of children are not potentially exposed to disease or chemicals which could have them develop autism or alternatively expose a non-vaccinated group to the diseases the triple antigen protects them from. There are experts in this field. I am no expert. However, in retrospect, I wish I knew that those three (measles, mumps and rubella) immunisations do not need to be administered simultaneously. Parents in Australia can choose to stagger the three relevant immunisations. Research also suggested at the time that if a predisposition to ASD existed, it was possible that ASD could be triggered by an external event (such as Streptococcus poisoning). That was vague information at best... I acknowledged Ed likely had genes which contributed to ASD. There were also a number of environmental factors which may have contributed. Clouded thinking...

One summer afternoon, I decided to give Francesca and Edison a play in a park on the way home from an outing. The park they played in was beside the Brookfield cemetery where my son is now buried. The furthest thing from my mind that afternoon was divorce or the death of a child. I was nine months pregnant at the time. As my eldest daughter's middle name Hope suggested, as a young mum, I forced myself habitually to focus on being optimistic. Some parents enjoy times shared in parks with their young children. At times, I joined the ranks of such parents. Much of the time though, experiences in parks with my children were taxing. For example, after pushing swings for what seemed like forever, I was delighted when, at around the age of nine years, Ed mastered the use of a park swing. This skill took thousands of hours to teach and it was more exciting to graduate from non-swing-pushing park parent than it was to graduate from university.

The children were playing on the park fort when Francesca decided to move along and read gravestones beside the park (she was an early reader). My attention disarmed for seconds was not focused on Edison who could no longer be seen playing on the fort. I searched after Edison and saw him running towards Brookfield Road in peak hour traffic. I screamed for him to stop and come back to me. He ignored me, throwing back his head in laughter. Running to catch him, I must have looked a sight. Waddling and screaming, I eventually caught up with him meagre metres from oncoming traffic. With a now empty bladder and urine soaking my legs, I hit my boy. I *really* hit him. I remember the motion and my fright of seeing him running into traffic. I remember being highly embarrassed about wetting myself. Seriously, one's bladder is the size of a pea at nine months pregnant. I hit him four times. I was furious. I hadn't hit my children before (nor since). I was appalled at my behaviour. Why didn't he listen to me and stop running?

Was Edison a bad, rebellious kid? Was I a terrible mother? Did Edison need his hearing tested? Why didn't he listen to me? Since his post immunisation decline, there were times where he didn't register the existence of others around him. He would lie in his cot and watch light dancing on the mobiles above him. He had developed selective listening. I have learnt this can be a life skill for many, not though, a helpful skill for an infant. Driving home, I decided to again visit a doctor, another new one who would hopefully help me to work out what was up with my boy. I told my husband about this pants-wetting waddle run an hour later when he returned home. I was humiliated and at the same time ashamed that I had hit my son. Being overly dramatic and not at all serious, I said to my husband, "*If Child Services had seen me, they would have taken the kids off us.*" With a wicked sense of humour, he immediately replied, "*Ask them to wait a week until the next bub arrives and ask them for two weeks parental leave so we can go to Fiji!*" Everyone has their qualities and those aspects of ourselves we need to work on. My children's father needed no tuition in humour. This was a memorable moment of shared adult humour.

Unwelcome change beckoned... I was getting nowhere in my fervent search to acquire a diagnosis that would explain Edison's behaviour as he continued to lose abilities and words which he had previously been proficient in. I couldn't fathom concurrently parenting three small children, working full-time and unravelling the Edison mystery. I also felt that if my husband became the sole income earner, he would feel more valued and that might go towards fixing our marriage. Something needed to give. I figured lowering our mortgage was achievable. I didn't like the notion of losing our dream home. Dreams can be motivational but at that point in my life, my best next move was to take a reality check. I disliked the possibility of losing our nuclear family unit more than losing a fantastical dream. It was a heart-breaking decision to sell the home we designed and then built on our forever land. I was apprehensive when I first introduced the idea of moving on to my husband. With a third child expected in March of 2005, I had some serious challenges to address. Another adjustment to my planning was required.

In my view, we needed to sell our forever home so that we both didn't have to service a large mortgage, one another and three children. Surely with a smaller mortgage, close neighbours and less land to manage, I could grasp towards my happy family ideal? I also thought that by living in suburbia, there would be a social motivation for my husband to be quieter when he was stressed and perhaps, also kinder. I hadn't grown up with raised voices in my childhood home and I did not wish to become accustomed to this. We had planned our first forever home with our combined incomes informing our budget. The first time my husband lost his job, he was unemployed for many months before finding a contract role as a teacher in a prison (which he was then also subsequently dismissed from). Individually, our earning capacity was decent. Jointly, we should have been able to accommodate our mortgage and family. Our motivation, however, was not congruent. I wished to enjoy the work-life balance I had strived for and toiled to achieve, for over a decade. He seemed comfortable for my earnings to keep us reliably afloat. Motivated to assist my husband in becoming re-employed, I created job applications for him with colour and creativity. He eventually found stable employment with a Catholic high school, which ironically, never checked his forcefully cancelled Teacher Registration status. It was interesting that the State Government authority deemed him unsuitable to teach, while the Catholic system did not do their homework.

My husband did not speak to me (literally) for 3 days when I proposed selling the home in order to put marriage and family as our highest priority. Maybe he eventually understood the pressure I was under servicing our family's expenses whilst also being the primary care giver for our children. Maybe he understood that his wife was strong willed and strategically minded and capitulation without an alternative option, was his best option. My plan involved, in addition to all the troubles I wished to escape, to be a housewife. To have my man feel needed seemed important to me. I pondered, *'Maybe if our home loan was small enough, I wouldn't have to work… I could serve him better? He'd feel important and that would feed his ego. That might help to fix this marriage…'* All the while, I was becoming a bull at a gate with my concerns regarding Edison's diminishing abilities which was clearly a major stress factor in all my thinking.

After many highly charged exchanges, we finally agreed to sell. We didn't plan for the auction of our home to occur on the same day that Freya-Grace arrived into the world. She's a determined child, and the timing was her choice. I was relieved when labour began at around 3:00 am. I set about finalising the presentation of the house for our auction. At sunrise, I called my parents and they dashed down to Brisbane to drive me to the hospital. With labour coinciding with the auction, my husband would not be able to attend the birth. He would be needed to sign contracts if the house sold under the hammer or in negotiations, shortly after. The marriage was in such a state of disarray that giving birth alone, from my perspective, was preferable to having him present. Things didn't go according to plan at that time either. Somehow, my parents and husband managed to orchestrate his attendance to the hospital, in time for the last few hours of labour. This was his child too. I mentally surrendered.

Freya-Grace was, and is, a beautiful child. As an infant, she had shocks of curly hair and like her two older siblings, she nourished her body from my breast. All three attached and suckled within a minute of being born. She was a love child – 'but for the grace of God'. My mother is of Swedish heritage and the name Freya was, as I understood it, the Norse god of love. Having three children so close together was the grace that had me realise the need to sell our Brookfield home and live within our means. Her name simply made sense. Freya-Grace lives up to her meaningful name daily. She was born on my maternal Nana's birthday. My Nana, Sylvia Walker was a devout, loving Christian woman. She would often cite, *"Jesus will return before the price of bread rises to a dollar."* I'm guessing Jesus' currency is not AUD. Should I have had any sense at the time of naming Freya-Grace, I would surely have included Sylvia into her name. I am somewhat consoled that I included in her name the Swedish heritage of her great-nana.

The house did not sell under the hammer. This was my third lesson in selling real estate. Auctions sell real estate agents' self-promotion on vendor's money; they don't necessarily sell houses. Some homes are perfect for selling via auction. Ours was not. The house did not sell for several months. These were trying months and I was not earning an income. Francesca had given up daytime naps and Edison had moved to a lunchtime only nap during the day, and of course Freya-Grace slept sporadically like a newborn. I don't remember sleeping but surely, I must have. My mothering duties were gruelling. Add to that having to live in a massive 'display home' with three young children, I was stir crazy to say the least. Toddler toys littered the 33-metre length of our home and proved a buyer hazard. I did my best to maintain a beautifully presented home. I was grateful on the days that my husband returned from work, offering to walk the two eldest in our double pram, to give me a break.

When Freya-Grace was around four months old, we finally sold our Brookfield forever home. The next major stress was packing, moving and finding another home with three young children in tow. Thank God for the internet. This was tough but tougher was around the corner when another major health crisis arose with Edison. One trying day, I found Ed coughing incessantly with croup. From my experience as a mother and an early childhood teacher, I knew that the dog-bark like cough of croup sounds worse than it indicates. I held on. Edison's health deteriorated quickly though and his breathing became stressed. Eventually, I could see Edison's struggle to breathe was serious. I asked three year old Francesca to keep a Ventolin vaporising nebuliser mask on her little brother's face while I called an ambulance and readied Freya-Grace to leave our for sale home. Fearing wasting taxpayers' money, but also living on 12 ½ acres, a long way from any hospital, I rang 000. The ambulance arrived and we were taken to the Royal Children's Hospital.

We remained in wait for five hours, being monitored intermittently. I sat in emergency for those hours with my children alone. This was a time when it would have been wonderful to have supportive and available family living in my city. What a sight we must have been! A mother perched in a cot with a three-year-old, a very sick and traumatised 22-month-old and a breast-fed baby. I continually called my husband's mobile phone to no avail. When, five hours later, he eventually answered, he agreed to visit us. He popped in but refused to stay as he had a work function to attend. Francesca rightfully needed out after five hours in a cot with her brother, infant sister and mother. Who of us didn't? He could see I was managing 'just fine' and he had no desire to stay. I didn't have the confidence to challenge his nonchalance in the middle of a hospital emergency room, however, I did attempt persuasion. After my best efforts, he agreed to take Francesca with him. Thankfully, that did make things more manageable. It was a Catholic school work-function my husband was due to attend. *'Surely, they could accommodate Francesca? Why was looking after one of his three children even questionable?'* I am amazed to this day what convincing I had to do to have my husband take our eldest that night. Perhaps I had disempowered him in his parenting? I don't think I had, but I can only speculate on his motivations on that night. Edison's father stayed for around 15 minutes at the hospital. He did not telephone that night to check our progress or status.

Emergency doctors noticed the escalating nature of my son's distress, and Edison was administered a fifth dose of adrenalin and perhaps more steroids – I wasn't monitoring the medication closely – that was the medics' job. Edison did not respond to the heavy medication administered to him in the emergency department. The doctors eventually noted this and finally considered his symptoms, a cause for concern. By that stage, we had been in emergency for 10 hours. Edison was going blue. *'Maaannn! What do you need to do to get attention around here? Good move, Edison!'* Eventually, Ed's 'trick' captured the medics' attention enough to motivate further action and he was admitted to the ICU. The staff were kind and diligent and I was allowed to stay with Freya-Grace to breastfeed her and play the role of comforter for my son. A frightening night in the ICU ensued.

Edison pulled through. The Royal Children's Hospital was a teaching hospital. As such, teams of doctors and doctors-in-training attended to Edison. By morning, my parents had arrived from Toowoomba to provide emotional and practical support. We overheard many murmured conversations speculating as to why Edison had not responded to the medication treatment typically. There were other conversations too. ICU doctors noted

Edison's head shaking, his inability to be comforted by anything other than me holding him tight, his lack of eye contact, lack of developmentally typical language and his anxiety. The looks of concern on teams of doctors' faces provided little comfort. We discussed whether I had taken Edison to a developmental paediatrician. I explained, *"Of course, I have – and many other doctors, all of whom tell me he is a typically developing boy. Please, what do you think?"* No answer nor advice was proffered. When Eddie was discharged, I was advised that it was most unusual that a child with croup would not respond to multiple doses of prednisolone. They gently added that although he was now stable, he was not responding to human interaction in a typical way. The doctors were concerned. The hospital doctors gave me no insight as to what Ed was going through, but their concern confirmed that this time, I wasn't the only one who noticed Edison's unusual traits confirmed a need for further investigation. This experience kick-started even more determination to pursue a diagnosis with the goal of a cure for Ed. What I was hoping to cure was an enigma. Through government funded tests and my self-funded quests, I had thus far only ruled out hearing loss.

Edison recovered from his severe bout of croup and I continued to see a new, 'poo-friendly', GP whose only consistent diagnosis was a mother's hyper-vigilance. Perhaps I was judged as displaying a tendency for dramatisation. I noted that most doctors with whom I consulted, thought Eddie was naughty. Ed didn't play with doctors' toys the way other kids did. Instead, he took great delight in destroying model displays and playing with toys in ways not expected. Ed found it entertaining to switch the fluorescent lights in doctors' consulting rooms on and off incessantly. I hastened my research for answers regarding my son's milestone deterioration. My concern was not shared with Edison's father, my parents nor my friends. The mantra remained unchanged, *'He's a boy, they develop slower'*. I continued to feel isolated in my concerns.

When finally, our forever house sold, I barely felt compensated for the loss of a dream. Our real-estate agent not only lied to us, he robbed us. He changed the contract price to a figure less than we agreed to over the phone. My husband didn't check the figure and signed for 30,000 dollars less than we verbally agreed to. The home was in my husband's name only because generally he either was unemployed or earned a lower risk income than I. He was less likely to be sued in his line of work and he was a union member. As such, my signature wasn't needed to sell the home. This 30K oversight was another bunch of cash I'd eventually have to re-earn. I later learnt our real-estate agent earnt his dodgy reputation. We were not the first vendors he pulled this 'fasty' on.

All three children were still under school age, hence, we could purchase our new forever home anywhere in Brisbane with a minimum of disruption to our routines. I determined that we could not afford a best suburb along with the other things we wanted. I drew up a wish list and asked for my husband's contribution. His requirements were simple. He wanted something close to an oval where he could run and a nearby gym with a 50-metre swimming pool. My list was longer and included good primary and high schools, close medical facilities, a double block, a character house, urban over suburban, a garden I could improve and a location close to a train station. Most of all, I needed to love my new abode, as home making was part of my fabric.

When provided the choice, I have never lived in houses, only homes. Long nights breastfeeding and googling to find a new home, and many days of drive-bys, were draining. Thankfully, my parents had also been glued to the internet day and night seeking out our next potential nest. With a 30-day settlement looming over our Brookfield property, the pressure to find a new abode increased. Research completed, I shortlisted two houses to show my husband. Dad was undergoing regular cancer treatment at the Wesley Hospital and he was very sick at this time. How my parents endured over a decade of the four-hour return journey for treatment, I do not know. Sometimes they stayed overnight in Brisbane to spend time with family. Looking back, they were very generous with their time. I witnessed my father suffer a lifetime of poor health. Despite this, he continued to put others first. Conveniently, my parents were in Brisbane for treatment during this house-hunting week, allowing Mum to help me choose our new residence. I was always delighted to see my parents as they often avoided our family during Brisbane based cancer treatment, due to the infection risks young children presented. One of my sisters, Kylie, was a single mum with older kids. With regards to possible germs and infection, her home was a safer option while Dad endured chemotherapy. Understandably, when staying overnight in Brisbane, my parents would select to stay with Kylie. The day we bought our Wooloowin home, Mum was there as a part of my executive functioning, coaching me in managing my husband through the purchase decision. Eventually, we procured an 1890s partially renovated Queenslander, on a double block in Wooloowin, only five minutes' walk to a train station and around five kilometres from the CBD. I managed to pull off my own checklist as well as my husband's. My husband was pleased that he had a local oval, pool and gym. Whilst it depleted my soul to lose my 360-degree outlook, I maintained a hopeful attitude settling into a new house that I could make a home. Privileges I had once enjoyed and now missed included a dishwasher, a garage, a walk-in robe and an en suite. Regardless, overall this new road-trip was looking rather positive.

With the Brookfield plan behind me, I carried baggages of loss. Fortunately, though, I welcomed the notion of becoming an urban mum. Originally, I had preferred rural living, but in my new situation I had decided on a 180-degree change, rejecting the option of becoming a suburban mum. The hooks and labels we attach our identity to, mystify me. Why would urban mum feel more authentic for me than suburban mum? I'd found a new forever home to turn my misery into a happy family and I was on my way with a newly planned future. Perhaps I was holding onto hope that I could become *one of us*… This new chapter provided me opportunities I had not anticipated. I was learning that no matter what life threw at me, I remained a planner.

Our new circumstances somehow saw many people who I used to be close friends with, drop out of our lives. Maybe losing some friends was a geographical thing. Maybe people just get busy. My husband appeared no happier. I asked myself whether I was simply choosing the wrong people. I had graduated last century, being recognised in the University of Queensland's Deans list (top 1%). Clearly, that psychology degree did not teach me well enough about humans, influence and power. It did teach me that I didn't want to spend the rest of my life categorising people on the (1990s) normal versus abnormal psychology scales. Post-graduation, in my mid-twenties, I read Dr M. Scott Peck's book *'People of the Lie'* in an effort to educate myself to mistrust certain people. The content didn't sink in as my nature was very trusting of others. Perhaps that's why I am such a slow learner when it comes to determining who shouldn't be in my life. In our new home, I went from a hopeful planner and dreamer to a powerless victim while my husband's cruelty escalated. Eroding hopes of becoming a content housewife were obliterated.

Chapter 8
Unwelcome Yet Sought Change

Moving to a new house was in the main, designed to achieve two goals. The first was to save my marriage and second goal was to have a mortgage we could sustain. We had managed to achieve the latter goal. Once moved into our new forever home, I set about finding yet another new GP. In the Wooloowin home, Edison turned two years. Once settled, I sought even more fervently to solve the puzzle of why, ten months or so earlier, my talking, bright, loving, affectionate, walking boy turned sad, less able, confused and rather violent. He had declined rapidly over weeks before my eyes. The massive change can be described as a terrifying spiral into a world that neither he nor I understood. My boy, whom mums' group mums once admired as advanced, was now scared. He turned in circles, made crazy non-word like noises and was clearly in a very frightening place. He cried, he bit, he was angry, he was lost. My prefect boy was behaving like an afraid, caged animal. I now think that was exactly what he was feeling as autism began to set upon him. But at that point, I still had no answers as to what had beset Edison.

When we first moved into our 1800s Wooloowin, wooden home, I was proactive regarding fire safety. I had never lived in an old wooden home before and I was keen to ensure our home was safe. A service that the fire department provided back then was a home fire safety check. I booked a review of our home in the knowledge that it would be deferred in the case of an emergency. The fireys turned up at the appointed time and talked us through where we should place additional fire alarms and educated us in training our children in a fire evacuation plan. Whilst we took this as a serious exercise, for Eddie, it was like first class entertainment had arrived on his doorstep. He admired the uniforms and one of the fire officers allowed him to play (supervised) on the fire engine during our fire safety review. He would have likely marked this as a '*good, good, good, very good day*'.

My husband was very motivated by exercise. He never finished his first degree, which was offered as a full scholarship to the University of Houston which had been awarded because of his athletic talents and achievements. He never abated with his exercise, which I both admired and resented. I see in retrospect that my resentment was based on envy. It was good for him to have a healthy outlet; something it would take me many years to develop. My husband did many things at 100%. Eating, outdoor work, football, running, cycling and couch surfing were all or none. We never stopped trying to change one another. A fruitless and stupid endeavour in any case to change anyone but one's self. Acceptance, again, was a challenge for me. Of course, I wouldn't accept the abuse that came hand in hand with my husband. He took like a fish to water all that gym membership offered him. I now see I could have made more of an effort to accept his less than considerate ways. I don't think my generation has the tolerance of my parents' generation. This can be both good and bad. What we learn or simply ponder...

Following the move, it took further months to find anyone who would recognise that my concerns about Edison were valid. Convincing a GP to provide a referral to yet another paediatrician continued to be a battle. Predictably, the assessment of '*he's a boy, they develop slower*' was parroted. My husband, my friends, my parents and countless GP's all continued to be unsupportive. I liken the experience to navigating a completely foreign world where everyone except Ed looked abnormal. The rest of my world was becoming unfamiliar and my life did not seem to make sense as I fervently upped the ante on connecting with Edison's experience. With a tough marriage, three essentially dependent children, no paid work and no local friends I became further isolated. I was ardent in my research and cries for help. The pace required for this journey was too fast to feel any depression, yet I would describe myself at that time, as desperate. My isolation proved a positive outcome from my husband's perspective. Isolated people lose their power. However, somehow I forged on.

My husband's sister, Sharlene, lived in a neighbouring suburb and was the mother of three children. I had a lot of time for Sharlene, and her partner was very likeable. She was kind and friendly and had made as many moves to have a positive relationship between our respective nuclear families, as I. We hoped for our kids to build strong cousin relationships. The odds were stacked against us with my husband displaying, at best, disdain for his family of origin. I remember, upon becoming engaged, cold-calling my fiancé's mum and dad (separately as they were divorced) to announce that their only son and their eldest child, was to be married. I was not disallowed to make these phone calls but I was certainly not encouraged. The phone calls were well received and fortunately, future encounters with my in-laws were positive. All of my husband's family came to Toowoomba for our wedding. I have since been told, this uniting of their family was a first and last, post the divorce of my in-laws. Clearly, my husband's family was more open to positive familial relationships than he. During my friendship with Sharlene, we both did what we could to foster family bonding, but in the long-term this proved to be yet another fantasy. Being relatively new to Wooloowin and having warmed to Sharlene, I sought out her local knowledge to assist in my quest of 'what was up with Ed'.

Sharlene recommended Dr Geoff Catton. Her children were older than ours and Dr Catton had been good to my nieces and Sharlene over the years. Upon making the initial appointment, I explained to the medical receptionist what I was seeking and that a long consultation was necessary. Dr Catton afforded us a whole hour. Dr Catton was generous with his time and he was the first medico directly consulted who shared my concerns about Edison's development. To this day, Dr Catton has been a rock for me. Doctor Catton thought Edison was suffering from something *deeper* than where my questioning was leading. I arrived at the appointment with a list of symptoms I had authored and categorised under the headings 'Physical, Emotional, Speech and Language and Other'. I was thinking ADSD, stress from my marriage, acting out or dyspraxia amongst many other potential concerns. Doctor Catton observed Edison as he interacted with his sisters in an unfamiliar environment while questioning me. Predictably, Edison flicked Dr Geoff's office lights on and off and attempted to post $50 notes through the air conditioner vents. No doubt Ed was emulating a scene from the movie *'The Polar Express'* where the train tickets resemble Australian $50 notes – and one is lost in a vent. I asked lots of questions. Should we revisit a need for grommets? Perhaps I need to eliminate certain substances from Ed's diet? Gravely, Dr Catton slowly shook his head and peered at me with kind eyes over his glasses, explaining again that he believed that there was something deeper underlying Edison's condition. Doctor Catton's *deeper* comment had a weighty effect on me. In that moment, my fears of something profound began to crystallise. I remember the moment like it was yesterday. I was very tearful driving my three kids home. Not my plan…

Upon arriving home, I opened and read the referral letter meant only for the referred specialist. The letter suggested Edison may have Mosaic Down Syndrome. A decade or so ago, I had taught some children with challenges (oppositional defiant disorder and ADHD for example), but I had never known a person who in my time, would definitively be described as having special needs. The notion that Edison wasn't sick but was 'special' was enormously confronting. At the time, the internet was young yet mature enough to feed my imagination, my ignorance and my fears. It would be over a month before I could see the referred specialist, and hopefully gain insight into why Edison was moving backwards. Whenever I could, I researched Mosaic Down Syndrome. I looked at Ed differently, asking questions of myself. *'Was the back of his neck flat in line with his skull? Did he have fine hair? I do, and he does. Does this mean Mosaic?'* I spent a long time studying Edison's palms. I could not conclusively decide whether he had a single crease across his palms. His major crease was big and continuous but there were others. I began to read parent support websites. I prayed the challenges these families faced were not ahead of me. The month between the Mosaic suggestion and meeting with the specialist developmental paediatrician was lonely while I lived in angst, now with a medical confirmation that Eddie wasn't quite right. Perhaps it was preparation for what was to come; a life which challenged my most basic life assumptions. I continued to face denial at home regarding Ed's condition. Not entirely alone, however, in the light of a doctor's opinion, my parents started to face the possibility that Edison wasn't typically developing. What would a mother know? I was yet to understand true social isolation.

I attended the referred specialist paediatrician appointment and was told within 20 minutes and with 100% certainty, zero comfort and no emotional sensitivity, *"Your child has Autism and he's not at the easy end of the spectrum. This is a life-long disability. Autism cannot be cured. Here's a brochure which will provide you more information. We also have a form which will allow you to seek assistance from physiotherapists, occupational therapists and the like."*

Given my degrees, how could I miss this? Hope, perhaps. Hope is important. The paediatricians gave me no hope nor comfort. It was like they had done this 100 times. I am sure that in reality, the paediatric team had experienced their own pain in delivering such news over one thousand times.

"Your son likely will not develop fully in gross motor, nor fine-motor skills... He's unlikely to be toilet trained; language will evade him. Your life will now change forever. Next please..."

There were no specific specialist referrals, nor a hug? A little more than a decade later, I do hope the medical profession has become more sensitive at the time of diagnosis. I cried and drove home with now autistic Ed in his safety seat, Francesca strapped in her booster seat and Freya-Grace in her baby seat. What would Edison's safety seat keep him safe from? There was no cure for being Edison.

I was angry and hurt. Today, I accept and understand Edison needed no cure. This understanding came only after a long and arduous journey. He was then, as perfect as the day he was born, but I could not see that at the time. I paced my backyard that afternoon, carrying Freya-Grace as the older two children busied themselves in the sandpit, oblivious to anything other than their discovery play at hand. That afternoon, I met only my children's needs and I disregarded their wants. My need for sanity, answers, hope, insight and strength far outweighed their wants in that hour. In my mind, I had just been informed that my son would never be married, would likely never have children, would not go to university, would not live independently, would not be able to…

Dreams shattered in a day. If my life had been kinder, this would have been the most devastating day of my life. It turns out life was yet to teach me total devastation.

I look back on this shattering diagnosis and realise the unconscious pressure and expectations we put on our children. At two and a half years of age, the dreams and expectations I had for my only son were crushed. What happens to parents who have typically developing kids raised in a loving home and find their child choosing a path they hadn't planned; drug addiction as teenagers for example? The dreams of those parents have been fostered and developed, modified and expanded for over a decade before being blown away. Surely, it must be harder for those parents?

I remained able to appreciate typical and humorous aspects of raising children amongst the fog of newly (for me) discovered autism. There were glimmers of joy to appreciate… With Freya-Grace being my youngest, I rarely corrected her speech in the manner I did her older siblings. She preferred to be as unclothed as possible at all times. It was a challenge to have her wear underwear and she would most often choose to wear her 'spare feet' when venturing out. Bare feet was her preference and her description of 'spare feet' warmed me so much so, that she was never corrected. At times, Freya-Grace would explain to me that she had an 'egg ache' when she wasn't feeling well. I would never allow my two eldest children to speak so mistakenly, yet poor little Freya-Grace had to grow herself out of cuteness, egg-aches and spare feet. Dark times were punctuated at times with joyous parental moments.

I was (and am) still growing. Presented to me along this unwanted autism diagnosis road-trip, was an opportunity for enlightenment, engagement and education. I learnt these lessons slowly and painfully. In time, the ASD diagnosis and what it taught me motivated a parenting style which empowered my children – respecting that they own their future. I learnt that I am a custodian only. It took a while for me to determine that I would not be the master of their dreams, hopes and aspirations. I would not write their plan. I would not become the parent who dictates academia, sport, music, heterosexuality, university, marriage, parenthood… My thinking started to turn inward, questioning my own choices. *'What's so good about being a wife, a mother, going to university a couple of times, having a bunch of kids and living in an urban community?'* This was me. I was supposed to be blissfully happy. *'Had I made the right choices? No?'* My marriage was a mess, I was tired. I was so very tired. Independence became a core value of my parenting and later became a core family value.

Chapter 9
Acceptance and Urban Family Life

A sleepless night ensued after I settled the children and prepared to face my new mental and emotional struggles. Around and around, my thoughts circulated in futility; '*I am an autistic mother*'. Privately, I have called myself an 'autistic mum' many times and I hope it doesn't hurt other people's feelings to read this. I know it's not accurate. It's just how I used to internally summarise a complex situation. Politically correct words can sometimes be elusive, especially in times of despair. The morning after Ed's diagnosis which I had so desperately pursued, I rose to prepare a cuppa to sip upon in my sunroom at sunrise, intending to beat the demands of the day and steal a precious moment for myself. I'd had a night to ponder our predicament whilst failing to achieve sought after quality sleep. My mind would not quieten. I was in turmoil with a trillion questions, concerns and fears running relentlessly through my head. I was in mourning for my lost son; processing, challenging myself to embrace this new son. The love I had for Edison did not cease. My focus that morning was on managing my grief. I did not recognise it as grief at the time. I was too consumed with emotion. I now recognise this grieving process forged an important and central new aspect of my identity. My focus that morning was on willing my mind into a new way of working, thinking, prioritising, parenting, existing… A massive challenge when I had not yet buried my last failed plan.

Bathing in the glorious, morning sunlight in the room of my reforming mind, my husband entered and noticed tears in my eyes.

"What the fuck is wrong with you?"

"I'm mourning. I don't need anything from you. I'm mourning the loss of my son. I'm processing."

"He's the same fuckin' kid he was yesterday. What the fuck's wrong with you?"

"You're right, I guess I'm lamenting a loss of my dreams for Ed and setting myself up to create new dreams."

"You're a fuckin' basket case."

"I'm just sitting in my sunroom thinking and if you don't like it, leave. If I can't have a tear and think at sunrise in my own home, asking nothing of anyone, we are in a pitiful state."

I don't know whether my husband experienced his own mourning, as he never discussed it with me but immediately following this interaction, he stormed off to the gym. I assumed then as I do now that the gym was his outlet, his way of coping... How could a father not grieve or at least take a little time to process an acceptance of such a significant diagnosis? Eddie's dad was very masculine. He had represented the country in athletics, played rugby union, received a USA college scholarship for sport, had a slim, high income trophy-wife, was a PE teacher, and at 6 foot 2 inches, he could bench press 120 kg. Surely, he too had dreams for his only son which had been crushed. If so, he didn't express any sentiment nor discuss it with me. Perhaps he had not prepared a mental template for receiving unwanted news regarding his son. Whilst in hindsight, it is clear to me that I spent the period of time leading up Ed's diagnosis bracing myself and developing a mental template of prospective loss, Ed's dad chose the path of complete denial. If he did mourn following the diagnosis, it presented as anger. He had his healthy outlets and that morning, I was thankful that he left me to cope alone. Perhaps in that marriage while I mused, and he exercised, I was too much head and he was too much body.

Once I began to come to terms with Edison's diagnosis, it was time for a call to action to give him the best possible outcomes. I set about rustling the support required as I began to intellectually accept Edison's diagnosis. In order, though, to provide all I could to allow Edison to blossom, I could not simply rollover in full acceptance. I came to terms with autism initially only by combating all that stood between Edison and potential opportunities lying ahead of him; opportunities which could allow him to lead, what I considered, a fulfilling life. My acceptance of Ed's autism gave birth to a formidable fighter. Deep down inside, I was sick of conflict and I didn't want to battle anyone nor anything. This was not about me though. I brought this child into the world. I was his protector, provider and nurturer. I now had an added job description – combatant for my son's rights – later more eloquently described as 'maternal autism advocate'. No matter what one calls it, when one lives it, this advocacy stuff is a political and social blood sport.

Our family dynamic was morphing. Despite my husband's cup of tea with a saucer reaction to the news of our growing family, our third child was indeed the apple of his eye. He loved his children, but with Freya-Grace being the youngest, she got away with misdemeanours the other children were unable to avoid the consequences of. The two eldest, Francesca and Edison would often behave like children – go figure. They would play, cry, be messy, be hungry, be cooperative, be rebellious... I observed that their father didn't demonstrate a natural inkling to fatherhood. He tried. I don't think he liked not being the centre of my attention. Feeding a mortgage, a toddler, an infant and a baby, I did my best. Life was difficult and we all tried. The children's father walked them at times and he read to them when they were good. He cooked most Sundays. He demanded that I slept in a separate room (when it wasn't time for sex), so that when I attended to their needs, I would not wake him. He sacrificed.

In the early days of willing myself into acceptance of my new life, I started a mostly work-from-home business. Despite this additional load, my new business led me down a path to becoming a far more satisfied person than I had been in my 10-month stint as a full-time housewife. I found myself back on fire in a good way. I had received many phone calls since leaving the workforce offering lucrative opportunities to re-join the IT industry. Each time, I declined, declaring my commitment to the housewife and mother role. My venture in creating a consultancy business started with a phone call from a stranger who offered me the improbable opportunity to do what I loved intellectually, coupled with flexibility. I refused the stranger's first two offers. Finally, he offered, *"You can charge what you want, work the hours that you want, work where you want, just please can you come and work with us and teach us your art?"* It went something like that anyway… 'My art', as this stranger put it, was in closing complex, and often multi-million dollar IT deals. One of the differentiators of my style was that I always saw deal closing as purchasing assistance, and not as sales.

Since graduating from university, I had attained qualifications in APICS – Supply Chain, Manufacturing and Logistics, and I was therefore able to walk into most businesses and understand why they had contacted me. I readily understood their shortfalls, the correlations or causes of their less than hoped for success trajectory or the big issues which needed to be fixed as a priority. I also had a decade or so of assisting NPF (Not-for-Profit and now, For-Purpose) organisations turn themselves around for the better. Many customers could not identify or articulate the causes of their business pain but were able to recognise help of some kind was required. Often the pain began with inefficient communication and hence better IT was sought. We can be like that as people – we are close to our own problems, but they can be tough to self-diagnose. Sometimes, we simply can't see our own big picture. In all complex human and business circumstances, an outside perspective is refreshing and useful. Some prospective customers were in a healthy financial state to invest in improved systems, so growth rather than pain was their motivator.

In my work, I always came from a place of integrity and respect for the prospective client and would qualify out before I'd close a deal which was anything short of valuable for all. Fortunately, the team which was employed by my first client shared my values, and with our combined skills, their business became more successful and client numbers grew as loyalty was both earned and fostered. It was Rob Cheesman who inadvertently set me upon this new business path. Today, he is a role model of an honourable and respectable man, for my family. He was also a pallbearer of my son's coffin.

My focus, apart from day to day activities involving marital issues, motherhood and work was consumed with unravelling the mysteries of Ed's autism. I found myself navigating overwhelming dialogue, research, chat-lines and literature. There was so much to learn and decipher. New, occasional work that I secured was a welcome distraction. I read, researched and attempted to distinguish between the witch doctors, western medical doctors and traditional therapies. My work afforded me luxuries. I was able to explore options which I did not understand yet offered hope. I had the funds to join Autism Queensland (AQ) and I was instantly disappointed with the little practical support they were positioned to offer. Their resources were stretched and they seemed more of a referral organisation at that time, than a support body. There was almost no government funding available so my hopes that AQ would provide a map of the autism rabbit hole were dashed. Yet again, I felt very alone and lost in a sea of confusion.

I mustered the strength to add intense observation and self-invented therapeutic tactics as a peripheral addition to work, mothering, Ed's conventional therapies and diet monitoring. As a mother of three, I observed and learnt, interacted and loved; always including the girls wherever I could. My children became my prime educators in all things useful regarding autism. It was Edison and his sisters who eventually taught me more than 100 text books could teach me about what autism meant for our family and most importantly, for Ed. Never the less, I continued to devour textbooks providing expert advice.

To gauge the severity of Edison's autism in preparation for formal education, I booked Ed in for an ADOS (Autism Diagnostic Observation Schedule) test. The focus of the ADOS was observation of social behaviour and communication which categorised a person as having Autism, Not Quite Autism (NQA) or Broad Spectrum Autism. Although the paediatricians told me Edison had autism, his documented diagnosis at that time was PDDNOS (Pervasive Developmental Disorder Not Other-wise Specified). Autism is (or was) a subset of PDDNOS. Some parents who face many challenges, learn after the ADOS that their child has an Asperger's (or high functioning autism) diagnosis. I hoped to be one of them... I learnt that a conclusive written diagnosis of autism was difficult to secure whilst the child was younger than three. Today, medicine has moved on and it seems the 'autism industry' is less reluctant to diagnose early. Thankfully, these days government funding is up for grabs even after the child turns 6 years of age. For us, no substantial financial support was on offer whilst wandering the wilderness of diagnosis and early intervention.

During the ADOS, Edison was observed intermittently by a physiotherapist, an occupational therapist and a doctor on one side of a one-way glass wall. They interacted with him one at a time. As I kept Francesca and Freya-Grace entertained on the observation side of the glass wall, I hoped Edison would get a score of under 5 or under 10 out of a total of 15. Edison's score was 12, indicating full-blown autism. Some not so comforting anecdotes... *"You should focus on having him toilet trained before he is an adult. He'll likely never speak, so you need to begin a whole new schedule of picture language. There are resources you can purchase to help you with that. Routines are extremely important. You need to train your entire family to function within routines so that Edison can cope and function as best he is able. His abilities won't improve after the age of six."* Another teary, long drive home with three hungry kids in tow, ensued. This was tough. It was tougher to have learnt that I was sitting on an autism time bomb and I was the only person to potentially disable the bomb. Where could I learn the skills to get Ed right before the age of six? I was compelled to disarm the bomb but I was at a loss of how to neutralise what was on my plate.

I found many sites on the internet that claimed autism was curable such as DAN (Defeat Autism Now). Tempting reading... Australian medical and allied-health practitioners whom I dealt with, were steadfast in their view of autism being incurable. Some gave hope of progress. Most welcomed me spending the tiny amount of government money I was eventually allocated for their services. I submitted our family to countless early treatments to fix or improve Ed's autism. I rejected more treatments than those I pursued. The autism fix menu was extensive and I knew clinically, that it would be wise to only take one bite at a time. It is an expensive and distressing exercise, treating a child with a disability, especially where the opinions of experts do not align. Over the years, I ultimately learned that teaching with, and learning from a child with autism could be an inexpensive and fulfilling exercise of love and encouragement. It took a long time and a fair deal of emotional and financial pain to build up the confidence to advocate as the adult expert in Edison's experience of autism.

Of the experts I consulted with, Dr Gary Deed provided useful advice and some promising results based on test results around allergies and gut flora. As a leader in his field, he had me courier samples of Edison's poo and urine to the United States for testing. The specimens were required in the US laboratory within 28 hours of leaving Edison's body. I won't even begin to explain the logistics of achieving this from a toilet at the international airport with three young children. The tests were run in the Sates and were eventually returned to Dr Deed. It turned out that Ed would function better not having salicylates, preservatives and a list of around 100 other components in his diet. I met parents of ASD patients who had followed strict new diets, left their jobs and were living rural, self-sustaining and off the grid as their autistic children flourished. Perhaps I was selfish or too materialistic to throw away my degrees, the work I hoped to re-enter as the children grew older, all to become a happy hippy with a slightly less autistic kid? There are degrees of autism, indeed ASD is a spectrum. By becoming a happy hippy, I wouldn't be able to hope for a cure. That recipe of escapism didn't gel with me. I had a husband who enjoyed his new work and I understood that I could not put more stress on the marriage. In addition, I had two typically (if not giftedly) developing daughters and I had no intention of having Edison's autism come between opportunities for my husband and my daughters. I would not open avenues which may prevent them from being the best who they could be. The hippy life was ruled out and the diet was considered.

Initially, I followed the recommended dietary changes vigorously. This was stressful on the entire family and it added an extra financial burden. At the time, Edison was doing weekly speech therapy and occupational therapy, my version of in-home ABA, Proloque2Go (a frustrating and expensive online, 30-minute, twice per day, supervised (by me) cognitive program, created specifically for young children with autism), along with many other treatments. Later, we tried Auditory Integration Training (AIT) which was an intense two times, one hour per day programme which ran over 14 days, requiring four hours of driving each day to attend. Adding more than one therapy or intervention at a time was my only option, given the 'six-year-old time bomb' expert theory. Of course, via my psychology degree, I knew that when adding a new trick to our autism fix-it bag, one can't identify which fix was working, if any. It is best to remove less effective therapies if those can be identified, one at a time. With time running out, I simply kept trying and applying. As such, the hours, treatments, therapies, diets and alternative interventions piled up layer on top of layer. At one point with an awareness I did not possess, my husband justifiably bemoaned his building frustration, anger and resentment. He spilled out: "*More, more, more autism stuff to fix a growing, growing, growing problem – where the fixes only add to our ever growing complications.*"

My tertiary education did not include concepts of neuroplasticity. In the early 2000s, neuroplasticity was not yet commonly accepted by the medical community I consulted with for autism advice. The pressure to pour everything I could into Edison's development before he turned six years of age was all consuming. Every expert expounded the *show* was pretty much over and the trajectory was set after an autistic child turned six years and one day. What a load of bullocks and unnecessary stress and expense we suffered from swallowing this falsehood! Were there alternatives? What worked? I couldn't know as I was doing so many things simultaneously, and eventually I gave up on the strict diet which excluded one of Ed's staples – vegemite. Vegemite was a food group in itself for Edison and giving it up created new behavioural issues which caused major day-to-day disruptions. As behaviour management was also a priority, I was very tough on Edison as he managed to do the hard work of putting up with me.

Chapter 10
Tremendous Adjustments

I began more intently to focus on Edison as a person and what made him tick, as opposed to all the medical noise. One thing Eddie was obsessed with was his favourite children's TV shows. He mimicked, acted out and repeated all he could from his favourite shows. I knew that his favourite 'Wiggles' moment was always intently watching the big red car accompanying The Wiggles drive off into a sunset under a rainbow. This favourite of Ed's will never leave me. Eddie loved his sunsets. I drew upon observing Eddie's obsession with various children's entertainment shows. Via *'Thomas the Tank Engine'*, I learned that things go wrong when 'it's windy'. When *'it's very windy'* viaducts self-destruct, sheep become homeless, trains can't get home to the Fat Controller and trees fall over train tracks… All manner of horrible things happen as a result of windy conditions. Early on, when Ed would accidentally break crockery or spill something, he would exclaim in tears, *'It's VERY windy!'* Connecting with his internal dialogue and his interpretation of the world helped me immensely in fine-tuning my perspective of Ed's needs and supports. His obsessive relationship with favoured DVD's, TV shows, book characters and the like provided a window into his way of being.

I had been taught that routine was very important to children with autism and although we had a predictable routine in our home, I set about mixing things up for Edison several times a day. I figured if people with autism couldn't cope with changes in routine (as the textbooks and the experts expounded), Ed and his ASD peers couldn't cope with life. At the time, in the ASD community, parents and carers were criticised if we weren't providing predictability for those on the spectrum whom loved. I wanted Ed to cope with life. Life rarely goes according to plan. Autism wasn't going to control my world nor the larger world outside our home. This was reality, and Ed needed to get used to being mucked up early in life. The rest of the world was not studying, changing and adapting to accommodate Eddie. Ed would have to accommodate a few billion peoples' manner of living with one another and navigate societal norms instead. The family unit was the priority, and that included my husband and my daughters as equally valuable individuals as all others, including Ed – but perhaps not me. My sense of self-worth was dangerously low. I paid no attention to that. I knew my family, and teaching Edison to accommodate change was of high importance. In order to teach Eddie acceptance of the new and unexpected, I made small and unforeseen changes such as setting him in the wrong seat, giving him the wrong plate, putting the wrong Thomas the Tank engine carriages together and so forth… Ed didn't rise to these challenges gracefully. He was as pig headed as his mother, however, I was not prone to bang my head, pull family members' hair or vomit when things didn't go my way.

Another less than desirable behaviour that Eddie engaged in was playing with his faeces. It took some creative thinking to extinguish this behaviour. Because there is lots of sunshine in Australia, many of our kids wear body suits for swimming. Body suits are one-piece nylon swimming costumes which enclose the wearer from neck to mid-thigh. Through the encouragement of one of my mother's friends who was a former occupational therapist, I committed to having Ed wear an all-in-one full body swimsuit, all day every day – plus nights. The body swimsuits were put on Edison backwards so that he couldn't unzip nor un-button them. He wore these suits under day care clothes and pyjamas. The key was that so long as he was wearing one of these suits, he could not access his bottom – therefore he could not get to his poo. If you can't touch your poo – you can't smear it. After a meagre nine months of dedication to all day and every day swimsuit wearing, we managed to cut the challenging poo smearing habit. Walls and furniture became stench free and clean. All behaviour has a purpose. In my attempt to extinguish the smearing, I introduced salami (a strong smelling and sensory heightening element), textual stimulants to sand play and introduced what I could, to accommodate Ed's need for strong smells and stimulating textures. I also tried basic options such as playdough, which proved useless but provided sustenance when Eddie was hungry.

Ed and I were often engaged in a war in which we respected one another. His role in this war was living as peacefully as he could with the challenges that autism presented. My role, in part, was to test him so that he could master any skills he could possibly achieve. I didn't know his limitations, and trial and error taught me what he was and was not capable of learning. We knew we belonged together in our war and we found space for one another when friction became too much. The bond of love, territory, frustration and co-existence became invincible. Edison's therapists were horrified that I deliberately messed with Edison's comfort zones and routines. I did not enjoy this chapter of parenting, yet I employed zero tolerance and eventually, in most instances, I won. In my mind, it was clear that if I won, Ed won too. My assaults on Ed's societally unacceptable behaviour and his peaceful withdrawal from others, was justified. Having Edison learn skills to embrace life independently was primary. It was a constant under-current in my parenting, that my battles to educate Ed would be tougher when he was over 6 foot tall. All the pain of tough love was centred around the adulthood I wanted Edison to enjoy. I have no idea, outside of the objective of 'a happy adult Ed', where I drew the strength to win the hundreds of battles Edison and I fought head-to-head. It was no simple task to teach him an understanding that he wasn't the centre of the world. Eventually, after a couple of years and with some clever tricks, Edison was typing proficiently and requesting using basic spoken words. Pleasingly, the floor was freed from fresh 'back-of-Ed-skull' dints caused by self-imposed cranial protests. Roald Dahl's children's book *'The Enormous Crocodile'* was a favourite of ours, which taught us clever tricks and perseverance. Ed and I played out these lessons to a variety of music. Hard work, abstinence and a deep desire to see my son flourish paid off. By the time Edison was the age of five, I observed my boy quite tolerant and adaptable to change – yet we remained still wound up in opposing clever tricks…

Somewhere along the line, I enrolled the children in day care for two days a week to allow predictable hours to build my business and earn an income. The local day care centres would not take Edison without government funded one-on-one adult support for six hours a day. Six hours was the maximum time I intended them to be in day care and so this seemed entirely reasonable until they warned me the highest funding ever approved in the state of Queensland, to their knowledge at that time, was for three hours a day, a couple of days a week. They were proud that they had managed to secure two hours funding three days a week for another child on the spectrum who presented as less challenging than my son. The fact that I had to fight to secure government legislated funding was unacceptable to me. I considered it a possibility that, *'Child care management must not be trying hard enough, or the system was broken – or both.'* I proposed that I draft the funding application and centre staff review the application and make any necessary modifications before signing off. The childcare centre management and owner were supportive and agreed to this in principle.

I set about reading thousands of pages of government policy on the educational support of autistic children. The documentation was full of loopholes (presumably designed for the government's benefit) and the legislation was vague and light-on in definitions. It took me a few months of research to prepare an application. During this time, I paid a nanny to be with Ed whilst I worked with clients and looked after day-to-day responsibilities. Concurrently, I was paying for two kids in day care with zero government subsidy. Thankfully, today the Australian government is generous and somewhat flexible in the funding they provide to families nurturing children (and adults) with special needs. Even typically developing children are funded for day care these days. The three months preparing our funding application cost me around $800 per week for two, six-hour days of three children in care. Given that motherhood remained my primary role and I was not a high-income earner, I doubt I broke even between childcare and after tax income. With a little pride and less hope in the outcomes of my work, I finally submitted my draft application. The day care centre management weren't glowingly optimistic, however thankfully, they were encouraging. The application was a couple of centimetres thick. Part of my strategy was to drown the government bureaucrats back in exposing unclear or inconsistent terminology. I used a few of their strategies against them. For example, I made up definitions where policy terms were conveniently vague and made sure Ed suited the maximum support requirements, as defined by me – referencing citations I had researched. I was later informed that we won the first ever six-hour government daily support for a Queensland ASD child, by using the government's lack of clarity in their policies against them. Loopholes were clarified by our submission. Eventually, funding policy changed. Small victories… I was quietly delighted that my actions had set down a path for other parents yet to walk in my shoes. Day care for their ASD child was now attainable too.

The first day of day care for Edison, we walked 150 metres to our local centre. Walking in unfamiliar territory was a massive challenge. The 150-metre journey took 45 minutes, as Edison vomited, stopped to lick the pavement, protesting and demonstrating that he was terrified in this new circumstance. Upon arrival, the day care director took one look at the four of us and immediately had one of her employees take crying Freya-Grace from my arms, another staff member took Francesca, a third ushered Edison to Thomas the Tank Engine toys. The director then asked me how I had my coffee as she opened the door to her office. I was a nervous wreck. The profession of day care worker is a lower than should be paid occupation, as such staff turnover is high. The team that supported us for those first few months was stable, creative and caring and they worked very hard with me, adapting activities to include Edison in day-to-day routines. I had created a library of around 1000 cut and laminated photos of people, places, emotions and activities to support Ed's communication. On the back of each photo, I placed velcro so that they could be ordered into storyboards. I had velcro on the inside of kitchen cupboards, Edison's wardrobe and all over the play room at home, including the side of the piano. A special velcro picture library was also created for day care and although Edison and I communicated best without the pictures, or with the pictures as supports only, the picture cues proved valuable resources for others wishing to communicate with Edison. I made storyboard mounts for day care to use in communicating with Ed via their personalised picture library. Over time, I added to the various libraries drawings. I enjoyed drawing and I am a somewhat talented artist. The goal of adding drawings to the photos was to assist in developing Edison's abstract mind. A drawing of a dog is very different than a photograph of a dog, in particular, in the minds of many people with autism.

During the day care years, Freya-Grace befriended a little girl by the name of Fuschia. She seemed a lovely child. She was there when I dropped Freya-Grace at day care on the way to school drop-off. Fuschia was also there when I picked Eddie and Freya-Grace up at around 3:15 pm. A few months of witnessing Fuschia not so happy elapsed before I met Fuschia's mum and after a few times running into one another, I offered up a bizarre proposition. Fuschia wasn't all that happy when I took her friend Freya-Grace home in the afternoon. I proposed that perhaps, when I pick Freya-Grace up from day care, I could also take Fuschia. Fuschia could have afternoon tea and dinner with us and then her mother could pick Fuschia up on her way home and relax with a fed, bathed daughter after a hard day's work. I told Fuschia's mum that I was early childhood trained and used to be a teacher but I didn't have a blue card or any formal child safety clearance. I offered that if she wanted to pop around for a cuppa one time and check out our home and family, I'd welcome her. I really can't remember exactly how the whole Fuschia being a part of our family three afternoons a week started, yet I recall her parents doing their homework to ensure Fuschia was in good hands. It worked beautifully, and all my kids hit it off with the newcomer. Eventually, Fuschia spent some regular mornings with us too. Fuschia was a happy child and knew her mind. The four children played well together, and it was good to mix up our routines with a new little friend.

In time, I became good friends with Fuschia's parents, Nat and Sheree and a little brother joined their clan. I remember one holiday shared together on Moreton Island fondly. Late in 2016, when returning home from Fuschia's family's Christmas party, my daughters commented to me how comfortable they felt with Nat and Sheree, *"That whole family is like a part of our family."* Friends such as these who reciprocally welcome us as family, are a precious gift. Many years on, Fuschia's parents were extremely loving and practical in their support. As it eventuated, Fuschia's parents and I ended up living a one-hour return journey apart. Never the less, when I was destined to be alone for a birthday, when we ended up homeless, when I felt that I had no one on my side, Nat and Sheree stayed solid. I remind myself yet again, to never under-value loyal friends.

Ed slowly morphed into a content child as those who loved him, accepted him and as he became accustomed to his developing autism. Learning from Eddie's perseverance at re-learning so many skills (such as language) which had developed effortlessly before late onset autism, inspired my perseverance in the face of challenges. One of my goals for Eddie as he shared some of his time between a special education pre-prep school programme and day care was to make sure that by the time he reached prep, he could type. I was determined that Ed's prep teachers didn't equate autism with stupidity (which sadly many people did with regards to Ed.) Ed was a fantastic speller. For example, at the age of three, he could spell *'crocodile'* but speaking the word was indecipherable to most. The laptop I bought for Ed for his third birthday prompted his passion for technology. I made Google the home page for internet searches and made this search engine pop-up during start-up. For a couple of years when I couldn't get Ed to verbally tell me what he wanted, he would type his requests. I taught him syntax and grammar in addition to spelling. Most sentences, therefore ended with *'full-stop press enter'*. Technology can be a wonderful tool in facilitating communication for us all and can have specific advantages for those with ASD.

I have recently enjoyed reading the somewhat controversial book *'To Siri with Love'* by Judith Newman. I don't feel the author meant to be controversial in her authoring. In my reading, I felt that she simply documented her perspective and experiences raising two children, one of whom is diagnosed with ASD. In my opinion, Judith was honest and generous in her sharing. Regardless of her caring and honest intentions, some of her views have been highly criticised. Her bravery rewarded her with an acclaimed book which attracted criticism from certain subsets of the community. Most of us upset someone at some point when we publicly and honestly share our perspective, experiences or opinions. As a listener or reader of another person's story, when honesty is paired with generosity, I attempt to withhold negative judgement. Instead, I focus on the intent of the person who is sharing. In Judith's book, her ASD son employs Apple's Siri technology to advance his communication.

I admire Judith's son's use of voice recognition technology to help him learn and communicate. Back when I was Ed's partner in early childhood development, technology was less advanced. Regardless of the fact that technology in the first decade of this century wasn't as advanced as it is today, Ed's language began to slowly pick up with the IT we had available to us. For around six months after the entry of Ed's laptop into his life, when he started to verbally request, his spoken requests were always finished by, "*Full-stop, press enter.*" To my delight and amusement, Ed would speak, for example, "*Vegemite sandwich, please, full stop, press enter.*" I learned to be careful of what to teach Ed as he was so extremely literal in his interpretation of most things. I observed some new, less desirable skills were hard to unlearn. Much of the therapy I conducted with Ed brought out my impatience. Ed didn't like a fair bit of this activity either – but he never gave up. He deserves the lion's share of the praise which I receive, for how far he progressed.

Chapter 11
One of Them

Grocery shopping was an extreme sport. Grocery stores are full of smells, sounds, advertising and strangers which all compete for our attention. For Edison, this was too much. Sensory overload was an ongoing issue with Ed. My daughters and I came to calling him 'superman' as we observed his reactions to sounds we could not hear and odours we could not smell. Coles supermarket shopping was a nightmare. Many experiences were loud, colourful, smelly, busy, crowded and overstimulating for my boy. When an Aldi, offering a less in your face, sensory shopping experience opened near-by, the challenge of grocery shopping was mildly alleviated. Shopping as the only adult with three small children is trying for any parent. Edison added to our grocery purchase outings a few extra challenges. He vomited due to overstimulation while we passed through every second isle; he licked the floor and played with items by pulling them off the shelves to stack them on the floor in a more aesthetically pleasing arrangement. Often, I bought many items I didn't need to appease Edison and allow us to exit stage-right relatively quickly. The kind, empathetic team at Aldi would follow us with a mop and bucket and they would open a checkout just for us when it came time to pay. For this, I remain extremely grateful. I persisted in my efforts of horrendous, basic shopping outings in the hope they would serve to provide skills for Ed into the future. To teach a child over six-foot-tall these coping mechanisms would be far more challenging down the track. I figured that one day Edison would need to buy toilet paper and other basics. I hoped that by starting the lesson of shopping at age three, I had a head-start, and he might be able to graduate to independent loo paper purchases by the age of 18.

Another difficult outing with Eddie, was to the geneticist practise which was attached to the Royal Children's Hospital. Our paediatrician had recommended we visit, initially to make sure Ed was typical from a genetic perspective. There is a saying about difficulty which refers to drawing blood from a stone... Edison was very challenging to draw blood from. Not quite a stone, but it did take four adults to hold him down each visit in order to extract five vials of blood. The stress he endured during these visits was extremely confronting. I found this ongoing process traumatic. Our first appointment revealed that Eddie was genetically normal. I challenged my paediatrician and the geneticist as to the reasons why we should continue to make such torturous geneticist visits once we had learned what we'd originally set out to discover. It was explained to me that the main reason was to help with research. My Ed was no research bunny, especially if the research was accompanied by pain and fear. We did not return.

With my arm firmly twisted behind my back by 'ists' (occupational therap*ists*, educational*ists*, speech therap*ists* etcetera), I enrolled Edison in special state school pre-prep. Once day care funding had been secured, Eddie eventually spent two days a week at special-ed and two at the day care centre. He was in care more than I wanted, but at that point, I was trusting that the experts (the 'ists') knew better than I and that professionals could do a better job with Edison than his mother. That assumption was wrong, but they tried and did no harm. The first day of special-ed was another confronting day. I was faced again with a personal challenge of acceptance. Why did the other parents and staff have no trouble accepting that their children belonged in special education whilst this burned against the core of who I was as the mother of Ed? I experienced extreme angst grappling with societally driven norms which excluded my reality. I wasn't racist, I wasn't classist, I wasn't anti-inclusion; I was accepting of those with special needs and I loved my special Edison. Why was I then in turmoil? There is a part of society that judges others based on the school we send our children to. I really don't like that part of how we relate to one another, yet sadly it remains a building block of where one is placed in societal ranks. I've always been a person who sees school up-one-ship as shallow and I despise it. Yet, I couldn't find it in myself to answer the question of where my kids go to school including the word 'special' in my answer. Another weakness in my character was exposed. Thankfully, Ed, my daughters and my marriage were the priority, so somehow I forged on while discovering bigotry in myself, which I did not welcome.

What was wrong with me that I just could not leave my special kid in special education for 13 years and trust the system? Why did I have to always fight? I still have no answers to these questions. After taking Ed to his first day of special-ed, I drove home with a head spinning with thoughts and emotions. I recall chastising myself... '*Why did I call him Edison?*' I lamented that it may not take long before primary school peers learnt to tease him with the name 'Special Ed'. Later, I was delightfully disproven on this presupposition. Over the years, in the main, Edison's peers were more supportive than many adults in his life. Upon arrival at special education, I nearly vomited with emotional turmoil controlling my gut. Sandra, who ran the pre-prep group was extremely, professional and empathetic. She and her staff were skilled and went above and beyond in educating their students. I had no rational basis upon which to justify my conflicting emotions. Eventually, Eddie left special education and whilst I was sad to bid farewell to supportive staff, I was pleased to leave that system.

As a teacher in Mackay many years earlier, I took on a few extra roles, as teachers do. I was the verse-speaking teacher, the Aboriginal and Torres Strait Islander homework coordinator and the union representative. In the union role, I was to represent union views to staff and staff views to the union. I had always been interested in politics and I was excited about the union rep role. When I had attended university for the first time, I ordered copies of major political party policies. At no cost to me, wads of paper (in pre-internet days) were posted to me. I had contacted the three dominant political parties with an objective of determining which party I would actively support. I read each and every document. The policies of the two major parties were almost identical in my opinion, and I preferred at the time, the democrats' policies and thus became a member of their party. At one point, I ventured on a two-night young democrats conference held in Canberra. It was a positive learning experience, including individual lessons offered by Kerry O'Brien on mastering the role of being the interviewee during political interviews. On the journey home, I learned more than I had anticipated about politics. I was the driver of a borrowed senator's car, traveling with three, strong-minded, male, young democrat passengers. A long, open, straight road unfolded, golden canola flowers glistening on each side. It was a gloriously clear and sunny, winter day. The speed limit was 100 kilometres per hour and the car in front was travelling at 80 kilometres per hour towing a caravan. I made the decision to overtake the car in front, seeing a truck on the horizon about one kilometre ahead oncoming in the opposite lane. My passengers began to debate the action that my indicator signalled. I clearly intended to overtake and they called for a vote as to whether it was safe to overtake or not. That was democracy gone mad, in my humble opinion. I switched lanes for the time required to pass the car ahead of us safely, counting out loud to 15 before the oncoming truck passed us in the opposite lane. Democracy which doesn't understand the importance of leadership is not my style of politics. I was the leader as the driver of the car, for that role and that moment. The leader of the democrat party at the time was Cheryl Kernot. Although she was an astute leader and one of the first professional women who inspired me, my life as a democrat was short lived.

Taking on the role of union representative as a teacher, I expected to be an advocate *for* teachers to the education department via the union. Being young and naïve, I learned union traffic travelled, in the main, one way. The traffic ushered union agendas to staff, to media and to politicians. Messages and requests of teachers never, it seemed, flowed back to the union. I held a junior position, and perhaps I simply didn't know what I didn't know. In this position of prospective advocacy, I attended a course at Great Kepple Island entitled *'How to Represent your Union and Your Staff'*. A mother spoke at one of the keynotes about her fight to have her autistic daughter attend mainstream school. During the early 1990s, teaching was a tough enough gig. Ignorantly, I had a mind-set which rejected the notion of adding special needs children to mainstream schooling. Warming my island conference room seat, I was at best sceptical as I waited to hear what this mother had to say. Not a dry eye could be seen when she finished her brave keynote. Still having never met a special needs child in my early 20s and knowing there were no known special relatives in my family tree, I was surprised at the impact this woman and her message had on me. Of course, if her crusade succeeded (which it did), I would have special kids in my classrooms. I expected that the impact would stop there and affect my professional life only. I never imagined this lady's speech, her plight and her passion would over a decade later, fuel my own plight and advocacy for a society which included the Edisons from all walks of life. This lady helped to pave the way for me. She helped my son, his sisters, his teachers, his peers and their parents for generations to come. She inspired my resilience and advocacy. I trust my system-focused fights have made the journey for others who walk in similar shoes easier. We all need role models to assist in navigating foreign circumstances.

The year following the Great Kepple island keynote, I had three special needs children in my classroom of 24 five-year-olds. The three weren't as disabled as my son to be. My not-typically developing students were quirky. I did not perceive them as any more challenged nor any more special than my other students. They were certainly differently challenged, but I didn't think of them as odd – hence claiming (inaccurately, as I feel now), that Ed was the first special kid I met. ASD is a spectrum. Normal or just plain special, is also a spectrum. We live in spectrums – skinny to fat, sporty to not so sporty, musically gifted to those like me, vestibular issues to I-can-walk-a-type-rope… Life with Edison taught me that our differences are far richer than I had once assumed. With the introduction of mainstreaming special children, the Education Department provided four hours (in total) of teacher aide time a week. I came to experience many complications involved in teaching special and typically developing kids, side-by-side in a single classroom. I was surprised that no additional funding nor support came forth from the government for the diagnosed special kids nor their peers whose education would likely be compromised. They were trying times, juggling a new classroom formula – but it was manageable. I learned a decade or so later that Ed was a more difficult student to manage than my quirky past students. There were moments during my time teaching when I relied upon humour to get through the day. Sometimes the children provided a giggle for me. The first day of teaching year one, a young lady raised her hand to comment on my nose ring (now long gone!).

"Miss Ginn, you look like a bull."
"How so, Jamie?"
"My dad has a bull with a ring in his nose. I'm going to ask Dad to make the bull's a diamond one because your stud looks prettier."

During my short teaching career, the term 'special needs' introduced me to political correctness gone mad. This terminology became another place where I decided to foster humour as my chosen modus operandi. After being introduced to the politically correct term of 'non-typically developing child', and after Edison's diagnosis, I would introduce myself in educational settings as a non-typically developing parent. I think I was the only one who laughed but hey, some experiences needed lightening up. Indeed, I was a non-typically developing parent and I remain so today. There is much that goes under the radar and much we don't know about what goes on behind closed doors. Over time, Edison taught me that we are all *one of us* and *one of them*. Tolerance and an understanding of people's lives I could not relate to became something I began to actively foster.

Chapter 12
School Entry?

In 2006, it was time to begin interviewing with local primary schools which would suit the needs of all three children. My preference was for the local state school. Our local school had a swimming pool, abundant resources, was 250 metres down the road and attracted a mixed demographic. We lived in a fairly affluent suburb and it was important to me that my children were exposed as much as possible, to a mix of high, medium and lower income earners; people of different ethnic backgrounds and a variety of belief systems. I wanted my children's' school world to reflect as best as possible, the Australia they would become adults in and I didn't want them to be praised or criticised about the car they were dropped off in. The local state school was close to a train station which fed a diverse, multi-cultural school community. My husband and I interviewed with the relief (temporary) principal of our local state school. Our interview may not have been indicative of the school's culture, but it certainly demonstrated the relief principal's biases against inclusive education. His sister had suffered from cerebral palsy and he explained the terrible negative effects of attending the same school as her. In explaining how the teasing of his peers' and associated subsequent ostracism contributed to his suffering, he was a little self-absorbed. We were advised that Edison's basic needs would be met in the school but that his education would largely be ignored, as Ed was just too special to be included. Additionally, I was assured my daughters would suffer should they attend the same school as their brother. Years later, I learnt that the local state school was indeed positioned to provide a rich education for my children, but back then, after the local school interview I needed to investigate other options.

My geographically next closest alternative was the local Catholic school. I was Christian but not Catholic. I had issues with praying to dead people (saints) and could not stomach a patriarchal system which allowed men of the cloth to be a vehicle to forgive sins on behalf of God, thus claiming they had a status closer to God than the rest of us humans. The idea of being married to Jesus as a nun was so opposed to my understanding of Christianity that it was a huge leap to even consider a Catholic school education for my children. Neither my husband nor myself were Catholic, hence the chances of the school accepting us, I assumed were slim. Add to the mix acceptance of an autistic child, I felt successful enrolment was highly unlikely. I was obstinate in my view that the three children attend the same school. After all, at the age of four, Edison could spell big words and although he was on the spectrum, he also was gifted in certain areas. When properly motivated, he could count and perform all sorts of tricks most four-year-olds would find problematic. Not yet toilet trained and grossly immature in his social development, my rose-coloured glasses overlooked simple deficits. A little research conducted on the local Catholic school unveiled many positive attributes. The interview process with the local Catholic school impressed me and my biased attitude diluted into hope that we would be accepted.

Life was stressful, to say the least, but my business was doing well, the girls were blossoming and my husband was seemingly content in his life which played out parallel to mine. As the new plan for our little family unfolded, reality began to appear bearable. Living was made more tolerable by my modern day 'mother's little helper'. My choice of support was wine, chardonnay, to be specific. I would manage through the trials of the day, momentous dinners, bath time, storybook, song and prayer times before rewarding myself with a glass or two of vino. Dinnertime was especially stressful for a number of reasons. I had it in my wee-mind that dinnertime should be a peaceful family gathering, as it had been throughout my childhood. (That awful *should* word again!). In the family I had now formed, dinner rarely eventuated as a joyful, nor a conflict-free experience. Edison refused not only to have certain food on his plate; additionally he would instinctively gag or vomit if an item such as broccoli was on the plate of a family member sitting beside him. Adding to the stress, Edison did not allow edible items to touch one another with the exception of spaghetti bolognaise. The occupational therapy involved in teaching Edison to use cutlery was another nightly hurdle. Ed's father found Edison's meal demands and my resistance to our son's demands overwhelmingly stressful. Given our circumstances, dinnertime was anything other than family bliss or a positive moment shared. I assumed at the time, that my husband treasured similar happy 1970s dinner memories from his own upbringing. He had a right to be confronted and cranky. The fact that I did not lower my standards, my expectations and my hopes regarding family dinners, likely did not help.

My life choices remained governed by looming certainty that Edison would one day grow into an adult much taller and stronger than I. I was determined that Edison be included in all our family activities. Paradoxically, I did all I could to prevent Eddie from becoming *one of them*. Top of mind was that Francesca and Freya-Grace would grow to be adults too. All three children deserved loving sibling and parent relationships. Playing heavy on my heart were initiatives I could peruse to avoid the possibility of my girls becoming carers for their brother. I did not want Edison's warm relationship with his sisters to become a hierarchical, responsibility-based role. Hence, I never participated in activities which excluded Ed's involvement. I attempted to fashion a tight unit, centred on family, not autism. In my endeavours to ensure Eddie wasn't considered as a social outcast, I discovered inclusion and exclusion are not antonyms. My inclusion value demanded that I exclude activities in our lives which rejected autistic people… I reduced our life experiences to only involve opportunities where Edison could contribute and be accepted. In my mind, our special needs' family journey was a two-way street; we all needed to step up. I refused to use any *one of them* respite funding to relieve us of Edison. Relieving me of Edison (or Eddie of us) may have formed a roadblock in the path to forgoing deeper love and understanding in our family unit. No counselling nor respite time away could scratch the surface of what I was trying to build. My husband didn't think the same way. It must have been challenging to be married to such an obstinate individual as I.

One year after buying the Wooloowin home, we decided to put a swimming pool in the back yard. We had a close friendship with our back neighbours in so much that we constructed a gate to adjoin our bordering back yards. The gate was used regularly on weekends to access afternoon drinks and was used more often by our six collective offspring, for play. Our neighbours were kind in allowing earth moving machinery access to our back yard, via their yard to construct our swimming pool. Before the Brisbane City Council would allow a pool to be filled with water, we needed to obtain a pool safety certificate. I remember the day the safety inspector visited. As he certified the pool as safe, we watched four-year-old Edison climb the pool fence, no props needed, plying himself safely on the other side of the fence. Ed proved the local pool safety council regulations weren't good enough for our family. With Ed unable to swim, yet positioned on the waterside of the fence, I received my pool safety certificate. I needed my own version of security with my pool and understandably, I didn't trust the paper certificate. As such, the day after we filled the swimming pool with water, I stayed home from work, and Edison did not attend day care. Single-minded in ensuring that my boy would be pool-safe by the end of the day, I drilled, trained and taught my son. By morning tea, Ed could make his way to the edge of the pool independently and use the stairs or the shallow ledge which ran along one side of the pool as a safe island. By lunchtime, he could paddle a lap. After lunch, I dressed him in jeans, boots, a long sleeve shirt and a heavy jacket and we practised water safety drills. By the time Eddie and I were ready to pick the girls up from school and day care, Edison was pool-safe, even whilst wearing weighty boots and clothing. Eddie was a bath-time, water-loving baby at birth. Our swimming pool confirmed that water was a preferred element in Edison's self-soothing.

As school selection progressed, I attempted to occasionally rouse some kind of personal social life. 2007 was the year of my 20-year high school reunion. It was a fun night and it was pleasantly surprising to see how easily old school friends picked up from a couple of decades of almost no contact. There was a man at the reunion whom I did not recognise. He was wheel chair bound and was being pushed by an older lady. It seemed the man could not speak and I asked the wheel chair pusher who he was.

"*David Lee,*" I was told. Jan, who was pushing the chair, was David's mother. She asked if I was friends with him back in our high school days. David Lee had been a prefect and he hung out with the good kids, the academic kids, the straight kids, many of them also the Christian kids. I could have formed myself quite easily into being a part of that peer group. In the main, they were kind, decent people. Becoming part of that friendship group never eventuated. After being bullied during my first year of high school for being a little nerdy, I turned to a less academic crowd. Ironically, the girl who was the lead bully ended up being the school captain in my senior year. My early teen choices were not based on wisdom and were fed by a lack of self-confidence. With a focus on fitting in, education had no place in my teenage hierarchy of needs. An avoidance of bullying became a diversion which dominated some of my life's less than optimal choices. I was not David's friend in high school. I wasn't a mean girl, just a survivor... David Lee's mother explained to me how David came to his injury. He was in his final year of studying medicine when a horse riding accident occurred, rendering him an almost paraplegic with an acquired brain injury. I asked David's mum, Jan, whether any school peers or university friends were active in David's life. As we chatted, I learnt that no one continued to be involved in David's life other than his family. All David's friends had dropped off – every single one. They made efforts early on and then maybe, they became busy. I made a commitment to Jan that night that I would visit David and we swapped telephone numbers.

I called Jan the following week and learned that the Acquired Brain Injury Centre where David spent his weekdays was only a 50-minute return drive from my Wooloowin home. Jan told me which days she visited, which days David had water therapy and so forth. Together, we set about agreeing a fortnightly visiting schedule which would coincide with a day when David had nothing else on. I agreed to the schedule with good intentions, completely ignorant of what I was to undertake. I anticipated conversation was going to be tough visiting a person who could not speak. David and I shared no memories and I didn't know his family. I didn't know him. The extent of his communication was facial expressions, laughter, indecipherable noises and a slight raise of the left hand up for '*yes*' and down for '*no*'. My children were young and without prejudice. The visits were not confronting for them. My first visit to the Acquired Brain Injury Centre was challenging, to say the least. It was clear upon arrival that this was a place few children visited. Some more able patients were allowed outside, unsupervised in the courtyard entrance. Patients' eyes lit up as they watched my children bustling one another to gain entrance to the centre. My children billowed through the gate, carrying props of trains, dolls and balls – hand in hand with innocence. Upon our first visit, I reported to reception and was greeted with quizzical curiosity as to who I was visiting and why.

"No, I'm not a former friend, I'm a former acquaintance. I went to school with David."
"Then what is the purpose of your visit?"
"Kindness."

Years later, Jan informed me that the nursing staff thought I had some kind of odd crush on David. I wore a wedding ring at the time. It is beyond me how anyone could draw that conclusion. Our first visit was relatively short, around 30 minutes, an excruciatingly long half hour. I felt physically sick seeing a tall, once handsome, intelligent, capable man now unable to feed himself and unable to manage almost all his bodily functions independently. During the drive home, the children and I discussed our Acquired Brain Injury Centre visit. My children were upbeat and positive, declaring, *"We can't believe David's real friends don't visit him."*

The journey to the Acquired Brain Injury Centre was always daunting, yet the visitations remained a priority. Driving to see David, I'd summon my mind to draw upon stories and day-to-day events which I could talk with him about. On several occasions, I took David out so that he could experience nature which was a complete contrast to the clinical hospital-style room in which he lived. Imagine a mum with three children under six-years of age (and Edison's escapee ways), pushing in a wheel chair an over six-foot-tall, almost paraplegic man cross-country… There were scary moments when I was forced to choose whether to chase my runaway toddler, or risk having David left with my young daughters as his temporary carers. As it turned out during each outdoor adventure, Ed enjoyed his escapism and David remained safe, never having to rely on my daughters. I now realise that I took on more on those visits, than maybe was sensible. Thankfully, my heart was in the right place and the outcomes were always positive. The drives home from visiting David became joyous as I realised that he treasured his time with us, and that the another-side-of-life exposure I was providing to my children would grow them emotionally. I was revealing to them a world right next door, which most of us choose to ignore. Putting a positive and caring spark in David's day was worth the effort, for him and for us. The visits also grounded me in the fortunes that my life provided.

Perhaps my tendency to show care for others was founded in my Christian upbringing. My childhood home was often full of all sorts of different characters who my parents supported. I remember feeling a little cool when my parents hosted a bunch of men overnight in the lounge and their eight Harley Davidsons in our driveway. During my early years of parent-hood, I reached out to others when I could and sporadically attempted church attendance. A memorable conversation took place during a service conducted at the church associated with my husband's new work place. I sat warming church pews with my children and no father present, waiting for an unfamiliar Catholic service to begin. My young children were interested in the new experience. As we waited for the commencement of the service, Freya-Grace, then three years of age, asked me whether God had turned up yet. I explained that God was everywhere.

"Is he in the pretty coloured windows?"

"Well, perhaps he inspired them." The data projector turned on, providing the congregation an order of service.

"Is that big screen God, Mama?"
"No, sweety, that's just a data projector telling us what's about to happen."
"What's about to happen?"
"Church."
"Does God have skin?"
"I don't think so, hon, but I don't really know."

"If he's everywhere, then why haven't you been able to see if he has skin or not?"

"Well, I can't actually see God." Pause.

"Does God have blood and guts like us?"

"I doubt it, sweetie. There are just some things I don't know."

"I hope he doesn't have blood and guts, because if he doesn't have skin, there would be mess everywhere and he'd have nothing to hold his guts in."

Introducing children to a connection with their spiritual side is perhaps better done via demonstrating care in action than warming a church pew.

I remained conscious that regardless of the adult height Ed would reach, he would be physically stronger than me before he reached his teens. This encouraged me to only ever discipline (apart from the Brookfield Road incident), with words, tone of voice and body language. My teaching experience had well equipped me for this approach. As a teacher of primary school children who needed a hug, encouragement or soothing, I had learnt to modulate my voice to impart care. Touching one's students was not allowed. There were times as a teacher when yelling or hitting-out as a response to obstinance, disobedience or rudeness was a natural urge. Following through on this urge was not allowed nor was a hug when my heart urged me to provide a hug. I had learned not to become the yelling, hitting teacher and subsequently this discipline became a positive aspect of my parenting style. My teaching experience taught me that a quiet teacher voice proved to be more effective discipline than a loud, fear inducing tone. That professional experience taught that I could effectively express love, discipline and care without physical contact. Thank goodness, I was allowed to hug and encourage my offspring and provide them nurturing touch. Once my children ventured into their teens, I aptly applied basic communication such as active listening and attendance to body language to show care when a hug was not any longer going to help. Ed's father and I differed in our discipline and care approach. We often locked heads as a result. There was little in our life that ran smoothly, yet we did our best to provide fun family times, including the year we were Sea World members.

Even those outings though, were not drama-free and inadvertently reminded us that we were not a typically developing family.

Back when there was a suggestion that Eddie might have Mosaic Downs, I learned that Downs' kids often have an IQ ceiling. Although it was difficult coming to terms with Eddie potentially having Mosaic Downs, I found comfort in his IQ trajectory being limited and predictable. I was comforted somewhat to learn that if raised with love, it is likely that people who have Downs live fulfilling lives and often grow to become extremely loving individuals. Once Ed was diagnosed on the spectrum, the internet revealed to me that it was possible that Ed might be severely intellectually disabled – alternatively he could be savant-like gifted. In the autism world, we talk about spikes in abilities. Early paediatric and other expert predictions for Ed's seemingly unquestionable lack of ability to ever live independently, let alone self-toilet, may have been realistic yet they may also have been completely wrong. I learned that many world-changing leaders and major contributors in invention, art, music and politics, were also deemed to have been autistic. I contemplated which end of the genius versus not-so-capable spectrum, did Ed sit within? This wrestle in my mind was un-relenting and I questioned myself whether my most important role with Ed would be to influence change and challenge him.

Competing with this thinking was a motherly love to simply foster Eddie's happiness and accept an unknown nor understood ceiling. With Edison's potential a mystery, where was I to invest my autism-focused energy? In selecting a school, I felt angst in holding the keys to more therapy doors than I could afford, nor had time to open. Determining which options to pursue which may or may not assist in Ed's growth continued to be confusing and mentally draining. Daily balancing a happy-mediocre Ed, with a potentially world-changing brilliant Ed, proved a conundrum. I did not need or want Ed to be a prodigy. Equally, I was content to love and attend to a less able Eddie. I opened myself to being a parent who provided opportunities for Edison to grow into a Rain Main like savant, should this be his destiny. Determining my child's potential and what I needed to do to nurture this potential, was an endless struggle which competed with my ignorance of the extent of his disability. In time, Eddie taught me that my focus needed to be purely focused on loving, educating and accepting my beautiful boy.

Resoundingly, I was strongly encouraged to use respite time to have a stranger look after Ed whilst the rest of us could experience a normal life (as *one of us*). What would be normal about leaving Edison with a stranger? There are people like the resilient David, who keep going and showing the care (which he is able to express), whilst wheel chair bound. As resilient and disabled as David is, no one will argue that he truly requires and deserves government-funded institutionalised care. There are families where autism is such a mammoth challenge that leaving one's ASD kid in care whilst the rest of the family re-groups, is a healthy choice. Fortunately, Ed's challenges gave me respite choices and when I could include Edison, I always would. Never once did I capitulate to rejecting Edison from our family. I added *inclusion* to our family values. I now fight for inclusion, independence, encouragement, co-operation and kindness where the values our family can demonstrate such ideals. It's tiring, this fighting. I fight too much but there's always more fight left in me. I accept too little... We can only do our best with the tool-kit we have at any particular time. I am still being educated, enlightened and empowered. I still, at times fail.

Chapter 13
A Challenged Marriage

Marriage is hard work, as it requires constant re-adjustment of one's views and behaviour to accommodate our chosen spouse. Children add another dimension to necessary modifications. Optimally, parenting within marriage requires that parents come to agreement on rules, discipline, family values and priorities. Add ASD into this mix, marriage becomes infinitely more complex, perhaps because there are so many unknown or unpredictable and unexpected challenges. There are many couples who are able to meet such challenges whilst raising an ASD child with grace. Such couples admirably manage to hold together a functioning and successful family unit. However, I am not alone in ASD becoming a straw that assisted to break my marriage. The early years of working through Ed's head banging, scratching, poo smearing and involuntary vomiting as a response to anything new or confronting were hard-hitting. There are no villains in my marital breakdown. There are two people who didn't manage to hold all the balls up in the air, when there were simply, for us, too many to balls to juggle with the lack of tools and support we had available.

My choice of wine to ease the pain went on over the years to become a nemesis. It was a slow demise from a couple of glasses to relax and unwind, to becoming a person who abused the substance for a time, after my work-life fell apart in 2016. I wouldn't say I ever became an alcoholic. Some-how I functioned exceedingly well. I am not proud that I drank more than what was healthy as I battled my various crises, via self-medication. My wine consumption worked for me in the short term. It was readily accessible, controllable and non-destructive to the kids. Additionally, wine was exceedingly affordable being less costly than prescription medicine and it could be enjoyed in privacy and without the burden of therapy. Most of my friends who were mothers of young children, behaved similarly to me by waiting until their kids were in bed, for their 'reward'. At that time, Australia boasted number three within the OECD world, in per-capita drinking ranks. I wasn't on my own. Time-consuming coping mechanisms such as exercise, yoga and psychological therapy or counselling were all beyond me with everything I had to manage. There was simply too much on my plate. Time was the one currency where choice was severely restricted. I also perceived that I had no alcohol related problem. Seeking help for a fictionally perceived problem, would have been ridiculous. Clearly, the motivations behind my priorities centred around my family unit and I neglected to acknowledge for a long time, that part of the focus of building a healthy family required that I treat myself well.

Following on from our not so positive experience investigating the local state school, I was pleased to learn the Catholic school, Holy Cross, had accepted us. When my husband told me that the Catholic school served wine at their welcoming event for new families, I decided Catholics might not be so bad after all. I write this tongue in cheek. I have friends who are Catholic, atheist or agnostics and others who subscribe to differing spiritual beliefs or religions. I do not judge others' spiritual beliefs, so it was acceptable for me to embrace a school that purported denominational beliefs that differed from my own. The principal of Holy Cross at the time of our acceptance had recently abolished the special unit in favour of inclusion of special kids within mainstream classrooms. During the interview process, I overcame my nervousness by being forthright and standing strong on my values, standards and pedagogy. I made it clear that if the school would not accept Edison the year after Francesca began schooling, we would find another school for Francesca. As such, the school evaluated both Francesca and Edison as part of the enrolment evaluation for my eldest. I was elated when the children were accepted. The school enrolled no more than 300 students and I soon learned that the school fostered a warm and considerate community. Pleasingly, I found that it is easy to settle into a new school when your child starts in prep with other new-to-the-school parents, amongst established school parents.

During the years that my children attended Holy Cross, each and every year I hosted a birthday party for each of my kids inviting every child in each of their school-class. We had a grand home in need of costly renovations we could not afford. Never-the-less our house layout lent itself to entertainment. The parties were frequent and I became close friends with many of the Holy Cross parents. Most enjoyed their wine and by and large I felt accepted. Only one of Eddie's peers ever invited him for a play (on the condition that I tagged along), and he was never once in his life invited to a classmate's birthday party. Yet we were welcome, as a family at a few people's homes. I enjoyed getting to know people in my home which provided comfort without upsetting friends' children when Ed was around. I tried not to take a lack of reciprocal invitations from the majority, as rejection. I certainly appreciated and enjoyed the two families which hosted us in their homes.

I made two big mistakes as a mother, at that school. The first mistake was to be honest with Francesca's prep teacher over one particular incident. Francesca had been acting-out at school and responsibly the teacher called me in for a meeting. Things were not pleasant on the home front and often Francesca wore the brunt of her father's anger. Daily, Francesca would apologise for whatever childish misdemeanour she had performed never being granted her father's forgiveness. She loved her father but it was very difficult for her to please him. At times, when Edison exhibited extreme autistic behaviour around his dad, the result was akin to pouring oil on a fire. Eventually through circumstances which do not need to be disclosed, I learned I could not leave the children alone at home with their father. In the meeting with Francesca's prep teacher, I had the choice of labelling my child unstable in some way or divulging the truth that things were not rosy on the home front – and our home life was affecting Francesca's emotional stability. I opted for the truth. The school nun was then brought in as counsel. The nun was a sweet and sincere lady who had absolutely no idea how to support us nor any understanding of the family dynamics we faced. Her 'help' became another burden to carry.

My second big mistake was being honest with the counsellor nun one afternoon. Bundling three kids into the car during school pick-up, she stopped me abruptly and asked how I was going. I decided to work with her offer of care and potential support and be honest. *"I'm stressed, completely over the school going on about inclusion and not actioning it. I am tired and I need to get three kids home and cook dinner… Thanks for asking and providing no practical support!"* My emotional and invited outburst could have been worded with more consideration, yet an outburst doesn't generally employ a pause-and-think play button. The next day, I was instructed to attend the principal's office. I was accustomed to principal-hosted meetings, involving a minimum ratio of 5 of them to one of me. Of the hundreds of meetings I attended with the school regarding Edison, this was my husband's second. I was severely scolded for expressing to the nun the issues I had shared and at the same time, I was berated for not sharing my concerns directly with the school. The fact that I had raised my lack-of-inclusion qualms politely, verbally and in writing several times, was not acknowledged. The tirade, discipline and criticism school administrative staff fired at me brought me to tears. I do not break easily. I was pleasantly surprised when my husband stepped up and defended me and advocated for the good fight I was trying to have with the school and not against the school. I almost learnt to shut my mouth. I certainly learnt not to speak with the nun.

Two weeks before I forced my husband to leave our marriage, my 4-year-old daughter opened my eyes. In addition to prayers, reading books and singing each of my children to sleep, on occasions that required it, I would often make up fantasy stories. On one particular night, our time around the family dinner table was oppressive. That night, we all cried except my then husband. As I tucked my youngest into bed following the routine of prayers, songs and reading, I made up a story for her. *"We are fairies. I am dressed in orange, my favourite colour, and you are dressed in blue, your favourite colour, and we are riding, flying on the back of butterflies with wings matching our favourite colours. We are flying towards a mountaintop to have a picnic of strawberries, mangoes and our favourite foods. We tell each other stories and laugh and play until sunset before we fly home and tuck ourselves into snug, warm beds."*

Freya-Grace looked up at me and said, *"You're so good at making everything feel right Mummy – so I have a story for you… We are all having dinner and you are in an orange dress and we are having dinner, and no one is crying."*

It hit me that my four-year-olds' comfort fantasy story created to soothe me was about a family who has dinner where no one cries. I was raising a broken family whilst married. I would not allow this situation to become my children's normal. I had decided earlier that year that if the marriage didn't take a serious turn for the better, then it would be over. I gave it until September. I didn't share this with my husband as I didn't want to play a game of threats. Instead, I beseeched him to enter marital counselling which he reluctantly agreed to. That was a waste of time as he wasn't honest and painted me as an incapable alcoholic and himself as the perfect father and husband. Neither were true. During our marital counselling, I aired my dirty laundry because the stakes were high, and I really wanted our marriage to work. I figured feeding the counsellor lies would prevent healing. My truth though, didn't help her to help us. At that time, I remained the main income earner. Even though my husband worked school hours, he never dropped the kids at school nor picked them up and he was verbally, emotionally and physically abusive. I was still enjoying my mother's little helper at night but by no means was I in danger with alcohol at the time. From the counsellor's perspective, I was the she-devil and he was the long-suffering, perfect husband and father. The counsellor took a liking to my spouse and devoured his stories hook, line and sinker. The counselling, which was clearly unproductive, ceased.

My marriage to my children's father may not have lasted a decade had I not been married once before. Once upon a time, I was determined to not be a two times divorcee (nor ever a divorcee). In my mid-20s, I was married for 12 weeks to a man who had achieved a black-belt in karate. He was 9 years older than me and I felt I was marrying a real man. I was young and stupid. It was during the honeymoon (for want of a better term) that I learnt my first husband's dabbling in marijuana was an addiction and he coupled with that, addictions to pornography and booze. I am very anti-porn. I also wasn't a huge drinker and I didn't smoke pot. I soon learned we didn't have as much in common as I'd initially been led to believe. After the honeymoon, one evening during a party, he became very abusive. At some point, we left the party and arrived home. I was tired and unaware that he was in fight mode. While sitting on the toilet, I verbally defended myself from a tirade of his insults. My verbal self-defence resulted in receiving the side of his black-belt karate foot, slashing my nose and cheek. His onslaught of violence continued a while before I escaped behind a locked bathroom door with a mobile phone in hand. I called my folks. During the phone call to my parents, Dad asked me to look into the mirror and tell him what I saw. I explained my face was covered in blood and that my leg and abdomen hurt. Dad questioned whether he should be calling an ambulance before he and my mother packed their bags on what was to become a far too regular rescue mission. My mind was not stable. I asked them to come to me and I stayed barricaded in the bathroom. *'Breathe in, breathe out...'*

At the time, I wasn't aware the police had been called by my parents, but it was somewhat comforting to hear their knock on the bathroom door. Upon attendance, the police coaxed me from the bathroom before informing me that it was not within their power to remove either one of us from our home. The then husband was coerced to leave and not long after my parents arrived to support me, in the middle of the night. At the breakfast table the next day, my father announced that my marriage was over. I argued that I had stood before God only 12 weeks earlier and had sworn my marital vows before my creator. Dad was convinced that I wasn't in the kind of marriage that God would condone and within days, I was living alone in a rental in Spring Hill. I find this aspect of my history embarrassing. Not many people know I've been married twice. It is not a thing to boast of. I declared to myself, *'If you ever get married again, Jillian, you must make it work.'* I passionately wanted to be a mother and to my thinking, a second marriage was therefore not off the table. A second failed marriage though, was not an option in my young mind.

Between my decisions to try super-hard on my real marriage – marriage number two, I wrote poetry to my husband and beseeched him to give our relationship the best he had. I more than once went down on my knees before him and begged him to treat the children and I as well and respectfully as he did the students and staff at the school that employed him. I pleaded, *"If you won't love us, then could you at least please be kind?"* Kindness became a further consolidated value. Independence, inclusion, kindness, co-operation and respect became a parenting mantra… With these values in abundance, surely life would be grand? My poems and pleadings directed towards my children's father fell on deaf ears. Perhaps he saw me as plain pathetic with my beseeching. My low sense of worth was transparent. He certainly contributed to my lack of self-respect, but he was not responsible for it. How I felt about me, was my responsibility.

As I saw the end of our marriage clearly written on the wall, I reduced my alcohol intake, bought a special reading light and began each night after the children were tucked into bed, setting about reading the bible. I guess I was searching… I was pleased with my grown-up behaviour in the face of the tragedy of my marriage falling apart. I gathered strength and recognised my need to follow through with the plan of separation. I don't think the bible helped at the time, but I think discipline in living and exercising responsible routines assisted. My plan was to make it through another couple of weeks – to when my husband would be on long service leave. I wanted to give him time to adjust when he wouldn't have to front up to work after being informed of the end of our marriage. I had organised the downstairs granny flat of a nearby friend for my ex to stay in until he found his feet. I specifically chose to be caring and protective towards the father of my children. I aimed to be one of those divorced couples who meet together with new happy families in a park for birthdays and special occasions. I wanted to become the single parents who actioned shared care; just how John Howard imagined it. John Howard is a former Australian Prime Minister who courageously advocated for father's equal rights and made shared care the norm for split families.

One heated night, two weeks before my husband's long service leave and the planned execution of my separation announcement, I faced my husband yelling at me at around 6:30. My husband had been out all day. He had begun his day venturing out on a one-hour journey on a $7000 bicycle which we could not afford. Later that morning, he returned home cranky about something that happened during his ride. Next, fresh, exercised and showered, he headed back out of his home to escape his family and hand out election how-to-vote cards. He arrived back briefly to yell at me as the TomTom GPS couldn't instruct him on where to go. Soon, my children's father stormed off again as I handed him a paperbound UBD book of maps to follow. When he was angry, negativity seemed to permeate the entire home. With my heart on the floor, noticing the children afraid, I put on some favourite music to cheer us all up. I cooked breakfast attempting to instil as much happiness as I could after a sad and stressful start to the day. Picking up the pieces was always tiresome, but that morning brought me close to my breaking point. The children displayed various responses to their father's nastiness. My eldest often blamed herself, my youngest was resilient and Edison became more autistic (if that's a thing). It was a busy day, and by 6:00 pm, with three children fed and bathing, I was ready to pack in the day as soon as our bedtime routine was completed. It was around that time that my husband came home and declared we all needed to get ready for movie night. Movie night involved lots of popcorn and a massive data projected to screen, and was often enjoyed on weekends.

I had already told the kids that it was going to be an early night for us all. They were content with this. Their father though was not content. I explained to him upon his arrival that I did not have the energy for movie night. He suggested I go to bed so he could do movie night with the kids alone. I exclaimed, *"Seriously? What about the children's safety?"* I asked what would happen when Edison decided to be autistic. We both knew autism and Ed's father were not a great combination. As the discussion heated, I implored my husband to support me and I explained that the kids were already primed to be tucked into bed early. *"Please just let this go…"* In a fog of drying kids clean from a bath and dressing them in pyjamas, I muttered to my husband, *"Can't you see this isn't working?"*

"What's not working?"

"Us. You and me. We're just not working. Can't you see it?" I was calm. I was exhausted. He had fight in him.

"What do you want, bitch?"

It spilled out of me. I wasn't supposed to declare myself for two more weeks and not like this…

"I want a divorce as of now. I don't want a separation. I want a divorce. As of now, I am a single mum. You have until 8:00 to leave. If you are still here, I'll call the police."

Holy dooly, did I just say that? Wow! I gave him 90 minutes to get out. That was a long 90 minutes. I set about putting the children to bed and packing my husband's essentials between prayers, songs and stories. I told him that I had arranged accommodation with neighbours and that he could stay with friends if he didn't like the neighbour idea. I offered to make phone calls for him, while demanding that he absolutely must leave. Confronting and emotionally charged initial protests and denial ensued before he left. I was quite brave taking this on a six-foot-two-inch, 120 kg bench-pressing, angry and broken spouse. I guess he wasn't the only one in the picture who was angry and broken.

My husband was back the next day, begging to be reinstated. In February that year (six months earlier), I had purchased tickets for two adults and three children to see the stage show 'Mama Mia'. Edison loved music as such we planned to attend the musical for his birthday. I booked a matinee show, especially selecting a back-aisle so that I could dance with Ed without disturbing others, should Ed not be able to sit still through the ABBA inspired musical. Half a year ago, upon paying for the tickets, my husband insisted that he was not interested in joining the family for the play. As such, I had invited my mother to attend the show with us in celebration of Edison's sixth birthday. My parents arrived from Toowoomba the morning we were to see Mama Mia (the day after I had declared my marriage was over). My father was extremely sick with cancer, undergoing another round of chemotherapy and was content to stay and read newspapers while listening to ABC radio in our sun room whilst Mum, the kids and I headed off to Southbank for the musical. My husband arrived at our home soon after we left and stayed in the house until we returned home. Apparently, not a word was spoken between my Dad and my ex for the entire time we were gone… an odd hold-up of sorts.

Returning home from Mama Mia, I was confronted by my husband who was vehement in his refusal to accept our separation. I stood steadfast in my decision to end the marriage. For about an hour, my husband pleaded, he begged, he cried; just as I had for a decade. At the time, my father was crippled with Multiple Myeloma (cancer of the skeletal system). After decades of ill health, standing his tallest, my father no longer reached my

167 centimetres in height. Amongst pending chaos, slowly, Dad raised himself off the sofa and stood face to chest with his son-in-law, calmly ordering him to leave. My ex didn't give in easily but by nightfall, he was gone. What a mess. I didn't get married to get a divorce. Again, life wasn't co-operating with my plan. I worked towards and hoped for a stress free divorce; a miracle not bestowed on me. Over years, high emotions and drama abounded while I summoned the strength towards an acceptance of events I could not control. I repeated inwardly, mantra-like, *'Accept what's going on'.* It was a long time before I came to terms with my failed marriage and our failed attempts of shared parenting.

Chapter 14
Single Mum 101

August 30, 2009, I was a single mum. It was so very hard being married. Surely, this newfound singledom was going to be fun and easy... Initially, I felt invincible; no one could take me down. The first six months or so after separating, my husband was either in Cairns or someplace else and he sporadically contacted us. I paid his credit card and phone bills, foolishly predicting financial support may pave a way towards divorce peace. He saw the children a few times for an hour or two in those early months and Pink's music became my friend. The kids and I would boogie, and I did everything I could to be a super-mum and give them the best possible experiences I could provide. It's incredible how at different chapters in life, music helps to heal by matching our emotional rhythms. Some music that resonated with me during this period, included *'I Get Knocked Down, But I Get Up Again'*, *'I Will Survive'*, *'So What'*, and for some reason *'Son of a Preacher Man'*. Music and dance strengthened positive energy. Edison was more content than I'd seen him since the cloud of autism had set upon him. He and our now family of four, were content and initially we adjusted well. When my ex took the marital bed, the children and I delighted in using the replacement floor-bound mattress as an indoor trampoline. The girls and I hollered and danced to music while Ed flapped, swaggered and jumped. We were the ages of 38, 7, 6 and 4 and we became quite the song and dance, bedroom troop.

When my ex decided to settle back into Brisbane, the time for division of our belongings loomed. I packed up all our possessions which I thought were rightfully now his. I piled into the sunroom, boxes of gifts that I had bought for him over the past decade, along with the few items he had brought into the relationship. I ensured wedding guests' presents from his side were in his bundle along with ample linen and of course his clothing. We then arranged a day where the kids would be in care or school and when I would be at work, so that my ex-husband could collect his packed items, along with anything else he wanted. I didn't want to be around that day as I was resolute that furniture and other belongings which had been lovingly purchased together, would not become a source of conflict.

There was only one piece he took which was justifiably mine and it irked me that he claimed it. I believe to this day, that he seized that item to spite me and it worked. If he hadn't have taken this prized possession, it would be burnt now anyhow (given the way my life panned out). Today, I harbour zero spite with regards to belongings or anything related to that man... The piece in question which I felt he stole was a fish light. An odd thing to covet, one may think. Before children, I had won an award from Microsoft for exceptional performance and the prize awarded was an all-expenses paid three-day trip for two to anywhere in Australia of my choice. Launceston in Tasmania was the chosen destination. Over many years, I had developed a ritual of purchasing art from every location I visited. In Launceston, I stumbled across an incredible, metal-fabricated, prehistoric looking fish lamp which shed an impressive pattern of light. I won that trip and I chose that lamp. He shouldn't have taken it. I purchased other arty lamps and set my mind to a positive future.

When I was confidant to explain to Edison that Dad was never going to live with us again, Eddie stopped wetting his bed and running away. This extraordinary change in Ed's behaviour, which I had fought to overcome for years, arrived overnight. There were many positive social and emotional changes we subsequently experienced. Most remarkable was the change in Edison's improved ability to accommodate change. He settled easily to bed and focused on his interests in coding, computers, The Wiggles, Hive Five, music in general and his favourite, Thomas the Tank Engine. The girls were also more settled, and tears became a rarity in the home. The children's quality of life undeniably improved when their father left. I believe none the less that the children and their father had a love for one another. It haunts me that Ed didn't mention his father for six years, but only one week before his death, I heard him muttering, *"Daddy.*

Daddy. See Daddy." Hearing this, I remembered the trauma the kids and I had experienced as a result of their father's cruelty. Listening to my son's murmuring, I was conflicted. I sought my father's advice yet again. I told my dad that Edison was potentially asking to see his father. Dad was strong in his stance and response. *"Stick with the court decisions. Those orders are there to protect you and the kids. If your children's father ever re-enters your lives, he needs to earn it. They can't have you reintroduce him on a whim. Respect the court orders, Jillian."*

Still, my mind wrestled with the notion of reconnecting Eddie with his father. Ed's spoken vocabulary was limited and so it was difficult for him to express many of his intentions clearly. Ultimately, I submitted to my dad's advice. I purposefully ignored Ed's few dad-centred mumblings mitigating the risk of emotional pain for us all. I may have made the wrong decision. I certainly made a safe decision.

The joys of being single began to evaporate as my ex became nastier and nastier several months into our separation. This nastiness dragged on for many years. I had not expected the isolation I experienced as a single mum with three young kids, including one with pronounced special needs. My marriage had been rife with anger, but it was full. My single life, outside of expensive lawyers, necessary work and parental responsibilities became empty. Some interesting social nuances came as a surprise. As a married person, I had never separated my wedded friends from my single or divorced friends. I continued to host large and frequent social gatherings, but I felt alone. Several people going through stressful times would visit and sit at our kitchen island sipping tea or coffee, chatting away their trials, and less often, tribulations. Those interjections of company were welcome, yet my open-door policy was not reciprocated. Once single, I stopped being invited to other people's get-togethers and when I invited a family over, the father would most often not attend. I was thrown into a woman's social world. Thank goodness, my work in IT was male dominated. I have always enjoyed the company of men and my relative isolation would have been almost unbearable without my work.

In my endeavour to connect with community, I learnt about an organisation who took families with special needs children camping. My children were too young for me to attempt camping as the only adult present, and so I eagerly signed up. After missing months of agreed dad visits, the Friday morning which was scheduled for our first camp out night, the children's father called me. He informed that me he would arrive for his two hours a fortnight, that afternoon. I asked him to please wait until next week or choose a different day for the visit, explaining that because we hadn't heard from him for over a month, I had booked a camping trip. He denied my reasonable request. His lawyer telephoned me. Subsequently, I called the happy camper group and cancelled our adventure. The children were extremely disappointed when dropped home by their father at 6:00 pm, to find that their camping weekend was not to be. The next day, we went shopping and purchased an outdoor furnace, marshmallows to toast and a bunch of camping gear. We set up a tent in the back yard that night and camped at home. It takes a little creativity at times to overcome disappointment.

With Edison's train obsession, many an outing was locomotive centred. There were regular visits to the Ipswich Train Museum, weekend steam train adventures and outings with other train aficionados. Train enthusiasts and friends, Pam and Daryl invited us to fun family days, riding little replica engines in the country. Fabulous memories were planted.

Once, back when we were a family of five, we attended a train expo at the Brisbane Exhibition Grounds. This proved to be a heavenly outing for Ed. By and large, the expo was dominated by retired engineers, sharing and exhibiting their expensive model trains and landscapes. One section of the expo was more child centric in displays and merchandise. A father and son team from Toowoomba had an impressive Thomas the Tank Engine display, and they also had many second-hand Thomas items for sale. I wanted to purchase everything they had on offer. New Thomas merchandise was expensive. Thomas paraphernalia provided a helpful teaching, communication and play aide for Ed. Observing Ed's clear obsession, the family kindly offered us the whole lot that they had for sale for a reasonable price. We drove home with boxes and boxes of tracks, sheds, engines, figurines, tunnels, sheep, carriages, books and DVD's which I could not possibly have afforded should they have been purchased at retail prices. I remain grateful for their generosity.

A few years later, we returned to the train expo shed, to attend the Royal Brisbane show, fondly referred to by locals as the Ekka. Edison's excitement was palpable as we approached the pavilion in which years ago, we had purchased so many of his loved Thomas toys, books and videos. As we entered, the pavilion now sheltering an exhibition of thousands of fowl, Eddie had a meltdown. Initially, I suspected the noise and stench of the birds may have set Eddie off. I quickly exited, noting Ed's limited verbal communication as he moaned, '*Thomas, Thomas, Thomas.*' At some point, I realised I had interpreted Eddie's stress inaccurately. Although I didn't initially recall the train expo from three years prior, held in that same location, Ed's photographic memory was intact. He was deeply distressed that there were no trains to see. His experience had taught him trains should be found in that shed, not chickens and geese.

In life, some people get lucky. I don't tend to be one who wins the raffle, spurious competitions or a predictable and tranquil life. Yet, I did get lucky once. I entered a competition when Eddie was eight-years-old, hoping to win a family pass to a Thomas, the Tank Engine stage show. In thirty words or less, I explained why our family deserved free tickets to the concert. I posted in the mail, a ditty describing how Ed had learnt his colours, numbers, geometry and a range of emotions from Thomas stories. We won! It was difficult to watch the stage during the performance, as Edison's lit up face was so much more entertaining. Thomas' eyes moved and he talked – all our friends were there, including The Fat Controller, sheep, Percy and even some of the baddies such as Diesel. Things don't get more real than that! There were many aspects of Ed's ASD which enriched our lives.

Autism also played a part in the seclusion of our family. Edison destroyed more than one child's prized Lego construction over the years. With the friends I had left, we learned that it was predictably safer to meet up at my place rather than theirs. I have an issue with modern day Lego kits. During my childhood, we had a massive bucket of Lego pieces and we would construct our own creations, allowing imaginations to run wild. Our constructions perhaps lasted a few days and no tears were shed when the pieces were returned to the Lego box. Today's Lego is instruction based, which has its own intrinsic value. As a nonconformist, I value imagination over instruction. I refuse to follow a cooking recipe for example. I will seek inspiration from recipes and pictures of delightfully presented food, but I will not follow someone else's instructions to the tee. Some would see this as a deficit in my personality. I accept this characteristic of slight rebellion as a part of who I am. A psychologist I saw for a few sessions once challenged me by suggesting that at 46 years of age, I should be able to follow some rules. She was likely correct. I do follow road rules and the law... Eight years after adjusting our lives to respect other children's Lego, with Edison no longer a problem for others, I am more predictably and reciprocally invited to friends' homes. It's sad to know that losing my only son, has allowed freedoms I would not have the opportunity to experience, should my beautiful boy still be with us.

Another problem Edison caused socially was theft. Experts expound that a key attribute of autism is a lack of theory of mind. In laymen's terms, this means that an autistic person necessarily lacks insight into the perspective of others. I disagree with this as a blanket claim. Edison didn't lack theory of mind. When the opportunity arose, he was sometimes a thief. He stole play dough from school and dinosaur figurines from cousins. Without theory of mind, Eddie's theft would have been difficult to detect. Edison, however, would often bury his stolen prizes deep in my handbag and when discovered, he would not only express guilt at being caught out, but he would also show genuine empathy for the victims of his theft. Edison often mirrored my emotions; he offered compassion towards me when I was sad. Searching through photos for Eddie's funeral, I found that in every single photo which included Eddie and me, we were touching one another, emulating the same emotion. Daily, I miss that other half of me more than words can express.

One of Eddie's favourite places was our Moreton Island villa which is perched on the beach shoreline. Post-divorce, the bank owned the villa and the kids and I owned the doorknobs and keys. The villa was part of a resort. It was a wonderful family beach house which was rented out when we were not using it. It was purchased prior to divorce to feed my ex-husband's ego and provide Edison predictable holidays and a place where Ed could experience safe freedom. At school, Edison was often hovered over by adults, afraid that he may impulsively explode (or something like that). At the villa which was three stories high, I could relax on one of the decks and observe Edison, for approximately one kilometre in either direction. I revelled in watching the freedom he enjoyed playing and exploring the beach. There is no bridge from the mainland to Moreton Island. The trip to the island must be made by boat; the 'flyer', barge or private water transport. With water transport being the only option to travel on or off the island, I felt my children were relatively safe from predators. One of the beauties of Moreton Island is its relative inaccessibility. Over 90% of the island is National Park territory. On our visits, once the barge arrived at Moreton Island, I'd drive the kids and (most often) our guests in our 4WD, across the beach and then park close to the villa. We'd cart our food and luggage to up to the villa and unlock our getaway before opening all the lockable storage and unpacking. In our private storage, there were boogie boards, beach buckets and spades, trains, board games, beach towels, snorkelling gear and many other props to round out an easy, relaxed beach holiday. The ocean on our side of the island was calm, and because the kids were all excellent swimmers, they were in no danger in the water. We knew the long-term resort staff and many of the other villa owners and so I had many extra pairs of eyes watching out for Ed. The first thing Edison would do upon arrival would be to grab a kite from storage and run straight to the beach, squealing with delight in the freedom he found being at one with nature and no one else.

It truly warmed my heart to watch Edison on those holidays. I remember, one late afternoon during a visit (whilst I was still married), freezing on the beach in the rain, supervising Ed swimming in the ocean. No matter the time of year, Edison was compelled to swim when it rained. On that particular afternoon, the rain was pouring down hard and so visibility of the beach and Edison was hindered from either of the villa decks. I walked down to the beach to supervise Ed closely. Even in calm waters, heavy rain can proffer potential risks. At all times during our villa holidays, I prioritised visibility of my children. Supervising Ed that afternoon, in winter and chilled by the rain, I felt resentful that holiday supervision jobs always fell to me alone. Ed's father was tucked up inside warm and dry watching football on TV.

The resentment didn't last long. I began to focus instead on Edison's delight. He was literally screaming with happiness. Turning around and around in circles, arms splayed – hands slipping over the water's surface like mini water skis. Years of post-divorce villa holidays were enjoyed. Edison was in his element, within the elements.

The walk from the villa to the only resort shop was around a two-kilometre return journey. The walk was a daily holiday ritual, always including some kind of jewellery or food treat. Always, the sporadic stop, run, walk and keep pace with Edison was my role alone when I was married. These times frustrated me as often as I enjoyed them. Once single, my sole supervision role no longer bothered me. Perhaps had I been more mature, I wouldn't have felt resentment for a lack of supervision support during my marriage. I learned that it was an honour to supervise Ed. I am so pleased I have those memories to treasure; both the fulfilling memories and those when frustration won me over. Frustration versus acceptance again became an unwelcome theme that played on my mind. Capitulation was not my nature, but when encouraged, acceptance reliably provided a positive and enlightened way of being.

When staying at the villa, the beach provided a rich therapy classroom. For years, I walked along the beach with the children, writing words using a stick in the sand as Eddie spelled mostly nouns out loud for me. Often, I would also draw an object or animal he had spoken of or spelled. After a couple of hundred metres of sand writing, our reward was building sand castles, sculpturing dolphins, turtles and terrifying crocodiles in sand with other fossicked beach treasure which provided decoration. On such holidays, we went fishing from the end of the jetty on a regular basis. The first time I took Ed fishing was hilarious. His only exposure to fishing before this was from a 'Winnie, the Pooh' book. In a favoured book, Pooh went fishing and immediately caught a fish. There was no waiting in Pooh's fishing, only catching. As I taught the children to bait their hooks, Ed's baited first, Eddie pulled up a fish on his line within seconds. The girl's hooks had not yet even been baited when Ed caught his first fish. Ed announced to us, "*Fishing done. Swimming now.*" Everything was so very literal in Eddie's life.

Fishing was about catching a fish, not experiencing family time by the water and learning to wait.

One of the friends I made during our Morton Island experiences, who was also a villa owner, was a divorcee. Soon after my separation, my new friend shared with me that his divorce took over three years to finalise. I found this incredulous and confidently I explained to him that my ex and I weren't like that. I explained to him that we would be done and dusted quickly, and we would share-parent well, whilst the money and assets would eventually fall fairly. How wrong was I? My divorce journey was unbearably painful, time consuming, brutal, abusive and expensive. My children's father was on a mission to destroy me and he very nearly succeeded. The lies that he told were unbelievable and included construing me as an unfit mother, arising from an abusive childhood. My childhood was idyllic. My parents were loving, and they loved one another. There was simply no basis for the vast majority of claims contained in his sworn affidavits. At one point, he put a caveat on my home, which the court, as a result of one of his first legal battles, had appointed ownership to me. The home was for sale at the time and that caveat (later overturned in another court), cost me another small fortune. An offer to purchase our home was forcefully withdrawn as a result of the eventually failed caveat. My ex was such a pathological liar, I have at times, wondered whether he came to believe his own fabrications. Many of those lies are filed in legal archives – none of which were upheld as having any validity.

An atypical part of our divorce litigation journey was that the children's father contrived an unexpected and unfair financial demand which was conditional on him spending time with his children. The condition was that he would not take on any debt from the marriage. Foolishly, I agreed to take on all our debt. We owed more than we owned but I wanted to keep the children in their routine and give them as much continuity as I could manage. This included keeping the children in their home. For Ed, this acceptance of my ex-husband's demand was particularly important. I hoped to wrangle my way out of my now, solely owned debt via hard work. It was a debt that two adults could afford which I later learnt, one adult, as the sole provider of three kids, could not. At around that same time, we partook in two separate family psychologist appointments to gain unbiased insight as to how the children, in particular, were dealing with our family dynamic. During the second psychologist appointment, I was asked by Freya-Grace, *"How do you spell taipan?"*

"Why, sweetie?"

"Well, this form wants me to fill out what animal I think of when I think of you or Dad – and I'm up to the Dad answer."

Freya-Grace was aged six at the time. With regards to her taipan question, she was likely drawing upon a memory I had shared with my children, which had occurred during my primary school teaching years. Over a decade earlier, I was faced with the terrifying task of being forced to kill a taipan (one of the world's most deadly snakes), during school lunch duty. My weasel of a principal handed me a rake and a shovel for the kill and stood back shaking. I am a person, as my kids know, who doesn't kill. I avoid stepping on ants and put spiders and cockroaches outside rather than spraying them. I avidly avoid killing any life. The taipan incident was different though. Taipans are territorial animals and the school was set amongst sugar-cane fields. The snake would return. Hundreds of kids were in the care of the schools' staff and I knew the children's lives were more important than a snake's life. When I placed the rake over the snake's neck and chopped its head off with the shovel, my primitive mind, my amygdala and associated brain stem systems took over. I had relayed this story to my kids to teach them that no matter how smart, spiritual or athletic you ever will be; we are still animals. Freud would have had a field day with Freya-Grace's 'what animal' query. I simply noted it with surprise.

An aspect of the court related divorce process which really surprised me, was the time involved in affidavits. I kept a log of all interactions with the children's father for years, which included screen dumps of texts and not so kind emails. I authored more affidavits than it would take to author a decent book. Eventually, financial and time demands forced a change of lawyers to a firm that allowed me to act, where practical, as paralegal in family feuds. Litigation via correspondence reduced and my wishes and opinions were respected. The new to me principal lawyer, Fiona, was able to advocate in court and as such, in practical terms she doubled as a family lawyer and she could also act in a Federal Court, in a barrister-role. Fiona's empathy, determination and sense of justice was exemplary, and her focus never wavered from the children's best interests. The children were her firm's highest priority.

One afternoon, I returned home from court unable to make it further than Freya-Grace's bedroom which was the second room down the hall to our left. Something had overcome me which I could not control. I struggled to Freya-Grace's bed, convulsing all over, feeling like I was being cut open alive. My stomach and feet were in agony and my whole body shook. My parents who had attended court with me that day, wrapped me in blankets and tried to calm me. I was scared, experiencing excruciating unfamiliar pain. This 'attack' lasted around 20 minutes. It was terrifying. Was it a panic attack? Was it a mental breakdown? I had no idea, but from my perspective those things happened to other people who were not as strong as I. I don't know the medical term to describe what I experienced that day. After my collapse, I felt vulnerable and I was devastated to learn how little control I had over my body when stress overwhelmed me. Maybe I was allowing myself to be *one of them?* Perhaps after so much divorce related conflict, my body inadvertently collapsed in the comfort of subconsciously acknowledging that my parents were there as a backup for my children…

Many evenings, I was awake way past midnight, preparing legal documentation and drafting responses to my former husband's lawyer. I once thought having three children within three years and one week whilst working was tough. But this period of my life, consumed by legal conflict, was soul destroying. Back when I was in my 20s, I asked God, if I really had to be strong. I prayed, *"I really don't want to be this strong God. I hope I'm not becoming strong for a reason. What could take more strength than this?"* I was somewhat comfortable with prayer, but I was more comfortable with logic. Years earlier, I had adopted a saying I would repeat to myself for decades to come, *'Trust in God, but lock your car'*. I was infinitely aware that my spiritual life was important; but I could only do my best by exercising common sense and employing my brain, my abilities and self-determination. Conceivably, the traumas of my teens and 20s ended up providing a platform of faith and strength

119

to draw upon as my life unfolded. Little did I know what was yet to come.

Final custody decisions were made by a Federal Magistrate who ruled that I have sole parental custody, hand-in-hand with a few provisos. My children's father would need to jump through a bunch of hurdles before being allowed time with his children. Although it was relieving to know my children would be safe, I experienced the court victory with a sinking feeling in my stomach. Not my plan. I accurately predicted that my ex would not execute the many actions that the court required for him to be able to spend time with his children. I wanted our children safe, but I had never set out for them to be fatherless. Although my lawyers won and set precedent, no one else won that day. How divorced or separated men and women raise children together, with traditional roles no longer being the norm is a complex wonder. Healthy co-parenting provided by people no longer in an intimate relationship, is truly admirable. My ex-husband has seen his children once since the day the Federal Court appointed me solely responsible for our children, which was around nine years ago. Sadly, the last time he saw his children was at his son's funeral where he was not allowed to approach his daughters.

Whilst navigating my messy life, I served on the board of Women In Technology (WIT). Feminism wasn't my cause. I appreciated what my foremothers had fought for and the benefits I received as a result of their good fights. None the less, I also had a heart for men and I questioned where their identity belonged in this new society where women had a voice, could earn money, have children without male-female intercourse and often dominated matters of the home. Respecting the rights of all people, I felt my arm was twisted as I considered the WIT board-member invitation. After much consideration, I agreed to serve on the board of WIT, hoping my service would do no harm. I was pleasantly surprised. In developing rapport with the other board members, I discovered that they were in the main, inspirational, balanced and successful women who were also juggling family challenges. At one point, WIT asked me to conduct a workshop with women who had left the workforce and wished to re-enter employment post raising children, after surviving cancer or a bunch of other work interrupters… I was honoured to accept.

I introduced the workshop by throwing into the audience 30 tennis balls labelled with life responsibilities, potential opportunities and various choices. Unmarked tennis balls had been delivered on my doorstep by the Canadian friend I had met in a park many years earlier. We chatted often on the phone. The night before the WIT event during one of our many phone calls, she encouraged me in my endeavour to support others. She supported me in what I was attempting to do, and delivered to my doorstep overnight, a package of 30 tennis balls. I set about labelling the tennis balls. The labels included, '*TV, work, friends, parenting, marriage, house-work, income earning, spiritual-time, pets, children, cooking, gardening*' and so forth. After dropping the kids at school, I made my way to the workshop in the city. Once the audience had been pummelled with my tennis balls, I asked, *"How many of you caught a ball?"* I witnessed a show of around 10 hands.

"How many of you picked up a dropped ball?" A show of more hands…

"How many of you didn't try?" No hands. Amusingly, those who didn't try to catch a ball also did not try to raise their hand. My message was one of learning to catch and juggle the balls you value and choosing to drop unimportant, or less necessary, metaphorical balls. It was a long workshop and as such, this anecdote is a meagre summary. Way back then I was applauded for my sharing and teaching. Yet over a decade later, I am still learning what to juggle, how much I can juggle, and I am discovering that my ethics don't change, but some of my ideals do. I still drop balls I'd prefer to juggle.

In Edison's final year at Holy Cross, there was a new school principal. The new principal had entirely different views to his predecessor regarding inclusion and where special kids belonged. Subsequently, Edison was relegated to a window free, student free prison with two kind and talented special education teachers who did their level best to advance Edison within the impossible parameters which constrained them. My lack of ability to accept mistreatment of Ed caused problems. Edison was moving backwards in his academic performance, his social skills were suffering and I noticed a decline in his self-esteem.

Somehow, through the many fights I had with those representing the education system over the years, I always remained calm. I never raised my voice, I never sought to blame and I always searched for collectively construed ways to move forward. In the end, my advocacy for Edison's inclusion had Holy Cross demand that Edison leave the school. They might have tolerated him for a year or so longer had I not expected more of them. Those were difficult times. They were also days in which I was meandering my way through single-motherhood status with no shared care, nor any practical community or government support. Again, I longed to have supportive extended family living close to us.

Chapter 15
Moving

In 2012, I found myself tasked with the job of finding a school suitable for my daughters who were high academic, musical and sporting achievers. I sought a school which would also foster Edison's talents and abilities while assisting him to be his best in the areas that autism proved most challenging for him. I narrowed the search down to three public schools; Brookfield State School, Indooroopilly State School and Jindalee State School. After interviewing with all three schools, I selected Jindalee State School (JSS). I wrote to the children's father requesting his input but there was no opinion forthcoming. A deal breaker for me was that back then, JSS did not just specialise in speech and language disorders, it was also a suburb which I could afford to live in. Edison had verbal dyspraxia as well as autism and it was therefore perfect for us that JSS Special Needs Unit also specialised in ASD and Speech and Language disorders. JSS boasted a BYOD (bring your own device) programme, better than average academic results, inclusion of special needs children (where possible) and they had a great track record in sport. The school was large, with over 1000 students and I felt a school with a large student population would provide an opportunity for the girls to explore their personalities and friendship groups in an environment where their brother wasn't *the* special needs child in the school. I was also looking forward to a life of relative anonymity in a new suburb, with my children attending a large public school.

At Holy Cross, we were labelled a 'broken' family. We were perceived as having the highest needs child in the school, we were non-Catholic and because I was involved with the school, we were quite visible. The children began attending JSS at the beginning of semester two, 2012. I soon learned that I was needlessly concerned about the children's ability to cope with a change of school, home, friendships and location mid-year. Before the end of their first week attending the new school, all three children had settled into their new environment happily. I noticed that my children were more resilient than I. Years on, observing their youthful resilience, I was pleased at how well they took extreme change in their stride.

Within the first week of arriving at Jindalee, I saw a near-by neighbourhood Police Beat sign and I decided to introduce Edison to the local police officer whom I later learnt was associated with our new school. With Edison's former runaway track-record, I wanted local authorities to know we had arrived. Although Ed hadn't 'done a runner' for a long time, I knew that I likely needed community support to keep Ed safe. One notable time when Edison had run away from home (back when I was married), a good Samaritan blew the whistle. Edison had left our home naked at the age of five and set out for a wander which took him to a very busy intersection where Kedron Park Hotel is situated. When Edison was found, approximately 20 minutes after he went missing, he was attempting to cross a very busy six-lane intersection on Lutwyche Road. The unknown to me gentlemen who raised the alarm, stopped his car, pulling up on the curb of the pub's pavement and gently stopped Edison in his tracks. The man then halted an oncoming female driver in the traffic. The police who delivered Ed home that day informed me that the hero who'd saved Ed didn't want to be seen putting a naked five-year-old in his car (to keep Eddie safe). The brave man didn't want to jeopardise his motivation of simply keeping an unclothed, runaway child safe. I was told that Ed's rescuer explained to his female, fellow motorist, *"I don't know this child, but I just found him trying to cross that busy road. He has a phone number on his bracelet. Can you please keep the boy in your car whilst I called the police first, and then the phone number on the bracelet, if necessary?"* What a fast-thinking and caring man he was. It's a shame a man so brave had to protect himself from public judgment in rescuing a naked young boy, just to do the right thing. Edison was delivered draped in a grey blanket to our home minutes after his rescue. As would be expected, the police interviewed me to ensure I was a fit parent, ensuring that they were not returning my boy to an unsafe home. Potential trauma was averted.

Ed only ever adventured alone out of site once after his father left. This occurred during a villa holiday when I believe he wasn't running away but was simply enjoying a bush walk-about. The experience of losing Ed to Australian bush was terrifying. As dusk approached, four hours of no Edison passed. The resort staff helped locate Eddie on that occasion. As a child, I would venture out with my siblings and neighbourhood children every Saturday. We would be gone from breakfast time to dinnertime. Back in those days, no one panicked when children were gone for hours. Societal norms are not stagnant. Outside of death, Ed's villa walk-about was the last time I lost him. Never the less, community support remained essential in raising Ed. When his desire to adventure alone dissipated and his location became reliably predictable, I had one less worry. At the time of my Jindalee Police Beat introduction, Ed was a low runaway risk. Regardless, it was reassuring to know that the local police were aware that my son and I now belonged in their precinct.

I put more energy than was healthy into motherhood during those first post-divorce years. I revelled in no adult Jillian-centred pleasures, ensuring my children were denied very little. Our home was always a zoo – full of pets and Homo sapiens. I am unsure of whether I have a real love for animals or whether I am just a true sucker for providing my children a rich life... A life filled with lessons in drama, voice, violin, piano, performance with a side-dish of swimming pool parties, ICAS exams, film and production agencies, birthday parties, parties generally, thousands of sleep-overs, iDevice everything, Netflix, sport (especially basketball) and a procession of pets resulted. It is likely that I was over-accommodating for a lack of a father in my children's lives while compensating for the *one of them* consequences of autism and divorce. Guilt appeasement was probably also a factor... I hadn't been able to provide my children with the *us* life I had imagined.

A by-product of moving to Jindalee was that it was no longer practical to visit David Lee, whom I used to go to high school with and subsequently two decades on, regularly visited with, at an Acquired Brain Injury Centre. David's parents lived close by in Kenmore and so we were able to maintain semi-regular contact via weekend visits, when David stayed with his parents. We were always warmly welcomed by David's family. David's father, Ernie is an astute businessman and when we have a chance to talk, I most often learn a thing or two. He is warm and caring and I sought his advice regarding work-stress more than once. I enjoyed having what seemed a little like an adopted family, only 10 minutes from where I lived. My sister, Kylie lived closer than this, but she also was a single mum and her ex-husband lived abroad, consequentially providing no shared care. She worked full-time and had somehow managed to build a full and positive social life. Understandably, I didn't see a lot of Kylie. It's a time in our lives, our 30s and often 40s, where most people with young children are relegated to a life of parenting, surrounded by children's friends' parents, while immersed in school and children's extra-curricular activities. David's mum, Jan is a chatterbox and could be relied upon for good phone banter. I enjoyed her company and would telephone her when we hadn't seen David for a while to ensure David knew he was in our thoughts. There is always someone whose adversity is greater than your own. Admirably, David most often put a smile on his dial, and mustered a positive attitude regardless of the physical adversity he suffered. His parents didn't just soldier-on; they proved a great example of people who choose to thrive rather than survive.

Post the Global Financial Crisis (GFC) which occurred about a nanosecond after we bought the Moreton Island villa, I couldn't sell the property without facing financial destruction. The sale of the property would destroy us, keeping the property would have the same net fiscal result. As a consequence of divorce, I inherited the villa and the associated debt. The mortgage was larger than the property's value post GFC. When financial institutions began to refuse loans for properties on islands, my gloomy financial status seemed unmanageable. I needed to live in the JSS catchment area to enrol the children in the school of my choice. This marked the beginning of three extremely financially challenging years. I was paying legal fees galore, paying to sell my Wooloowin home, paying $600/week in rent and servicing a massive loan on the villa, along with a large mortgage on the children's former home. Additionally, I was not regularly receiving child support. I could have declared bankruptcy as my first family lawyer recommended. As a director of a business, bankruptcy didn't sit well with me. Additionally, if unnecessary bankruptcy was an ethical non-option. Some people don't have the opportunity to exercise such ethics. I refused to compromise the children's activities, and so piano lessons and other child-centred extra-curricular activities were maintained. My hair grew longer as I could no longer afford haircuts, and my wardrobe stayed the same as I could not afford new clothes for myself. The children did not go without, and potentially, partially out of guilt, I added Cub Scouts, more basketball and all manner of other activities to our schedule. Previously, I was a mother who intentionally minimised children's extra-curricular activities. I somehow found myself going completely in the other (equally unhealthy) direction.

It wasn't easy to find a suitable rental in the JSS catchment for our family. I needed a swimming pool to cater for Edison's proprioceptive and vestibular needs, a place that would take two dogs and two cats, a place that would accept a single mum (and single income earner) and a place large enough to accommodate a family of four. The home needed to be fenced and have room for a trampoline where Edison could jump in privacy (as clothing was not a necessary accessory for Ed's trampolining). Ideally, it would be quiet (it was not) and preferably it would be a little rundown so that I wasn't in constant cleaning mode to ensure a full return of my bond. Eventually, I found a place where I could live with several compromises. We planted ourselves there for the 18 months it took to try to sell, then rent, then sell the Wooloowin home. The kids were happy and thrived in the new school. I helped out with reading groups in Freya-Grace's year-2 class, and tried to get to know fellow JSS parents. There was a mum from Freya-Grace's class, Lisa, who was particularly warm and welcoming and who ended up playing a pivotal role in our lives. Of course, the fiscal and time-consuming burden of Edison's therapies, medications, specialist visits and so forth, did not abate. I was one busy lady. I had a solution. I worked harder and slept less.

Moving suburbs meant moving support providers. Understandably, Disability Services Queensland (DSQ) had regions to manage and our move required DSQ reassessment and reassignment. Around a year before moving to Jindalee, I had managed to secure a small additional amount of government funding to go towards expenses associated with Ed's needs. I remember that the Carer's Allowance was $110/fortnight. I mentally referred to that government contribution as a Band-Aid for an amputation. Regardless of the meagre sum, I didn't reject the Band-Aid. There was also a small respite budget which was not enough, yet extremely appreciated. Although I had opted for self-directed funding, respite needed to be channelled through an organisation which covered our new post-code.

The research required to find a new agency which would administer self-directed funding in the area of our new abode was not simple. There were lots of on-hold phone calls and many dead ends. In addition, to moving DSQ regions, we were due for a new DSQ funding review to allow them to ascertain whether we were still valid for receiving funds. When we were initially deemed in need of support, DSQ was required to, every few years, review what level of funding (if any) should be provided to the families they supported. I remember specialists teaching me '*autism is a life-long disorder*' and I wondered why government disability services needed to check whether I'd fixed Ed yet. I set a date for the DSQ caseworker assigned to us to visit our home. They liked to observe real life within the DSQ customer's home. For example, they preferred to observe and document how life was, getting ready to go to school, the routine upon returning home from school or dinner/bedtime.

Those were the golden years before the NDIS (National Disability Insurance Scheme). The DSQ approach back then was as unobtrusive as possible. It was fair and the process trusted that carers could think. The system was designed to help and it did not prop up a false economy of therapists, paper-work administrators and unqualified 'care and objective planning counsellors'. There was, thankfully, a high priority placed on family independence. Privacy was also respected. DSQ was a three-letter word while in my opinion, NDIS was unfolding (in the planning phase) as a four-letter word. For our DSQ review, we agreed on a morning appointment with a 7:30 start. The time slot agreed would give the DSQ caseworker an hour of observation and if required, I could spend a little time with her alone, after the kids were safely at school. Our review morning

128

occurred during 'book week' on book-character dress up day. Not planned! The girls had readied their costumes the night before and I had a few ideas to try on for Ed. I was up early on the observation morning in the hope that I'd be showered and fully ready in time for the DSQ lady's arrival. Instead at 7:15, the doorbell rang as Freya-Grace showed up in my upstairs en suite to tell me, *"You have to come downstairs now Mum, there's paint everywhere and I think there is a stranger at the front door!"*

I threw some clothes on as fast as I could, catching a glimpse in horror, of the main bathroom on my way to our entrance. I hastily welcomed my DSQ guest and explained that I had a developing disaster to avert. I knew I needed to clean up, yet I had no idea the extent of what I had to clean. I encouraged our visitor to make herself comfortable before I sought my boy. I felt slightly calmer when I found Edison naked in the main bathroom, once pale-skinned, now blue. The shower was blue, the basin was blue. Edison was blue. I ushered Eddie into the shower, checking that the water temperature wouldn't scold him as I would have liked to do. With Ed safe in the shower, I traced the blue footprints to the living room to find my Persian rug, sporting a good whack of blue paint. My observations revealed blue paint everywhere. Even the inside of Ed's mouth was blue. Perhaps blue paint tastes good. I did not want to find out first-hand. The DSQ lady was friendly and non-judgmental as she watched the show unfold. The girls organised their own breakfast and finalised their book week costumes. There were a few debates; one in which, in my parental wisdom, I shared, *"Yes, the Harry Potter series was certainly a bunch of books before they were movies and Francesca has read them all. Her outfit is valid."*

Edison could not clean himself in the shower independently. He could shower himself but self-cleaning was another matter. Fully clothed and doing what I could to ensure that the girls were looking after the DSQ employee, I scrubbed, cleaned and comforted my distressed son. Ed was disturbed in his realisation that he may have done something wrong and there-by may have disrupted our morning. Even with limited words, he was able to express that he was sorry as he succumbed to my fix-it fervour. Edison's demeanour that morning demonstrated his possession of theory-of-mind. Un-be-known to Eddie and me, while cleaning the blues in the main bathroom, his sisters were doing just fine. They even managed to offer our guest a cuppa. Upset Ed, was never easy to manage so that morning comfort, physical safety, emotional welfare and big-picture management modes kicked-in simultaneously. Edison was an ethical and caring boy who sometimes behaved badly. I didn't want to send a distressed and literally blue son off to school. Spinning saucers… Oddly, whilst trying to show off my capability as a parent to Ms DSQ, I felt comforted that she was in the kitchen being hosted by my daughters. Eventually Edison finished his shower and was dressed. He wanted to wear his school uniform. A school uniform was part of his routine. Mucking-up our routine albeit occasionally part of my 'therapy' wasn't easy for Ed. I did consider the fact that the JSS' formal school uniform sported blue shorts and a blue shirt to match his still blue arms, legs and face. Finally getting close to piling the kids in the car, I grabbed a toy trumpet and passed it to Eddie asking his sisters to tell the teachers upon school arrival, that their brother was dressed as 'Little Boy Blue'. I thought to myself, '*Surely, Little Boy Blue has been published in a book somewhere. I am fairly certain it's a poem not a book. Whatever… I've done my best'.* The DSQ lady remained at my home while I finalised the school drop-off. I had a full day of work ahead of me and so I was eager to see the end of her assessment visit. We chatted and she didn't berate me for allowing my child to eat and smear the home with blue paint. A few weeks later, I received a notice that we were still eligible for funding and we had moved to the top funding bracket – another $20 a fortnight. The Carer's Allowance remained in place and our respite funding increased thankfully, and marginally. I never used the respite to have others spend time with Edison whilst trying to act like I had a normal life but the extra housework hands that the funds provided, were very appreciated.

Throughout my marriage, I had maintained contact with my children's paternal grandmother, Jan. I figured that once we were divorced, there was no reason that my former mother-in-law would be denied access to her grandchildren. (I was unable to establish contact with their paternal grandfather.) For years, she had been posting her grandchildren Christmas presents and she telephoned a few times a year. Back in the days of being married, when Jan called and her son answered the phone, he would hand the conversation straight over to me. In 2013 during one of our telephone catch-ups, Jan told me that her grandson, Brydehn, my ex-husband's nephew (whom I had met once as a young snapper), was moving to Brisbane with his girlfriend, to study engineering. I asked Jan if they had family in Brisbane to support them. I was informed that they did not. Our family set about socially fostering Brydehn and his stunning partner, Haley. They were an easy-to-take young couple who were old enough to show maturity and connect with our odd-bod family while being young enough to play with and interact with all three kids. My children grew to love Brydehn and Haley and they became a welcome part of our lives. I remember special times such as shared Christmas experiences. I was pleased my children knew and loved relatives on their mother and father's sides.

There were many ASD associated quirks which came out of left-field. One day in September 2012 whilst Freya-Grace was enjoying year two at school, I received a call from her concerned classroom teacher. The students had spent the afternoon making Father's Day cards which were to be laminated as presents for the forth-coming Sunday. Without a present father, 7-year-old Freya-Grace decided to make a card for her brother. On the card, she wrote something like *'I love you Eddie because you hit me. Happy Father's Day'*. The teacher was understandably alerted reading this and she organised a substitute supervisor so that she could go to the office and immediately telephone me to discuss her concerns. I listened to Freya-Grace's teacher describe her distress before explaining that Ed showed love to his favourite people by pulling hair or hitting his favoured person. At the time, Freya-Grace was Ed's favourite person, hence she was his affection and minor violence victim. I assured Freya-Grace's teacher that her student was safe. Goodness knows how she felt when I justified to her that it was completely valid for my daughter to love her brother, in part, because he hit her.

Late in 2012, without warning, the children's dad turned up at school on a Friday 30 minutes before pick-up time to collect the children for the weekend. He hadn't seen his children for around a year. He had telephoned them about 10 months earlier to apologise to his children, that they didn't have a father anymore. During that phone call, he told them he would never see them again. He was sorry… At the time of that phone conversation, the court had not denied him access to his children and the rejection of them, was his decision alone. I was working towards a manageable and safe parenting proposition which would include him. I had remained hopeful that in collaboration with my ex, we could move towards positive shared-parenting. I have never been negative with my kids when speaking about their dad. When their father telephoned to inform the children of his desertion, it came as a shock to us all. After the telephone call, the girls were distraught – particularly our eldest. I can't imagine the state of despair their father experienced as he considered total abandonment of his children. I knew he loved them. These were dark times for us all…

The January of the abandonment phone call, we were on holiday at the villa and the lady who owned the adjacent villa stepped up a gear or 10 to support us as we worked through the wake of how young children respond to being told over the phone that they no longer have a father. Our villa decks are around 2–3 metres apart. As such, if so desired, day and night conversation is easily accessible from neighbouring decks. Sometimes, especially when howling children are involved, privacy between villa neighbours can be compromised. My villa neighbour was Sally and she was the first friend to offer me an unpaid break from my kids. Upon first meeting Sally a couple of years earlier, I was awe-struck when she called over from her deck to mine one afternoon, *"Hey, Jillian, why don't you have a break and send your kids over here for an hour or so? We are painting, I'm sure your kids will enjoy it."*

"You mean Ed too?"

"Of course."

"Wow, really? Wow, that's so kind. No one has ever offered that before. Yes! For sure…I'll bring them over in 5."

I can't remember what kind of break I had but I had a break and Sally has remained a true and dear friend. On the day of the 'kid's you don't have a father anymore' phone call, she was again holidaying next door and provided support for all of us. Edison didn't really comprehend the context of his father's rejection, but he loved his sister's and he was visibly challenged by their sorrow. Sally's kindness that afternoon demonstrated a generosity of spirit and self, which I acutely appreciated.

Later that same year when the children's father arrived un-expectantly to get the kids for the weekend at 2:30 pm from school, I received another un-welcome phone call. Knowing that the children hadn't seen their father all year, school administration telephoned me asking what they should do. I told them that the court orders allowed him access to the children every second weekend, that the children had never had a sleep over with their father and that they hadn't seen him for around a year but that neither the school nor I were in a position to over-ride court orders. I explained that if indeed, this particular Friday was one of 'his' weekends, he was entitled to take the kids. I concluded that the school would have to release the children to their father. There were new children's court orders at foot but the law respects current orders. Clearly, I wasn't happy about the children's circumstance. I was angry that the children's father's approach wasn't considerate of the children's feelings and did not cater for practical matters such as clothes, emotional well-being and pyjamas. Yet I wasn't about to break orders nor ask others to do such. The school made the decision to telephone the local police. I was asked to come down to the meet with police and school management. The school was put in shutdown for a while whilst our newest drama played out.

My ex and I were interviewed by police officers in two separate rooms. Then a decision was made which still shocks me today. Francesca at the time was only 10 years old and some police officer with seemingly no understanding of how a child's mind works made the daft decision to interview Francesca without the support of either parent or a trusted teacher. Our eldest was put in a position to speak for herself and on behalf of her siblings. I am pleased her opinion was sought but her time with the police could have been handled with more sensitivity. After the interview with Francesca and at around 5:45 pm, the police officers reported to me that the children did not want to go with their father but there was nothing in their power that they could do, to prevent him from taking them. A drama would have been spared had my advice been heeded hours earlier. They assured me that they would organise a couple of drive-bys that night and keep an eye on the home the children were to stay in.

The plan was that they would be delivered home lunchtime Sunday, in 2 days' time. The police did the best job they could in a difficult situation. I found that night troubling. Although the children were due to arrive home on the Sunday, their father dropped them at our rental early the next morning. I observed some obvious stress, but mostly the kids were happy to be home. I spent time settling them gauging and monitoring emotions, hoping I wasn't paying too much attention to their last 24 hours. I did my best to focus on our *now*. Francesca reported to me how terrified she was being interviewed alone by two male police officers. Our 10-year-old girl was justifiably afraid with no adult advocate nor a child protection representative present. Francesca sobbed, "*I could see their guns Mum, I was really scared.*" The day they were returned, Freya-Grace who does not sleep during the day, fell fast asleep in a heap on the floor of my home office, as I worked from my computer. The children had been looking forward to a swimming play-date that afternoon at our house, which they now wouldn't miss. It was decent of their father to ensure they didn't miss their play date. This fiasco was the first and final sleepover the children had with their father. Never again, it turned out, were they in his care. Life returned to our peculiar version of normal.

On the 12th of March 2013, I fronted up to the Federal Court of Australia for a revision of the Children's Orders which determined time spent with the children, for each parent. My former husband had taken me back to court for revised 'custody' orders and in the months prior to this, fresh Family Reports, affidavits and litigation via correspondence had dominated my mental landscape. It was a huge day for us all as my ex had seen the children once since December 2011 and had been largely uncooperative with regards to the Children's Order under review. The Magistrate presiding that day ordered on a final basis 16 items. The most important item was that I be granted sole parental responsibility. There were qualifications in place which in time, made life a little easier. For example, I was enabled to apply for passports for the children without the father's permission. The new orders also determined that he was not allowed to attend the children's schools nor their extra-curricular activities. The magistrate determined that the father could spend time with the children if he undertook a number of court appointed actions. He never undertook those actions and therefore to this day, does not see his children. I married a man with many positive qualities. I have no doubt that at some stage in the future, at least one of my children will want to get to know their father. There are times where I feel disappointment regarding how things turned out. Had we managed John Howard's vision of responsible shared parenting both my daughters would today be benefitting from his excellent mathematics tuition and his experience in athletics and basketball coaching. My daughters are very active. As I write, one is preparing for the Kokoda Challenge and the other is training for district athletics. Their father was an excellent sports coach; he possessed many talents which I did not. In 2017, Freya-Grace ranked the top basketball player in Brisbane, in her division. Had their father been present, he would be proud. He missed witnessing these achievements. Our kids, maybe missed out too.

Chapter 16
Bunkering Down and Finally Settling In

Year 2013 involved many weekend visits after basketball to the Wooloowin home in order for me to maintain the swimming pool and yard. At some stage, the tenants moved out and it was time to try to sell again. In preparation for the sale, I fixed stairs and gates, contracted to have the exterior painted, I painted 2/3s of the interior myself, paid to have the place styled and generally put all the energy I had left over from living duties into selling the home. Styling the home was a complete waste of money. The manner, in which the home had been decorated while we lived in it, was far more stylish than the stylist's outfit. I owned the copyright of my original photos but once again, I found myself influenced by a real estate agent to unnecessarily spend money. Although I wasn't contractually compelled to promote the agent and line her referral pockets, I was motivated by fear of further losses and so I spent money I didn't have on styling and over-marketing the home. Whether the real estate agent did a poor or good job is subject to one's perspective. I was desperate. In the end, I sold the house for 100K less than her estimate and 150K less than the predicted, estimated average I had been provided by other real estate agents. Money. Money. Money… doesn't make you happy, but a lack of it can sure make things stressful when there's mouths to feed, bodies to shelter and minds to educate.

Pleasingly, we were able, with a budget far smaller than I'd hoped, to purchase a new home. My parents kindly lent me around 90K towards the deposit which I managed to pay back fairly quickly. I realised that I was in a fortunate position being able to purchase a home of any sort and not rent forever. I've never taken for granted what comes with being educated,

Australian and other wonders such as benefitting from a stable upbringing. I regularly steal from A.B Facey, reminders of my fortunate life. Again, home selection criteria informed a rigorous search for a new home. Necessarily the property needed to include a swimming pool, four bedrooms and room for private trampoline jumping. Wants consisted of a character home, two living areas, a study/office (much of my work was conducted from home), a car port or garage, a garden or a blank canvas where I could create a garden, a cul-de-sac, other kids around, a fireplace and an abode I could make home and leave one day, in a box. We were in search of our new for-ever-ever home. After a couple of months of searching, the internet and the streets of postcode 4074, we purchased our Hilliup Street, Westlake home. It was my mother who found this house on the internet. I thought I had seen every possible 4074 home, but somehow she found this little gem waiting for us. It was tiny by the standards I was used to. It was quaint and it abounded character. It ticked nearly all my boxes and in January 2014, when we moved in, I madly set about nesting. Edison's bedroom was a shoebox with barely a foot at the end of his single bed and around a foot and a half between his bed and his wardrobe. He had a big yard of over $800m^2$ to play his golf, a pool, privacy and tolerant neighbours. Edison was generally pretty easy to please when he had access to an environment he could use for self-administered occupational therapy or fun.

The neighbours turned out to be more than tolerant. They were all friendly, accepting people. In every home in which we'd lived, including the Jindalee rental, we made an effort to get to know our neighbours. Moving into the Hilliup Street home in January provided an opportunity to meet neighbours on Australia day which occurs on January the 26th. The kids and I letterbox dropped the small cul-de-sac with a note, inviting neighbours to come for a drink and a snack at the end of the street at 3:00 pm, Monday, Australia Day Public Holiday. When the day came, the kids and I sat outside our front yard with eskies and fold up chairs for about 20 minutes before anyone arrived.

"This is so embarrassing, Mum. Everyone can look out their windows and see us by ourselves. No one is interested."

"Well, let's break open the treats and enjoy our Australia Day holiday with one another then. It will be great if neighbours turn up. If they don't, we can still hang out here a little longer." Within an hour, five other families joined us, and we enjoyed a bonding afternoon as we got to know one another. I asked if we could put our basketball hoop at the top of the cul-de-sac for the kids to share and all agreed. We learned that years ago, a previous generation of children in the street spent many happy afternoons during their suburban childhood around a basketball hoop in the same place. Our hoop was moved and enjoyed by many for a short while. Later, a neighbour complained about the hoop and it was placed back in our driveway. Never the less, the neighbourhood basketball was fun as a shared game, while it lasted. We became friends with one couple two doors up who had two young daughters. Francesca relates well to young children and with these neighbours embracing Edison and all his quirks, we regularly enjoyed reciprocal, entertaining social time. The family had another neighbour over the back who was a single mother of a young daughter. They joined our regular meet-ups. Many a happy Sunday afternoon was relished with these neighbours; swimming, chatting over an early BBQ dinner and enjoying the all year round, glorious Brisbane climate. I found myself again, content in my home and neighbourhood.

Relishing the warmth of my fireplace, one evening, I reminisced some experiences set in our past dwellings. Edison had his ninth birthday in our rental home and as was my way, I invited his whole class to his birthday party. He had been in the new school (JSS) for around two months and I was eager for him to make a friend. The party was a success and at least 40% of his peers attended. I was pleased with the new state school life that I had introduced to my children. I was excited about the notion of Edison finding a friend. As I was getting to know the new-to-me mums during Ed's party, Edison pulled out his penis and weed in the swimming pool. This was a major social faux pas, even in grade 4. Ed's chances of finding friends were looking slim. At JSS, Edison was also never invited for a play, for a sleepover or to a party. Having stated that, the co-hort of children he found himself amongst was supportive. There were many notable children who went above and beyond to include, look out for, and play with Edison. I don't know if I would have been that wonderful with a special kid like Edison when I was nine years old. Back then, we didn't get the chance to test such waters.

Edison had certain destinations, icons or shops in our new neighbourhood that he obsessed over. One of his favourite drive-by locations was the Mount Ommaney Fire Station. The façade of the station was adorned with massive roller doors, large enough to allow an emergency exit for a couple of fire engines. The roller doors were painted with a compelling image of a fire fighter rescuing a child from a threating blaze. Each and every time we passed the local fire station, Ed would comment, *"Fire man saves child."* He loved most transport vehicles, as many young children do. Years back, I was physically strong enough to carry Eddie, in terrifying, ecstatic excitement, each Wednesday morning, we would run to greet our garbage truck and driver. This routine, inspired by a large and scary automobile was a story shared with others. Edison was delighted when his Uncle Bruce, years later, sourced for him a replica mini-garbage truck. The mini-garbage truck found a home on a shelf in Ed's tiny bedroom as an icon of trepidation and glory. The glory piece reflected my son's ability to conquer the thrilling fear of large transport machines. Fire engines, garbage trucks and trains became revered, and no longer feared.

In moving homes, certain routines changed such as where we shopped. Woolworths was an easy walk away from our rental house at Jindalee. Our local Woolies was a small grocery store which suited shopping with Edison just fine. Our favourite checkout person was Sally. She was fond of Ed and all the staff were patient and supportive. I had many names for Ed; 'Mr Magoo', 'my little man' and quite often 'Eddie Spaghetti'. Given that our local Woolworths was a safe place where we were known, I didn't always have the children close at hand and both Ed and Freya-Grace had a tendency of running off to whatever isle was attractive to them. In an attempt to locate my kids, I would frequently be heard calling out, *'Eddie Spaghetti! Freya-Grace?'* Customers would sometimes hear, *'Where's the spaghetti? Fried Rice?'* and thinking me a little mad, would gently point to the pasta isle. 'A quick shop is a good shop' is one of my common sayings. I am not a wanderer in life, in shopping, nor in any way. I could likely benefit from learning to wander a little. For our big shops, we would visit Coles at Middle

Park. Again, the staff were just wonderful. Edison found Coles a hug worthy place and we encountered just about every reaction one could imagine when a stranger was offered a hug from a lanky, becoming-pimply, tall and not so verbal young man. Every so often, the nominated hugged stranger would let down his or her guard and return the hug, seemingly filling Ed's heart with joy.

Our third grocery hangout was Coles Jindalee. The girls attended piano and violin lessons close to this supermarket at the local music store for a couple of years, before we switched to in-home lessons. During the hour of their music tuition, Edison and I would enjoy shopping therapy. Not shopping therapy in the way a couple of 40-something strung-out mums may shop… Our therapy involved Edison reading, finding, choosing and counting products we needed in the home. This therapy-shop always occurred at the same time each week, and if we finished before the girls' lessons were completed, Edison was treated with McDonald's. During these therapy shopping excursions, we predictably came across an elderly man each week who was always kind to Eddie. He was a return-hugger. Often, he would be the one to initiate contact after the first time Edison had approached him. We came to know the man as Graham, and over time we co-shopped and Edison and I would help Graham put his groceries in the car. My guess was Graham was in his late 80s when we met him. When instrumental lessons began at home, I kept the weekly Jindalee Coles routine going and my daughters were introduced to Graham. Graham had retained his wit and intelligence. He was well over six-foot-tall but because he needed to use the shopping trolley as a walker, some grocery items were not easy to reach. Ed and I continued our therapy-shops whilst the girls would meet up with Graham, fetching high items for him, keeping him company, packing his groceries into his car before returning the trolley to then meet up with Ed and me at the checkout. We became friends with Graham and sometimes visited him in his welcoming Fig Tree Pocket home.

I shared with Graham aspects of my life and parenting dilemmas. I talked to him about experiences others may find minor. He used both his ears to listen and exuded patience. I complained about how Eddie experienced sensory input differently to me and lamented many challenges associated with

ASD. Edison found it extremely difficult, for example to tolerate haircuts. The only haircut I paid for, for Ed, was his last. Somehow, haircuts seemed painful. I don't know if it was the noise of clipping scissors, or actual pain or something else. I do know I did not enjoy being Ed's hairdresser. As I took on the barber role over many years, Eddie ended up with one of three hairstyles; very, very short, growing out, or surfy dude (which was my favourite because this style showed off his curls). Graham listened attentively to my minor challenges and provided wise counsel as he often responded with humour. I think it's a shame that modern society doesn't make more cross-generational efforts in connecting with one another. I have found that it's worth the risk to attempt connection with those we think are so very different to *us.*

A love of literature and probably too much time listening to the local ABC (Australian Broadcasting Corporation), radio station was something Graham and I had in common. I recognised that it was odd to form a friendship with a man around four decades my senior when we had no shared history nor friends. His companionship built new bridges. He wrote short stories for my kids and shared with us special times that he had experienced with his grandchildren. As with many children, my kids were not particularly comfortable around old people (who I think may feel at times like they are *one of them*). Graham's warmth and the care he took to have what he was physically able to prepare, to welcome us in his home, was admirable. We never left our visits with Graham feeling regret for reaching out to an old man who was kind and brave enough to hug Eddie back.

Pets remained part of our day-to-day life at Hilliup Street. Sadly, our lovable dog, Sam, who was purchased as a companion for Max when I was first engaged to be married, became very ill. He had to be carried outside to toilet and although the spark in his character never extinguished, I found it difficult to manage a sick, 16-year-old dog with everything else going on in my life. He no longer enjoyed a quality of life, and so I made the difficult decision to put him out of his misery. Killing Sam was confronting. The term, 'euthanasia' can have a wistful blameless ring to it. I will not touch on human euthanasia as it's an ethical minefield which do not have the experience nor education to tackle. Killing my beloved dog was no wistful venture. Most adults who are pet carers face this dreadful experience at one stage of their lives. I called my parents the night before I put Sam down to discuss my dilemma and seek guidance. My mother explained to me that not all vet kills are easy and that perhaps I should say *'bye-bye'* before the injection and avoid witnessing possible convulsions. I did not follow her advice. If Sam had to face death, the least I could do was hold him through the experience. It was not pleasant. While the girls were sad about Sam's passing, although Ed liked and had played with Sam often, he didn't seem to even notice Sam's absence.

Eventually, we adopted the 'dragon'. We had purchased our Cavoolde, Phoenix, in 2008 and he was another loyal dog. Phoenix sported a red, soft, wavy coat and a gentle nature. Francesca named him after the phoenix in the Harry Potter book she was reading at the time. A month or so after Sam's death, we set out to find a friend for Phoenix at the RSPCA animal shelter. I planned to adopt a male, strong dog. I reasoned that with three females in the family and no dad around, we were lacking testosterone in the home. I wanted Edison to have a powerful dog and illogically, I thought he might prefer a male pet. I also harboured a plan to source and train an intelligent dog as a useful companion for Ed. When setting out to adopt a dog from the RSPCA with three children in tow, one rarely leaves without a new family member (no matter the plan). Phoenix came with us to the animal shelter to ensure pet-pal characters were conducive. Upon arrival, we learned that there were no dogs available to fit the bill I had hoped for. We eventually came home with Lilly, the dragon.

Lilly was named Matilda when we adopted her. I didn't think that name suited her, and I reasoned with myself that her former owners would likely have called her Tilly at times. Renaming her Lilly, I believed, would not cause her trauma. Sometimes I do wonder at my thinking and what motivates it. Lilly was not male, not strong and would have given Max's bitchiness a run for her money. When we first brought Lilly home from the RSPCA, she was a fluffy, small, unresponsive dog who didn't seem to understand the role of being a pet. It took many months to teach her that she had a tail to wag, a friend to play with and people to care for her. Within six months, she began to resemble a pet, yet she carried with her defensiveness, likely born from whatever past she had experienced three years prior to becoming part of our family. Lilly was a runaway barking, killer Bichon Frise. Edison couldn't cross her – literally. Ed enjoyed holding the cats up to his face and giggled as their fur tickled him and often made him sneeze. He would jump all over Phoenix, but the relationship he developed with Lilly was not so congenial. He was so afraid of this fluffy, tiny dog that he dubbed her 'the dragon'. Edison would climb furniture before he would cross the dragon's path, always afraid of her next attack. Lilly only ever attacked Phoenix, myself and native animals, unfortunately, even killing a large goanna once. We were all in fear, to varying degrees, of Lilly's ferociousness. At approximately 25 centimetres tall, she was a terrifying power. I enjoyed observing Edison's different and appropriately modulated interactions with his pets. He seemed to have an innate ability to read animals and people.

By 2014, the children were old enough to spend some school holiday time in Toowoomba, independent of me. The kids cherished special trips to their grandparents' home and I enjoyed the freedom of being able to work without having to juggle children at home during school holidays 24x7. On one trip with Granny and Papa, Eddie went missing during a bush walk. My much-loved Aunty Dawn and mother had decided to take the kids on an ice-cream excursion to Picnic Point. After consuming ice-cream treats and playing a while in the park, my children implored their granny and great aunty to go exploring in the bush. Off the five of them set for a short and safe bush walk. The circular trek they set upon meandered through Australian vegetation at the foot of Picnic Point's waterfall. The track was a nature-inspired child's playground. There was bamboo to hide amongst and rocks which acted as stepping-stones over tame streams on which to jump. About halfway through the walking track loop, Granny and Aunty Dawn noticed Edison was missing. Aunty Dawn told me that it was around 10 minutes before they located him. They ended up spotting him about 15 metres, climbing up a cliff face that was approximately 30 metres tall. My girls and their adult carers called and called to Ed and at one point only, did he acknowledge their shouting. Edison continued to traverse the cliff face beside the waterfall. All the while, the bellowing of his sisters began to attract the attention of others. There was no way for anyone present to chase or rescue Ed. Indeed, I am sure Eddie felt no rescue was required. Diligently and with remarkable dexterity, Ed reached the top of the cliff face, only to be met with an obstacle he found challenging. At the top of the cliff was a safety rail and Eddie struggled to work out how to conquer the safety rail. How is that for ironic? A family who had heard the calls for Edison was situated on the safe side of the rail at the top of the waterfall. With a wife and three children in tow, the father managed to secure Edison safely over the rail and harboured him whilst Ed's sisters, granny and great aunt eventually made it back to him. My mother learnt yet another lesson on the vigilance required when Ed's safety was her responsibility. There were many times where Ed escaped near possible death experiences. I am thankful for the rich and adventurous holidays my children experienced as a result of the generosity and love of my parents.

Granny and Papa, with Aunty Dawn (who could never arrive anywhere without a treat in hand), risked taking the children out on many interesting adventures. One of the children's favourites was the Japanese Gardens of Toowoomba. Ed would relish in delight at feeding the turtles and all the children enjoyed exploring the myriad of walks throughout the gardens. The children also especially enjoyed a park with a flying fox. During these visits with Granny and Papa, Ed was able to enjoy a one-way trip on the flying fox but he could not propel himself on a return journey, as most children his age would be capable of doing. As such, my daughters lovingly helped Ed to fly back and forth, assisting Ed's propulsion as he delighted in being air-bound. When Eddie would arrive at my parents' home and upon my exit, he would find a photo of me on their fridge which he would keep with him, sleep with and even try to shower with. Edison decided that a photo of me needed to always be near when he wasn't with me. It was never easy for Eddie nor me to be physically apart.

Edison – the coder

In 2014, Edison's photographic memory became something people other than our immediate family noticed. Whilst staying at my parents' place, Edison wrote from memory the following:

Warning HIT VIDEO Kipper Brambly Hedge Percy the Park Keeper Amazing HIT FIB VHS VIDEO Barney's Let's Go To The Zoo HIT FIB VHS VIDEO Barney's Christmas Snow Tree HIT FIB VHS VIDEO Bob the Builder Scary Spud HIT FIB VHS VIDEO Bob the Builder Naughty Spud HIT FIB VHS VIDEO Bob the Builder Runways Roley HIT FIB VHS VIDEO Bob the Builder Bob the Framer HIT FIB VHS VIDEO Bob the Builder Spud The Polit HIT FIB VHS VIDEO Bob the Builder Lenged Spud's A Hand HIT FIB VHS VIDEO Bob the Builder Skat Borad Spud's HIT FIB VHS VIDEO Bob the Builder Spud's Big Supries HIT FIB VHS VIDEO Bob the Builder Spud The Spanner HIT FIB VHS VIDEO The Wiggles Wiggly Christmas VHS VIDEO Pal A Rare HIT FIB VHS VIDEO The Wiggles Splish Splash Big Red Boat HIT FIB VHS VIDEO The Wiggles Sailing Around The World HIT FIB VHS VIDEO The Wiggles Pumpkin Face! HIT FIB VHS VIDEO The Wiggles It's A Wiggly World HIT FIB VHS VIDEO The Wiggles Cold Spaghetti Western HIT FIB VHS VIDEO The Wiggles Top of the Tots HIT FIB VHS VIDEO HIT FIB VHS VIDEO The Wiggles The Wiggles The Wiggly Big Show! HIT FIB VHS VIDEO The Wiggles Wake Up Jeff! VHS VIDEO Pal A Rare HIT FIB VHS VIDEO The Wiggles Wiggly Safari HIT FIB VHS VIDEO The Wiggles Space Dancing! HIT FIB VHS VIDEO The Wiggles Toot! HIT FIB VHS VIDEO Santa's Rockin'! HIT FIB VHS VIDEO The Wiggles Wiggle Bay HIT FIB VHS VIDEO Hi-5 It's A Hi-5 Christmas HIT FIB VHS VIDEO Hi-5 Action Heroes HIT FIB VHS VIDEO Hi-5 Animals Adventures HIT FIB VHS VIDEO Hi-5 Star Dreaming HIT FIB VHS VIDEO Hi-5 Music Machines HIT FIB VHS VIDEO Hi-5 Surfing Safari HIT FIB VHS VIDEO Hi-5 Have Some Fun Hi-5 Happy House HIT FIB VHS VIDEO Hi-5 Summer Rainbows HIT FIB VHS VIDEO Hi-5 Move Your Body HIT FIB VHS VIDEO Hi-5 Travelling Circus HIT FIB VHS VIDEO Hi-5 Santa Is Coming! Claus HIT FIB VHS VIDEO And Other Stories VHS Part 1 3 4 5 6 7 and 8 Magic Key Animals Stories and Sheeep LBWalkdenVHS

A fatal error has been detected by the Java Runtime Environment:

EXCEPTION_ACCESS_VIOLATION (0xc0000005) at pc=0x49e3ec58, pid=4488, tid=4648
#
JRE version: 7.0_05-b05
Java VM: Java HotSpot(TM) Client VM (23.1-b03 mixed mode windows-x86)
Problematic frame:
C 0x49e3ec58
#
Failed to write core dump. Minidumps are not enabled by default on client versions of Windows
#
If you would like to submit a bug report, please visit:
http://bugreport.sun.com/bugreport/crash.jsp
The crash happened outside the Java Virtual Machine in native code.
See problematic frame for where to report the bug.
#

--------------- T H R E A D ---------------

Current thread (0x49b21800): JavaThread "Minecraft main thread" daemon [_thread_in_native, id=4648, stack(0x4b450000,0x4b4a0000)]

siginfo: ExceptionCode=0xc0000005, writing address 0x6eaa4014

Registers:
EAX=0x3e400000, EBX=0x00000000, ECX=0x3e2feb85, EDX=0x6eaa3ff8
ESP=0x4b49eb20, EBP=0x4b49eb68, ESI=0x4b49eb50, EDI=0x49b21800
EIP=0x49e3ec58, EFLAGS=0x00010206

Top of Stack: (sp=0x4b49eb20)
0x4b49eb20: 4ac27d26 3e2feb85 3e400000 018c10f7
0x4b49eb30: 49b21928 4b49eb50 3e2feb85 3e400000
0x4b49eb40: 737b1b80 00000000 00000000 737b1880
0x4b49eb50: 18e20ab0 4ff25f70 18e20ab0

0x4b49eb60: 4d916671 49b21800 4b49f7f8 01a99150
0x4b49eb70: 737b1b80 00000000 00000000 0196d933
0x4b49eb80: 49b21928 4b49eba0 00000de1 00000007
0x4b49eb90: 4b3e0000 4cc095e0 000084c0 4dc502f0
Instructions: (pc=0x49e3ec58)
0x49e3ec38: c0 ff 80 00 00 00 81 0d 6c 15 41 4b 00 01
0x49e3ec48: 00 00 8b 15 64 15 41 4b 8b 4c 24 04 8b 44 24 08
0x49e3ec58: 89 4a 1c 89 42 20 c2 08 00 00 00 00 00 00 00 00
0x49e3ec68: 00 00 00 00 00 00 00 00 00 00 00 00 00 00 00 00

Register to memory mapping:

EAX=0x3e400000 is an unallocated location in the heap
EBX=0x00000000 is an unknown value
ECX=0x3e2feb85 is an unallocated location in the heap
EDX=0x6eaa3ff8 is an unknown value
ESP=0x4b49eb20 is pointing into the stack for thread: 0x49b21800
EBP=0x4b49eb68 is pointing into the stack for thread: 0x49b21800
ESI=0x4b49eb50 is pointing into the stack for thread: 0x49b21800
EDI=0x49b21800 is a thread

Stack: [0x4b450000,0x4b4a0000], sp=0x4b49eb20, free space=314k
Native frames: (J=compiled Java code, j=interpreted, Vv=VM code, C=native code)
C 0x49e3ec58
J awv.a(IZ)F
v ~StubRoutines::call_stub
V [jvm.dll+0x12964a]
V [jvm.dll+0x1d851e]
V [jvm.dll+0x129833]
V [jvm.dll+0x129897]
V [jvm.dll+0xd24af]
V [jvm.dll+0x149977]
V [jvm.dll+0x149ae0]
V [jvm.dll+0x17e049]
C [msvcr100.dll+0x5c6de]

C [msvcr100.dll+0x5c788]
C [kernel32.dll+0x4ed6c]
C [ntdll.dll+0x6377b]
C [ntdll.dll+0x6374e]
Java frames: (J=compiled Java code, j=interpreted, Vv=VM code)
J org.lwjgl.opengl.GL11.nglTexCoord2f(FFJ)V
J awv.a(IZ)F
J awv.a(ICZ)F
J awv.a(Ljava/lang/String;Z)V
J awv.b(Ljava/lang/String;IIIZ)I
J awv.a(Ljava/lang/String;IIIZ)I
J bhi.a(Lawv;Lbge;Lwm;IILjava/lang/String;)V
J aww.a(IIIF)V
J aww.a(FZII)V
J bfq.b(F)V
J net.minecraft.client.Minecraft.K()V
J net.minecraft.client.Minecraft.run()V
j java.lang.Thread.run()V+11
v ~StubRoutines::call_stub

--------------- P R O C E S S ---------------

Java Threads: (=> current thread)
0x49b20c00   JavaThread   "Server   thread"   daemon
[_thread_blocked, id=4208, stack(0x59fd0000,0x5a020000)]
0x49b23800   JavaThread   "Snooper   Timer"   daemon
[_thread_blocked, id=6032, stack(0x53b20000,0x53b70000)]
0x49b22800   JavaThread   "File   IO   Thread"   daemon
[_thread_blocked, id=5444, stack(0x4b7b0000,0x4b800000)]
=>0x49b21800 JavaThread "Minecraft main thread" daemon
[_thread_in_native, id=4648, stack(0x4b450000,0x4b4a0000)]
0x49b21c00   JavaThread   "Timer   hack   thread"   daemon
[_thread_blocked, id=2264, stack(0x4b6c0000,0x4b710000)]
0x49b21000   JavaThread   "Snooper   Timer"   daemon
[_thread_blocked, id=2596, stack(0x4b530000,0x4b580000)]
0x49b23c00   JavaThread   "TimerQueue"   daemon
[_thread_blocked, id=5208, stack(0x4b600000,0x4b650000)]
0x49b20400 JavaThread "thread applet-net.minecraft.Launcher-1" [_thread_blocked, id=696, stack(0x4b340000,0x4b390000)]

0x49b1f000   JavaThread   "AWT-EventQueue-1"
[_thread_blocked, id=3520, stack(0x4b800000,0x4b850000)]
0x49b1fc00   JavaThread   "JVM[id=3]-Heartbeat"   daemon
[_thread_blocked, id=5640, stack(0x4b390000,0x4b3e0000)]
0x49b1f800   JavaThread   "AWT-EventQueue-2"
[_thread_blocked, id=3556, stack(0x49d90000,0x49de0000)]
0x49b1ec00 JavaThread "Applet 3 LiveConnect Worker
Thread"   [_thread_blocked,   id=4444,
stack(0x4b100000,0x4b150000)]
0x49b1d800 JavaThread "Browser Side Object Cleanup Thread"
[_thread_blocked, id=5872, stack(0x4b260000,0x4b2b0000)]
0x49b1e400   JavaThread   "CacheCleanUpThread"   daemon
[_thread_blocked, id=5700, stack(0x4b160000,0x4b1b0000)]
0x49b1e000   JavaThread   "CacheMemoryCleanUpThread"
daemon   [_thread_blocked,   id=4936,
stack(0x49ee0000,0x49f30000)]
0x49b1b000 JavaThread "SysExecutionTheadCreator" daemon
[_thread_blocked, id=3128, stack(0x4acb0000,0x4ad00000)]
0x49b10c00   JavaThread   "AWT-EventQueue-0"
[_thread_blocked, id=2412, stack(0x4a980000,0x4a9d0000)]
0x49b08400   JavaThread   "AWT-Windows"   daemon
[_thread_in_native, id=4128, stack(0x4a860000,0x4a8b0000)]
0x49af9800 JavaThread "AWT-Shutdown" [_thread_blocked,
id=4804, stack(0x49e90000,0x49ee0000)]
0x49af9000   JavaThread   "Java2D   Disposer"   daemon
[_thread_blocked, id=5788, stack(0x4a710000,0x4a760000)]
0x49aa3c00 JavaThread "Java Plug-In Pipe Worker Thread
(Client-Side)"   daemon   [_thread_in_native,   id=6072,
stack(0x4a570000,0x4a5c0000)]
0x49a57400 JavaThread "Timer-0" [_thread_blocked, id=4176,
stack(0x4a5c0000,0x4a610000)]
0x49a04000   JavaThread   "traceMsgQueueThread"   daemon
[_thread_blocked, id=4744, stack(0x4a150000,0x4a1a0000)]
0x499c7400   JavaThread   "Service   Thread"   daemon
[_thread_blocked, id=3508, stack(0x49bc0000,0x49c10000)]
0x499b9400   JavaThread   "C1   CompilerThread0"   daemon
[_thread_blocked, id=1544, stack(0x49f40000,0x49f90000)]
0x499b7000   JavaThread   "Attach   Listener"   daemon
[_thread_blocked, id=5796, stack(0x49d20000,0x49d70000)]

0x499b3c00 JavaThread "Signal Dispatcher" daemon [_thread_blocked, id=2024, stack(0x49e40000,0x49e90000)]
0x49969c00 JavaThread "Finaliser" daemon [_thread_blocked, id=668, stack(0x01610000,0x01660000)]
0x49965000 JavaThread "Reference Handler" daemon [_thread_blocked, id=5384, stack(0x49c90000,0x49ce0000)]
0x016bbc00 JavaThread "main" [_thread_blocked, id=4268, stack(0x01660000,0x016b0000)]

Other Threads:
0x4995f800 VMThread [stack: 0x49b70000,0x49bc0000] [id=5716]
0x499d8800 WatcherThread [stack: 0x49fb0000,0x4a000000] [id=5960]

VM state:not at safepoint (normal execution)

VM Mutex/Monitor currently owned by a thread: None

Heap
def new generation total 314560K, used 63895K [0x037c0000, 0x18d10000, 0x18d10000)
eden space 279616K, 14% used [0x037c0000, 0x0609f370, 0x148d0000)
from space 34944K, 63% used [0x148d0000, 0x15e56b28, 0x16af0000)
to space 34944K, 0% used [0x16af0000, 0x16af0000, 0x18d10000)
tenured generation total 699072K, used 416313K [0x18d10000, 0x437c0000, 0x437c0000)
the space 699072K, 59% used [0x18d10000, 0x3239e760, 0x3239e800, 0x437c0000)
compacting perm gen total 18432K, used 18424K [0x437c0000, 0x449c0000, 0x477c0000)
the space 18432K, 99% used [0x437c0000, 0x449be020, 0x449be200, 0x449c0000)
No shared spaces configured.

Code Cache [0x017c0000, 0x02088000, 0x037c0000)

total_blobs=4297   nmethods=3907   adapters=321
free_code_cache=23802Kb largest_free_block=24371456

Compilation events (10 events):
Event: 4219.812 Thread 0x499b9400 3897 awx::a (184 bytes)
Event: 4219.814 Thread 0x499b9400 nmethod 3897 0x0207ef88
code [0x0207f240, 0x0207fc70]
Event: 4239.659 Thread 0x499b9400 3898 ami::b (33 bytes)
Event: 4239.659   Thread   0x499b9400   nmethod   3898
0x02080d48 code [0x02080e60, 0x02080f78]
Event: 4562.697 Thread 0x499b9400 3899 ng::aZ (67 bytes)
Event: 4562.698   Thread   0x499b9400   nmethod   3899
0x02081088 code [0x020811a0, 0x0208131c]
Event: 4574.862 Thread 0x499b9400 3900 vr::a (34 bytes)
Event: 4574.863   Thread   0x499b9400   nmethod   3900
0x02081548 code [0x02081660, 0x02081750]
Event: 4576.998 Thread 0x499b9400 3901 so::d (136 bytes)
Event: 4576.999   Thread   0x499b9400   nmethod   3901
0x02081848 code [0x02081970, 0x02081b9c]

GC Heap History (10 events):
Event: 4203.301 GC heap before
{Heap before GC invocations=75 (full 8):
def new generation total 314560K, used 293937K [0x037c0000,
0x18d10000, 0x18d10000)
eden space 279616K, 100% used [0x037c0000, 0x148d0000,
0x148d0000)
from space 34944K, 40% used [0x16af0000, 0x178ec7f0,
0x18d10000)
to space 34944K, 0% used [0x148d0000, 0x148d0000,
0x16af0000)
tenured generation total 699072K, used 366935K [0x18d10000,
0x437c0000, 0x437c0000)
the space 699072K, 52% used [0x18d10000, 0x2f365f60,
0x2f366000, 0x437c0000)
compacting perm gen total 18432K, used 18424K [0x437c0000,
0x449c0000, 0x477c0000)
the space 18432K, 99% used [0x437c0000, 0x449be020,
0x449be200, 0x449c0000)
No shared spaces configured.

Event: 4203.336 GC heap after

Heap after GC invocations=76 (full 8):

def new generation total 314560K, used 28541K [0x037c0000, 0x18d10000, 0x18d10000)

eden space 279616K, 0% used [0x037c0000, 0x037c0000, 0x148d0000)

from space 34944K, 81% used [0x148d0000, 0x164af6a0, 0x16af0000)

to space 34944K, 0% used [0x16af0000, 0x16af0000, 0x18d10000)

tenured generation total 699072K, used 366935K [0x18d10000, 0x437c0000, 0x437c0000)

the space 699072K, 52% used [0x18d10000, 0x2f365f60, 0x2f366000, 0x437c0000)

compacting perm gen total 18432K, used 18424K [0x437c0000, 0x449c0000, 0x477c0000)

the space 18432K, 99% used [0x437c0000, 0x449be020, 0x449be200, 0x449c0000)

No shared spaces configured.

}

Event: 4311.493 GC heap before

{Heap before GC invocations=76 (full 8):

def new generation total 314560K, used 308157K [0x037c0000, 0x18d10000, 0x18d10000)

eden space 279616K, 100% used [0x037c0000, 0x148d0000, 0x148d0000)

from space 34944K, 81% used [0x148d0000, 0x164af6a0, 0x16af0000)

to space 34944K, 0% used [0x16af0000, 0x16af0000, 0x18d10000)

tenured generation total 699072K, used 366935K [0x18d10000, 0x437c0000, 0x437c0000)

the space 699072K, 52% used [0x18d10000, 0x2f365f60, 0x2f366000, 0x437c0000)

compacting perm gen total 18432K, used 18424K [0x437c0000, 0x449c0000, 0x477c0000)

the space 18432K, 99% used [0x437c0000, 0x449be020, 0x449be200, 0x449c0000)

No shared spaces configured.

Event: 4311.549 GC heap after

Heap after GC invocations=77 (full 8):
def new generation total 314560K, used 7584K [0x037c0000, 0x18d10000, 0x18d10000)
eden space 279616K, 0% used [0x037c0000, 0x037c0000, 0x148d0000)
from space 34944K, 21% used [0x16af0000, 0x17258318, 0x18d10000)
to space 34944K, 0% used [0x148d0000, 0x148d0000, 0x16af0000)
tenured generation total 699072K, used 390949K [0x18d10000, 0x437c0000, 0x437c0000)
the space 699072K, 55% used [0x18d10000, 0x30ad9678, 0x30ad9800, 0x437c0000)
compacting perm gen total 18432K, used 18424K [0x437c0000, 0x449c0000, 0x477c0000)
the space 18432K, 99% used [0x437c0000, 0x449be020, 0x449be200, 0x449c0000)
No shared spaces configured.
}
Event: 4427.678 GC heap before
{Heap before GC invocations=77 (full 8):
def new generation total 314560K, used 287200K [0x037c0000, 0x18d10000, 0x18d10000)
eden space 279616K, 100% used [0x037c0000, 0x148d0000, 0x148d0000)
from space 34944K, 21% used [0x16af0000, 0x17258318, 0x18d10000)
to space 34944K, 0% used [0x148d0000, 0x148d0000, 0x16af0000)
tenured generation total 699072K, used 390949K [0x18d10000, 0x437c0000, 0x437c0000)
the space 699072K, 55% used [0x18d10000, 0x30ad9678, 0x30ad9800, 0x437c0000)
compacting perm gen total 18432K, used 18424K [0x437c0000, 0x449c0000, 0x477c0000)
the space 18432K, 99% used [0x437c0000, 0x449be020, 0x449be200, 0x449c0000)
No shared spaces configured.
Event: 4427.696 GC heap after
Heap after GC invocations=78 (full 8):

def new generation total 314560K, used 12165K [0x037c0000, 0x18d10000, 0x18d10000)

eden space 279616K, 0% used [0x037c0000, 0x037c0000, 0x148d0000)

from space 34944K, 34% used [0x148d0000, 0x154b1710, 0x16af0000)

to space 34944K, 0% used [0x16af0000, 0x16af0000, 0x18d10000)

tenured generation total 699072K, used 390949K [0x18d10000, 0x437c0000, 0x437c0000)

the space 699072K, 55% used [0x18d10000, 0x30ad9678, 0x30ad9800, 0x437c0000)

compacting perm gen total 18432K, used 18424K [0x437c0000, 0x449c0000, 0x477c0000)

the space 18432K, 99% used [0x437c0000, 0x449be020, 0x449be200, 0x449c0000)

No shared spaces configured.
}
Event: 4504.470 GC heap before
{Heap before GC invocations=78 (full 8):

def new generation total 314560K, used 291781K [0x037c0000, 0x18d10000, 0x18d10000)

eden space 279616K, 100% used [0x037c0000, 0x148d0000, 0x148d0000)

from space 34944K, 34% used [0x148d0000, 0x154b1710, 0x16af0000)

to space 34944K, 0% used [0x16af0000, 0x16af0000, 0x18d10000)

tenured generation total 699072K, used 390949K [0x18d10000, 0x437c0000, 0x437c0000)

the space 699072K, 55% used [0x18d10000, 0x30ad9678, 0x30ad9800, 0x437c0000)

compacting perm gen total 18432K, used 18424K [0x437c0000, 0x449c0000, 0x477c0000)

the space 18432K, 99% used [0x437c0000, 0x449be020, 0x449be200, 0x449c0000)

No shared spaces configured.
Event: 4504.510 GC heap after
Heap after GC invocations=79 (full 8):

def new generation total 314560K, used 33781K [0x037c0000, 0x18d10000, 0x18d10000)
eden space 279616K, 0% used [0x037c0000, 0x037c0000, 0x148d0000)
from space 34944K, 96% used [0x16af0000, 0x18bed498, 0x18d10000)
to space 34944K, 0% used [0x148d0000, 0x148d0000, 0x16af0000)
tenured generation total 699072K, used 390949K [0x18d10000, 0x437c0000, 0x437c0000)
the space 699072K, 55% used [0x18d10000, 0x30ad9678, 0x30ad9800, 0x437c0000)
compacting perm gen total 18432K, used 18424K [0x437c0000, 0x449c0000, 0x477c0000)
the space 18432K, 99% used [0x437c0000, 0x449be020, 0x449be200, 0x449c0000)
No shared spaces configured.
}
Event: 4568.805 GC heap before
{Heap before GC invocations=79 (full 8):
def new generation total 314560K, used 313397K [0x037c0000, 0x18d10000, 0x18d10000)
eden space 279616K, 100% used [0x037c0000, 0x148d0000, 0x148d0000)
from space 34944K, 96% used [0x16af0000, 0x18bed498, 0x18d10000)
to space 34944K, 0% used [0x148d0000, 0x148d0000, 0x16af0000)
tenured generation total 699072K, used 390949K [0x18d10000, 0x437c0000, 0x437c0000)
the space 699072K, 55% used [0x18d10000, 0x30ad9678, 0x30ad9800, 0x437c0000)
compacting perm gen total 18432K, used 18424K [0x437c0000, 0x449c0000, 0x477c0000)
the space 18432K, 99% used [0x437c0000, 0x449be020, 0x449be200, 0x449c0000)
No shared spaces configured.
Event: 4568.873 GC heap after
Heap after GC invocations=80 (full 8):

def new generation total 314560K, used 22042K [0x037c0000, 0x18d10000, 0x18d10000)
eden space 279616K, 0% used [0x037c0000, 0x037c0000, 0x148d0000)
from space 34944K, 63% used [0x148d0000, 0x15e56b28, 0x16af0000)
to space 34944K, 0% used [0x16af0000, 0x16af0000, 0x18d10000)
tenured generation total 699072K, used 416313K [0x18d10000, 0x437c0000, 0x437c0000)
the space 699072K, 59% used [0x18d10000, 0x3239e760, 0x3239e800, 0x437c0000)
compacting perm gen total 18432K, used 18424K [0x437c0000, 0x449c0000, 0x477c0000)
the space 18432K, 99% used [0x437c0000, 0x449be020, 0x449be200, 0x449c0000)
No shared spaces configured.
}

Deoptimisation events (0 events):
No events

Internal exceptions (10 events):
Event: 2922.328 Thread 0x49b21800 Threw 0x0b9c9430 at C:\jdk7u5_32P\jdk7u5\hotspot\src\share\vm\prims\jvm.cpp:1166
Event: 2922.328 Thread 0x49b21800 Threw 0x0b9c96a8 at C:\jdk7u5_32P\jdk7u5\hotspot\src\share\vm\prims\jvm.cpp:1166
Event: 2922.329 Thread 0x49b21800 Threw 0x0b9cc048 at C:\jdk7u5_32P\jdk7u5\hotspot\src\share\vm\prims\jvm.cpp:1166
Event: 2922.329 Thread 0x49b21800 Threw 0x0b9cc4b0 at C:\jdk7u5_32P\jdk7u5\hotspot\src\share\vm\prims\jvm.cpp:1166
Event: 3468.656 Thread 0x49b20c00 Threw 0x144881a8 at C:\jdk7u5_32P\jdk7u5\hotspot\src\share\vm\prims\jvm.cpp:1166

Event: 3468.656 Thread 0x49b20c00 Threw 0x14488420 at
C:\jdk7u5_32P\jdk7u5\hotspot\src\share\vm\prims\jvm.cpp:116
6
Event: 3573.988 Thread 0x49b20c00 Threw 0x0d0bfe28 at
C:\jdk7u5_32P\jdk7u5\hotspot\src\share\vm\prims\jvm.cpp:116
6
Event: 3573.988 Thread 0x49b20c00 Threw 0x0d0c00a0 at
C:\jdk7u5_32P\jdk7u5\hotspot\src\share\vm\prims\jvm.cpp:116
6
Event: 3791.013 Thread 0x49b21800 Threw 0x0f4736a8 at
C:\jdk7u5_32P\jdk7u5\hotspot\src\share\vm\prims\jvm.cpp:116
6
Event: 3791.013 Thread 0x49b21800 Threw 0x0f473920 at
C:\jdk7u5_32P\jdk7u5\hotspot\src\share\vm\prims\jvm.cpp:116
6

Events (10 events):
Event: 4569.054 Executing VM operation: RevokeBias done
Event: 4569.054 Thread 0x49b24400 Thread exited:
0x49b24400
Event: 4573.817 Thread 0x49b24400 Thread added:
0x49b24400
Event: 4573.827 Executing VM operation: RevokeBias
Event: 4573.827 Executing VM operation: RevokeBias done
Event: 4573.827 Thread 0x49b24400 Thread exited:
0x49b24400
Event: 4578.796 Thread 0x49b24400 Thread added:
0x49b24400
Event: 4578.814 Executing VM operation: RevokeBias
Event: 4578.815 Executing VM operation: RevokeBias done
Event: 4578.816 Thread 0x49b24400 Thread exited:
0x49b24400

Dynamic libraries:
0x011a0000   -   0x011cf000   C:\Program
Files\Java\jre7\bin\java.exe
0x77b30000 - 0x77c6c000 C:\Windows\SYSTEM32\ntdll.dll
0x75ed0000 - 0x75fa4000 C:\Windows\system32\kernel32.dll
0x75da0000   -   0x75deb000
C:\Windows\system32\KERNELBASE.dll

0x762a0000 - 0x76340000 C:\Windows\system32\ADVAPI32.dll
0x771b0000 - 0x7725c000 C:\Windows\system32\msvcrt.dll
0x75fc0000 - 0x75fd9000 C:\Windows\SYSTEM32\sechost.dll
0x75ff0000 - 0x76091000 C:\Windows\system32\RPCRT4.dll
0x77900000 - 0x779c9000 C:\Windows\system32\USER32.dll
0x76340000 - 0x7638e000 C:\Windows\system32\GDI32.dll
0x75fb0000 - 0x75fba000 C:\Windows\system32\LPK.dll
0x763f0000 - 0x7648d000 C:\Windows\system32\USP10.dll
0x749d0000 - 0x74b6e000 C:\Windows\WinSxS\x86_microsoft.windows.common-controls_6595b64144ccf1df_6.0.7601.17514_none_41e6975e2bd6f2b2\COMCTL32.dll
0x774f0000 - 0x77547000 C:\Windows\system32\SHLWAPI.dll
0x75aa0000 - 0x75aec000 C:\Windows\system32\apphelp.dll
0x739b0000 - 0x73a3d000 C:\Windows\AppPatch\AcLayers.DLL
0x75a80000 - 0x75a9b000 C:\Windows\system32\SspiCli.dll
0x76560000 - 0x771aa000 C:\Windows\system32\SHELL32.dll
0x779d0000 - 0x77b2c000 C:\Windows\system32\ole32.dll
0x760a0000 - 0x7612f000 C:\Windows\system32\OLEAUT32.dll
0x75190000 - 0x751a7000 C:\Windows\system32\USERENV.dll
0x75b70000 - 0x75b7b000 C:\Windows\system32\profapi.dll
0x73fe0000 - 0x74031000 C:\Windows\system32\WINSPOOL.DRV
0x71bd0000 - 0x71be2000 C:\Windows\system32\MPR.dll
0x77d00000 - 0x77d1f000 C:\Windows\system32\IMM32.DLL
0x76490000 - 0x7655c000 C:\Windows\system32\MSCTF.dll
0x69c50000 - 0x69d0e000 C:\Program Files\Java\jre7\bin\msvcr100.dll
0x64210000 - 0x6455a000 C:\Program Files\Java\jre7\bin\client\jvm.dll
0x726b0000 - 0x726b7000 C:\Windows\system32\WSOCK32.dll
0x77d20000 - 0x77d55000 C:\Windows\system32\WS2_32.dll
0x77c70000 - 0x77c76000 C:\Windows\system32\NSI.dll
0x72b20000 - 0x72b52000 C:\Windows\system32\WINMM.dll

0x76260000 - 0x76265000 C:\Windows\system32\PSAPI.DLL

0x719a0000 - 0x719ac000 C:\Program Files\Java\jre7\bin\verify.dll

0x6e8f0000 - 0x6e910000 C:\Program Files\Java\jre7\bin\java.dll

0x6d5b0000 - 0x6d5c3000 C:\Program Files\Java\jre7\bin\zip.dll

0x73f00000 - 0x73f06000 C:\Program Files\Java\jre7\bin\jp2native.dll

0x69d80000 - 0x69dc8000 C:\Program Files\Java\jre7\bin\deploy.dll

0x74f10000 - 0x74f19000 C:\Windows\system32\VERSION.dll

0x775a0000 - 0x77758000 C:\Windows\system32\WININET.dll

0x75d90000 - 0x75d94000 C:\Windows\system32\api-ms-win-downlevel-user32-l1-1-0.dll

0x75c00000 - 0x75c05000 C:\Windows\system32\api-ms-win-downlevel-advapi32-l1-1-0.dll

0x75bf0000 - 0x75bf4000 C:\Windows\system32\api-ms-win-downlevel-shlwapi-l1-1-0.dll

0x75eb0000 - 0x75eb4000 C:\Windows\system32\api-ms-win-downlevel-version-l1-1-0.dll

0x75d30000 - 0x75d33000 C:\Windows\system32\api-ms-win-downlevel-normaliz-l1-1-0.dll

0x75fe0000 - 0x75fe3000 C:\Windows\system32\normaliz.DLL

0x77260000 - 0x77458000 C:\Windows\system32\iertutil.dll

0x76130000 - 0x76251000 C:\Windows\system32\urlmon.dll

0x75ec0000 - 0x75ec4000 C:\Windows\system32\api-ms-win-downlevel-ole32-l1-1-0.dll

0x6d220000 - 0x6d234000 C:\Program Files\Java\jre7\bin\net.dll

0x755e0000 - 0x7561c000 C:\Windows\system32\mswsock.dll

0x755d0000 - 0x755d6000 C:\Windows\System32\wship6.dll

0x6e8e0000 - 0x6e8ef000 C:\Program Files\Java\jre7\bin\nio.dll

0x735e0000 - 0x73722000 C:\Program Files\Java\jre7\bin\awt.dll

0x74850000 - 0x74890000 C:\Windows\system32\uxtheme.dll

0x74520000 - 0x74533000 C:\Windows\system32\dwmapi.dll

0x75af0000 - 0x75afc000 C:\Windows\system32\CRYPTBASE.dll

0x49ce0000 - 0x49d17000 C:\Program Files\Acer\Acer ePower Management\SysHook.dll

0x75940000 - 0x75948000 C:\Windows\system32\Secur32.dll

0x72670000 - 0x72674000 C:\Windows\system32\api-ms-win-downlevel-advapi32-l2-1-0.dll

0x730a0000 - 0x730bc000 C:\Windows\system32\IPHLPAPI.DLL

0x73090000 - 0x73097000 C:\Windows\system32\WINNSI.DLL

0x73a70000 - 0x73a9a000 C:\Program Files\Java\jre7\bin\fontmanager.dll

0x73990000 - 0x739b0000 C:\Program Files\Java\jre7\bin\sunec.dll

0x73a60000 - 0x73a69000 C:\Program Files\Java\jre7\bin\sunmscapi.dll

0x75c10000 - 0x75d2e000 C:\Windows\system32\CRYPT32.dll

0x75be0000 - 0x75bec000 C:\Windows\system32\MSASN1.dll

0x75620000 - 0x75636000 C:\Windows\system32\CRYPTSP.dll

0x753c0000 - 0x753fb000 C:\Windows\system32\rsaenh.dll

0x750c0000 - 0x750c5000 C:\Windows\System32\wshtcpip.dll

0x70100000 - 0x70127000 C:\Program Files\Common Files\Microsoft Shared\Windows Live\WLIDNSP.DLL

0x700d0000 - 0x700f1000 C:\Program Files\Bonjour\mdnsNSP.dll

0x754a0000 - 0x754e4000 C:\Windows\system32\DNSAPI.dll

0x700b0000 - 0x700b6000 C:\Windows\system32\rasadhlp.dll

0x72ec0000 - 0x72ef8000 C:\Windows\System32\fwpuclnt.dll

0x73e90000 - 0x73ea0000 C:\Windows\system32\NLAapi.dll

0x70160000 - 0x70170000 C:\Windows\system32\napinsp.dll

0x70140000 - 0x70152000 C:\Windows\system32\pnrpnsp.dll

0x70130000 - 0x7013d000 C:\Windows\system32\wshbth.dll

0x700c0000 - 0x700c8000 C:\Windows\System32\winrnr.dll

0x73960000 - 0x73984000 C:\Program Files\Java\jre7\bin\dcpr.dll

0x73920000 - 0x73951000 C:\Program Files\Java\jre7\bin\t2k.dll

0x77460000 - 0x774e3000 C:\Windows\system32\CLBCatQ.DLL

0x74240000   -   0x74370000
C:\Windows\system32\WindowsCodecs.dll
0x6df70000   -   0x6dfa1000
C:\Windows\system32\EhStorShell.dll
0x77760000   -   0x778fd000
C:\Windows\system32\SETUPAPI.dll
0x75d60000   -   0x75d87000
C:\Windows\system32\CFGMGR32.dll
0x75d40000 - 0x75d52000 C:\Windows\system32\DEVOBJ.dll
0x74890000   -   0x74985000
C:\Windows\system32\PROPSYS.dll
0x6df00000 - 0x6df6a000 C:\Windows\System32\cscui.dll
0x6def0000 - 0x6def9000 C:\Windows\System32\CSCDLL.dll
0x6ee80000 - 0x6ee8b000 C:\Windows\system32\CSCAPI.dll
0x6de80000 - 0x6def0000 C:\Windows\system32\ntshrui.dll
0x75810000 - 0x75829000 C:\Windows\system32\srvcli.dll
0x73450000 - 0x7345a000 C:\Windows\system32\slc.dll
0x4a100000   -   0x4a138000   C:\Program
Files\WIDCOMM\Bluetooth Software\btmmhook.dll
0x49c80000   -   0x49c87000   C:\Program
Files\ReferenceBoss_1p\bar\1.bin\1pbrstub.dll
0x4ac20000   -   0x4ac8b000
C:\Users\User\AppData\Roaming\.minecraft\bin\natives\lwjgl.d
ll
0x737b0000   -   0x73878000
C:\Windows\system32\OPENGL32.dll
0x738d0000 - 0x738f2000 C:\Windows\system32\GLU32.dll
0x734f0000 - 0x735d7000 C:\Windows\system32\DDRAW.dll
0x74040000   -   0x74046000
C:\Windows\system32\DCIMAN32.dll
0x738c0000   -   0x738c6000   C:\Program
Files\Java\jre7\bin\jawt.dll
0x4d910000   -   0x4e356000
C:\Windows\system32\nvoglv32.DLL
0x738b0000   -   0x738ba000   C:\Program
Files\Java\jre7\bin\management.dll
0x4b2f0000   -   0x4b311000   C:\Program
Files\WIDCOMM\Bluetooth Software\btkeyind.dll
VM Arguments:

jvm_args: -D__jvm_launched=9180914085   -D__applet_launched=9180911772   -Xbootclasspath/a:C:\\PROGRA~1\\Java\\jre7\\lib\\deploy.jar;C:\\PROGRA~1\\Java\\jre7\\lib\\javaws.jar;C:\\PROGRA~1\\Java\\jre7\\lib\\plugin.jar   -Dsun.awt.warmup=true   -Xmx1g   -Xms1024M   -Dsun.java2d.noddraw=true   -Dsun.awt.noerasebackground=true -Dsun.java2d.d3d=false   -Dsun.java2d.opengl=false

java_command: sun.plugin2.main.client.PluginMain write_pipe_name=jpi2_pid3488_pipe9,read_pipe_name=jpi2_pid3488_pipe8

Launcher Type: SUN_STANDARD

Environment Variables:

PATH=C:\Program   Files\Internet   Explorer;;C:\Program Files\Common   Files\Microsoft   Shared\Windows Live;C:\Windows\system32;C:\Windows;C:\Windows\System32\Wbem;C:\Windows\System32\WindowsPowerShell\v1.0\;C:\Program   Files\WIDCOMM\Bluetooth   Software\;C:\Program Files\Windows   Live\Shared;C:\Program Files\QuickTime\QTSystem\

USERNAME=User

OS=Windows_NT

PROCESSOR_IDENTIFIER=x86 Family 6 Model 23 Stepping 10, GenuineIntel

--------------- S Y S T E M ---------------

OS: Windows 7 Build 7601 Service Pack 1

CPU:total 2 (2 cores per cpu, 1 threads per core) family 6 model 23 stepping 10, cmov, cx8, fxsr, mmx, sse, sse2, sse3, ssse3, sse4.1, tsc

Memory: 4k page, physical 3109812k(808272k free), swap 6217872k(2355100k free)

vm_info: Java HotSpot(TM) Client VM (23.1-b03) for windows-x86 JRE (1.7.0_05-b05), built on May 15 2012 18:11:27 by "java_re" with unknown MS VC++:1600

time: Tue Jun 25 10:33:46 2013
elapsed time: 4580 seconds

My parents informed me that before typing this code, Ed's computer shutdown un-expectantly. He trance-like stared at the error text as the machine processed a reboot. For a long time after the blue-screen-of-death reboot, Ed, extremely focused, typed what he had read on the screen during shutdown. Go figure... the school and paediatricians wanted Ed on attention deficit drugs. His memory showed no deficient signs, in my opinion. Typing from memory, movie credits and other strings of words became one of Eddie's favourite pass-times. He spent hours either watching and mentally capturing words or typing them out. Here is another example...

01 Hi-5 Series 2 Theme Song
02 Hi-5 Fairies Land DVD Intro
03 Fairy Land Wish – Hi-5 – Season 2 Song of the Week
04 Hi-5 Charli Fairies Bed
05 Hi-5 Kellie Fairies Land Wish
07 Hi-5 Tim Going Shopping
08 Hi-5 Kathleen's Bed Time
09 Hi-5 Nathan's Brush Teeth
10 Hi-5 Sharing Stories – Fairy Dream
11 Fairy Dream – Hi-5 – Season 2 Song of the Week
12 Hi-5 Kellie Fairy Wish
13 Hi-5 Tim Music Night
14 Hi-5 Charli Fairy Wish
15 Hi-5 Nathan's Dreaming
16 Hi-5 Kellie Fairy Dream
17 Hi-5 Kathleen's Fairy Wish
18 Hi-5 Charli Fairy Dream
19 Hi-5 Sharing Stories – Fairies Land
20 Fairy Land – Hi-5 – Season 2 Song of the Week
21 Hi-5 Fairy Land End Credits

When we went to the movies as a family, we always had to stay through all the credits. Once the movie was finished, the best part for Ed began. He would run to the front of the cinema and dance around and around in circles to music, trying to adjust his eyes as to not miss one credit. Eddie and I would always share a monster box of popcorn during the movies. Special times... After Ed's death, I took my daughters to the cinema once. I felt so empty and confronted without my boy, that I have not since returned years later.

Enjoying a glorious afternoon at Hilliup one day, I found the time to enjoy the weather and relax on the back deck. I was working on the weekend. My kids were all under control. As I worked on my laptop, Edison arrived and announced, *"Hello, Mama."* I looked up from my screen to see my boy dressed in a pirate's vest, hat and boots, holding a plastic sword in his hand. I replied to Ed, *"Hello, pirate."*

His response was confusion and he tore off the pirate hat and repeated, *"Hello, Mama."*

"Hello, pirate." Edison removed his vest and threw his sword over the deck.

"Hello, Mama."

"Hello, pirate."

Edison, confused and frustrated, removed the costume boots also. I drew in a deep breath upon seeing my son, un-adorned in pirate gear and declared, *"Hello Edison."* Edison sighed in relief that his not-so-bright mum could finally recognise him. There were anomalies in Edison's predominantly literal interpretation of all things. He, for example, found it exasperating that I saw him as a pirate and not Ed. Maybe he didn't get my humour that day. Maybe he just expected more from me. He was a child prone to making other's laugh and he seemed to understand his version of humour more than he did many other things. Certain aspects of his makeup remain a mystery to me. His resilience and sense of humour, regardless of my lack of insight, will always be remembered with respect and deep love.

Early in 2014, the school conducted a parent teacher interview with Edison's grade 4 teacher, a Special Unit staff member and myself. Edison's grade 4 teacher had taught Francesca the year before and so we already had established positive rapport. I held respect for him as a teacher and a person. Ed's teacher had also coached my daughters in basketball and they really liked his tough style of coaching. *"She's not your friend! She's not your sister! Defend!"* I felt fortunate that the children had a strong and strict, yet likeable, male role model in their lives. Prior to the classroom interview, I had raised concerns with the Special Unit that the material Edison was covering was not challenging enough for him academically. As mentioned previously, he was equipped with a photographic memory and could spell words like elephant, giraffe and crocodile by the age of three. At JSS, the 'Unit' was teaching him the likes of 'cat, rat, mat'. He was coming along in his fine-motor and writing skills at JSS, but I certainly did not feel he was being challenged academically. I was satisfied somewhat with the work they were doing around numeracy. I always found it confronting and odd that I was never afforded a parent teacher interview one on one. In fact, outside of meetings with Mr McKinnon, Edison's final case manager, I do not remember one formal, planned school meeting where the ratio was 1:1 (staff to parent).

The day before this year 4 parent teacher interview, the head of the Special Unit had expressed to me some very derogatory statements regarding Edison's abilities and his future. I have since learned such statements are called 'life limiting statements' and such statements are not encouraged by the Queensland Education Department. The head of the Special Unit had made it clear to me that he was of the opinion that Edison would never live independently, would never acquire the social skills to venture into society alone and that his future was institutionalisation, for the rest of his life. This man had known Edison for a short chapter of his life and he had no idea of the baseline Edison had bravely and persistently grown himself from. In listening to this man's derogatory comments, my memory took me to Ed's early childhood years where I was told never to expect Ed to be toilet-trained etcetera. While day by day, I celebrated Ed's persistence and achievements, this school leader focused on Eddie's limitations, both real and imagined, with a hopeless bias I did not share. Needless to say, I went into the parent teacher interview the next day a little defensive.

The classroom teacher handled me well. Thankfully, the negative, biased head of the Special Unit was not present at the meeting. The special needs representative allocated to attend the parent teacher interview did not handle my advocacy of Edison so well. There were two major outcomes from this meeting. The first was, after being supplied verbal post-interview feedback from the Special Education Unit (SEU) representative, the head of the SEU wrote an email complaint to the school principal, copying all and sundry with regards to my demeanour. The second outcome was an agreement that Ed showed a higher level of ability in many domains at home than he displayed at school. The conclusion agreed to was that he either wasn't performing optimally at school because it was simply a different environment (to home) or that the school was not putting the right supports in place for Edison to flourish. Subsequently, we agreed that I would spend each Monday morning in the classroom so that I could get a first-hand view of how Edison behaved in the classroom and what his capable classroom teacher was up against. We were all aware that my presence might affect Eddie's performance, but as the classroom teacher and I were keen to collaborate, for the best interests of Edison and his peers, classroom assistance from Mum seemed a logical next step. I changed my work routine to accommodate weekly classroom support.

By assisting in Edison's learning Monday mornings, I learnt many things. I was already aware that the Monday morning routine began with each child reading a news article from the weekend's newspaper. During the first term of that year, Edison and I had spent Sunday afternoons practicing his news articles. In term 2, when I began helping in the classroom, I witnessed the results of our Sunday afternoon rehearsals. Each Sunday morning, I would give Ed two or three articles which I thought would be of interest to him to select from. He would select an article and then I would often summarise the piece and hand write the article out in large print to make it easier for Edison to read aloud. Edison was quite literate but his verbal dyspraxia made speech and reading aloud a tremendously difficult task. The Monday morning school routine, following news-article sharing included spelling. Edison had different words to the other kids. There was also a quiz that involved looking up various locations in an Atlas. On those Monday mornings, the teacher would often use a child's news story or two as the location to look up. He would facilitate discussion about various aspects of the location (climate, topography, demographics and so forth). It was relatively easy to adapt these tasks in a mainstream setting to suit Edison's needs. It was relatively easy because I was present. I realised quite early on the challenge that the classroom teacher faced by including Edison without a full-time teacher's aide. I developed a newfound empathy for the staff of the SEU and Edison's classroom teacher. Adjustments were made accordingly. I was quite impressed how the Special Unit included me in the very many modifications they made for Ed after my stint in the classroom. In the main, the staff were extremely dedicated and caring, always looking for new ways to accommodate and extend Edison without compromising the needs of his peers.

On about the fourth Monday of helping in the classroom, when it came Edison's turn to read his news article, one of the so-called cool kids sitting in front of Edison, began to snigger as Edison tried his best to read out loud his news article. The sniggering spread amongst a few of the kids (not all of them). The classroom teacher could see rage growing across my face as I noted disapproval growing on his expression. We locked eyes and I sensed the teacher was taking a big risk in letting me address the class once Edison had finished his reading. I was raging inside, a truly angry mama. On the outside, I was as cool as ice. I asked the teacher, *"May I?"* He nodded and I explained to Edison's peers what a feat my son had just accomplished. I asked the children how many of them had ever blown out candles on a cake at their birthday parties. *"Show of hands, please."* All hands shot up. I went on... *"When Edison was about one and a half years old, I noticed it was hard for him to make some sounds and do some things with his mouth. In noticing this, I added to his story, song and prayer routine each night, the blowing out of a candle. Each night until his sixth birthday, Edison practiced blowing out a candle. Do you know that it wasn't until Edison practised blowing out a candle for four and a half years that he successfully blew out the candles on his birthday cake? He practiced this thousands of times before he got it right. Now hold up your index finger like this. Imagine it is a candle and blow it out. Now, put up your hand if you think that was hard."* No hands. *"If my son has worked that hard to blow out a candle, can you imagine how hard he has worked to read out loud to you, a news article?"* Silence. *"When Edison next reads aloud in the classroom, can you please show him the respect he deserves and imagine one thing you've had to work at, as hard as he's worked to blow out a candle?"* A small approving smile from the classroom teacher was gratefully noted. I was so very appreciative that the teacher entrusted me to teach his class a simple lesson. We had added as a family, respect and encouragement to our values over the years. I was proud of the fact that my children knew our five core values better than the back of their hands. I hoped Edison's lesson to his peers that day when he was teased for being autistic, was one of respect.

Post the aforementioned parent teacher interview, the outcome of the email of complaint against me initiated a reply copying all, from me. As a result of various communications, including a bunch of hierarchical escalations, a subsequent 12 Education Queensland staff with one Jillian meeting was organised. I telephoned Autism Queensland, requesting a person to support me during the upcoming meeting. Thankfully, they agreed. A transfer of the head of Special Needs ensued along with a few other long-awaited changes. I don't know where the man who was transferred went, but I never discarded photographs of bruises on Eddie which I am sure that he had inflicted. Clearly, this process caused much stress and my summary does not do justice to the trauma such confrontation caused.

Chapter 17
Community Finds Us

Mid 2014, we attracted another drama. I wasn't doing well with my postcode 4074 planned anonymity. The 2013 school shut down caused by our family was the first event to put us on the map. I helped out in Freya-Grace's classroom for reading and in 2014 also worked the tuck-shop most Fridays. Edison was in a school of over 1000 kids, generally perceived as the highest need child in the school. He was very sociable but not always appropriately. He loved younger children and obsessed over caressing young girls' hair and providing unsolicited cuddles to younger children. I was overly conscience of working with the school to meet Edison's needs and as a parent and a former teacher, I aimed to encourage methods and processes, which whilst supporting Ed, would not compromise his typically developing peers. There had been many parent-led complaints about Ed. Unfortunately, most of them were reasonably grounded. There were many more social fire-extinguishing meetings than I had the appetite for. I found it tiring hearing how hard it was to, on-occasion, encounter my son. My son's social intentions, I believe, were always morally sound. Often though, his behaviours were understandably interpreted as mean, inappropriate or surreptitiously lacking in empathy by those unaware of Edison's challenges. I had developed into an autism educator, advocate and mediator with no desire for my son to cause the community stress. Despite the complaints about Ed, predominantly, the school community was kind, understanding and tolerant.

Community support came to a head the day that Freya-Grace was hit by a car outside the school. This incident occurred around Easter of 2014 when Freya-Grace, at the age of nine, was training for cross-country. She had a history of doing very well in cross-country and athletics generally and training occurred three mornings a week, beginning at 7:45. The routine during cross-country season was for Freya-Grace to be dropped at the oval adjacent to the school so that she could train. I then, would drop Francesca and Edison to a government supported BSC programme, before heading off to work in the city. Routinely, Freya-Grace was dropped off on the opposite side of the road to the training oval and we'd wait as she crossed the road to join her training team. It was a fairly straight road to cross with clear visibility of oncoming vehicles. The morning of the accident, Freya-Grace had waited quite a while to feel safe before crossing. If she saw a car 700 metres away, she would not cross, even though it would be safe to do so. I mentioned to her that if a car was right up at the school intersection (a long way away), it was ok to cross. Stupid mother. That statement thwarted her confidence and her own judgement in safely crossing a road. Hence, as she looked left and saw safety, she forgot to look right again before stepping out. Metres in front of us, Freya-Grace, within seconds of my safe crossing advice, was hit by a car. I was the first person to her side, somehow concurrently ordering Francesca and Edison to stay in the car.

When I reached Freya-Grace, she was unconscious. I thought she was dead. There was nothing else in my world in that moment. I wasn't a daughter, a worker, a mother of other children... My existence became consumed by my care and love for my limp daughter lying on the bitumen. I felt for her pulse and after some time, I felt a beat and realised she was alive. Soon, a small crowd gathered and were asking me for instructions. Clearly, I didn't need to ask anyone to call 000 as many had already contacted emergency services. Volunteers offered to move Freya-Grace off the road. I was First Aid qualified and with my mum's history, I knew a little about spines. I exclaimed, *"You cannot move her! No one is to touch Freya-Grace until the paramedics get here."* Pictures of a wheel chair bound Freya-Grace flashed before my eyes. Fire officers were the first on the scene and pretty soon after, paramedics and the police joined them. Freya-Grace regained consciousness whilst on the way to the emergency department of a hospital. By the time we arrived at the trauma unit, Freya-Grace was quite lucid.

The principal at JSS at the time was a warm man and an admirable leader. In the one year or so as a new to JSS principal, he instigated many positive changes. Unfortunately, many of his initiatives did not last, although they were well appreciated by the school community, whilst in place. Amongst well-intended onlookers and emergency services, the principal along with some of his staff who knew Edison and Francesca well, took on the role of comforting Francesca and Edison. Clearly, my other children were in shock having just witnessed their sister knocked to the road unconscious while their mother then treated them with relative abandonment. Before entering the ambulance with Freya-Grace, the principal assured me his staff would take care of Francesca and Edison and he provided me comfort. He asked if there was more he could do while the paramedics prepared Freya-Grace for the ambulance. I requested that he send staff to care for the lady who had driven the car that hit Freya-Grace. Clearly, she also had been traumatised by the event. From my peripheral vision, somehow, even in a state of tunnel-like attention, I noticed police around her but no parents or staff supporting her. Perhaps they were there but I didn't see them. That poor lady.

When hit by the car, Freya-Grace had bounced onto her left-hand side splatting onto bitumen. Most of the skin on her left arm, left hip and the upper half of her left leg had been ripped off. With her flesh exposed, trauma unit hospital staff treated her as a burn patient. Now, Freya-Grace is one tough cookie. Having a brother with autism meant the simplest of things, such as getting milk, was challenging. Since she was four-years-old, she had only one parent. Coupling her not-so-typical nine years of life experience with her character, it was not surprising that she was scared of little. Burn patients are treated with silver dressings, and my they hurt! As the trauma team of 12 staff fed Freya-Grace nitrous oxide (pain relieving gas), I could see the gas' effectiveness was not helpful. To this day, I cannot readily bring to mind, any other time where Freya-Grace has cried over physical pain. Whilst applying the silver bandages, she didn't so much as cry, she quietly sobbed into her own heart. It was horrible to see my beautiful, happy, tough nine-year-old daughter in so much pain. Eventually, we were moved to a ward and Freya-Grace was intermittently carted off for tests which would determine the extent of her injuries.

Lisa, the mum who had befriended me when Freya-Grace was in year two, was an early arrival on the scene of the accident and promptly went into a practical mode of assistance. She gently questioned and encouraged me. Eventually, Lisa learned how to break in to our house and where things were in my home which I may need whilst Freya-Grace was in hospital. She became our ambulance chaser and a comfort. After picking up certain supplies, Lisa followed us to the hospital and was by my side whilst Freya-Grace was treated in the emergency and trauma unit. Lisa, who was supposed to be at work that day, stayed with me throughout the day. There were moments when I couldn't quite take Freya-Grace's pain. I am ashamed to admit that I left the trauma room for around 10 minutes at one stage whilst Freya-Grace's dressings were being applied. I was shaking all over, likely from shock myself and I needed to be alone and breathe fresh air to regain strength in order to comfort my girl. Lisa was a rock. Late that afternoon, the doctors had run enough tests to provide news. I can't remember all the details of that day, but I do know that the community and medical staff who supported us were crucial to me coping.

After an MRI and other tests, an unknown doctor explained to me, *"Your daughter has suffered a mild brain injury..."* Oddly, not for the first time, I considered, *'It must be a challenging job to deliver that kind of news daily and never be remembered as an individual.'* Initially, no other medical information sank in. Fear played on my mind over and over. *'My daughter is now brain damaged? Not her brain!'* I am not a person with particularly high self-esteem and I really don't treat my body as well as I should, but my brain is one thing I treasure. All three of my children have incredible brains. Francesca with her academic and sporting achievements was also growing into a gifted artist. Edison could see, smell and hear matter I could not even perceive whilst his gift of memory was unlike anything I had ever encountered. Freya-Grace's mind and musical and sporting talents were no less remarkable, in my clearly bias opinion. Whilst comprehending our situation, hospital staff provided brochures outlining how a mild brain injury presents. The brochures included several statistics regarding possible recovery. I can't remember where Edison was that night. I think Lisa stayed overnight at our place while I slept on a hospital couch beside Freya-Grace. Friends brought Francesca to the hospital to see Freya-Grace. Freya-Grace was pretty high on painkillers when her sister visited with Freya-Grace's friend, Beth, alongside her mother, Jessica. Freya-Grace was happy to see Francesca and her friend, and the visit lifted Freya-Grace's spirit. Freya-Grace was not impressed when she learned that doctors had denied her returning to school the next day. She fought relentlessly to be let out of hospital so that she could be enabled to resume her somewhat normal life. To this day, Freya-Grace strives for a 100% school attendance record, and most years she is successful. The silver dressings used to treat Freya-Grace's bare flesh needed to stay moist and I needed to attend to them every two hours, day and night. Disappointingly for Freya-Grace, an immediate return to school was impractical.

Upon Freya-Grace's insistence, reluctant doctors checked us out of the hospital after agreeing with our local GP a schedule of visits. The school had arranged for counsellors, for Freya-Grace's fellow JSS students who were suffering as a result of Freya-Grace's accident. Notices had been sent home to hundreds of families associated with JSS on how to support their child through my daughter's brain injury incurring car accident. The notices were not blunt; they were worded and sent with care. My desired anonymity became a more difficult aim to pursue. Freya-Grace, it seems, was one of the least effected of the community by the accident. Upon her return to school, she was in pain, but like her papa, she never complained once. She fully rejected the notion of a brain injury whilst I counselled her older sister about behaviours and emotions we should look out for which may be forthcoming from Freya-Grace. Francesca and I alerted our attention to anything which was not typical and may be caused by Freya-Grace's brain injury. I had explained to Francesca all the facts (in age appropriate terminology) and we held onto the hope that Freya-Grace's brain would fully heal. Edison had favourites at different chapters of his life. Freya-Grace had been his favourite for around two years at that time and he was stupendously pleased to have her home. Being Edison's favourite required a fair deal of resilience. It meant he reserved his most annoying behaviour specifically for his chosen one.

Settling home from hospital, Freya-Grace took Ed's love in her stride.

Freya-Grace returned to school a mini-hero. Teachers were primed to look out for and accommodate signs of a brain injury. Much care and attention from our community was forthcoming, yet Freya-Grace stood steadfast in her attitude of business as usual. She did not like sympathetic attention and it became obvious that self-indulgence was not part of Freya-Grace's nature. One of the teachers confided in me that many staff called Freya-Grace 'rubber'. '*She even bounces off cars.*' I have learnt much about resilience as my children educate me in parenting positively. Kids are great teachers. It was difficult for me to treat Freya-Grace according to her wishes of no car accident related attention as I changed her dressings, and as inconspicuously as possible, monitored her brain injury related behaviour. This was a chapter of parenthood which again taught me the importance of respect. The accident wasn't mine. The injuries were not mine. They were Freya-Grace's events and the best way I could support her was to respect her wishes. For around five months there were behavioural signs of the brain injury, mostly by way of Freya-Grace's occasional atypical emotional outbursts. Within half a year, the symptoms fully receded and Freya-Grace's first report card after the car accident boasted A's and one B. It was near impossible to get an A in Physical Education at JSS, even if the student represented the school in several sports in regionals and districts, as did Freya-Grace, while also performing at A levels in PE academic subject matter. Her Physical Education B score was to me, still an A. Any best effort is an A. A big sigh – a big, '*Thank-you-my-creator-for-watching-over Freya-Grace.*'

Edison's 11th birthday fell on a day of the JSS annual school fete. None of us expected that his 11th would be his final birthday. Francesca was in her last year of primary school and had a wonderful teacher whose name is Selina; a lady who regularly stepped up to the role of MC each year for the fete. The JSS fete was no small affair and culminated in fireworks each year. Thousands of people attended. Logically, therefore there was a general rule that special birthday or anniversary announcements were not made over the loudspeaker system. In the full knowledge of this, my daughters never the less asked Selina if she could have the school sing '*Happy Birthday*' to Edison. This was the first and only birthday for which I had not thrown Edison a private birthday party. I had told him the morning of the fete that the whole school was having a party on his birthday and he would have favourite foods and rides galore – and if we were lucky, we might find some Wiggles or Toy Story treasures at the trash and treasure stall. Selina agreed to my daughters' request and on '*one, two, three*', thousands of people from our school and community sang happy birthday to Edison. His face lighted up and for Ed, the day was perfect. A special memory to treasure…

There are other memories of that day. There are memories of my jealousy towards parents who could relax on the grassy banks or enjoy the beer tent without having to ensure their child wouldn't be pushed out of a ride line-up. There are also memories of caring children. On Ed's birthday, around six hours into diligent Edison supervision, while also juggling turning up at my daughters' various performances, a little angle approached me. Her name was Rebecca. Eddie and I were lining up for a ride as Rebecca approached. We'd endured the line up for around 30 minutes before Rebecca arrived. Thirty minutes in a line-up with a hungry (always hungry) ASD child is a long wait. Rebecca introduced herself as one of Eddie's friends. She explained that she had been watching Ed and I, lining-up all day and she felt that I needed a break. She offered to watch and simultaneously protect Ed for an hour or so. I explained to the considerate and mature Rebecca that I appreciated her kindness but watching over Edison wasn't an easy task. She was as stubborn as me. She would not budge, explaining to me she knew something of special needs living with her own brother's challenges. She was firm, *"You are going to have a break."* Eventually, I capitulated to Edison's 11-year-old protector and enjoyed a light beer. Thank you, brazen, caring Rebecca. Ed might not have had sleepover friends but you, Rebecca, proved to be a friend.

Chapter 18
Day-to-Day Adjustments

I was confounded by the consequences of some rules that Edison's school had for everyone else which differed to the rules that applied specifically and only to us. I accepted and understood that people with pronounced differences can't necessarily conform to mainstream norms. An accommodation the school made for us, fuelled unwelcome conflict. The school pick-up routine required parents or carers to collect children from pick-up/drop-off safe zones. The zones had reasonable restrictions regarding their use. One restriction was that no vehicle could be in a safe zone for more than two minutes. Volunteers and staff were recruited to move latent cars along in order to keep the traffic flowing, ensuring student safety. If I wasn't there to pick Eddie up within a minute of a school day concluding, he would become extremely anxious and his behaviour would stress those around him. As a result, I was required by school administration to always arrive as close to first in line, as possible. I complied. Understandably, the parents of around 1000 kids who shared the pick-up safety zones were not informed that whilst I had been ordered to stay, everyone else was moved on. Often, the volunteer move-on-police were also not aware that the school had exclusive rules for Eddie and me. I did my best in managing this conundrum, yet many times, I was abused for not following 'the' rules. I was following special rules designed to protect all. I envied the freedom provided to the other parents. A predictable 15-minute window within which, to pick up children was a minor luxury which I was never afforded. I guess, in this situation, ignorant abuse is a consequence of uninformed entitlement. I lost one of my best friends over this matter. She simply could not accept that I was following Ed specific school rules which I did not like, nor request.

Our family doesn't celebrate all that is evil on Halloween. Yet it is fun to get dressed up, play trick-or-treat and unite community. At our Jindalee rental, we had two Halloweens where we'd invited the neighbours to trick-or-treat with us. The second Halloween at Jindalee, we had over 40 people turn up on our front lawn to door-knock together. We only had one Halloween at Hilliup Street and it was fun. The kids and I wrote up the invitations and printed them out before letterbox dropping them. The invitations read something like this, '*In the interest of celebrating our community, we invite the children of our neighbourhood to meet with us at sundown at the end of Hilliup Street on the 31st of October for a community trick or treating adventure. If you don't want to participate in trick or treating, that's OK, just don't answer your door and there will be no tricks. We hope to see you for an evening of fun.*' Our invitation attracted quite a crowd. After our Halloween adventure that evening, the small crowd came back to our Hilliup home, to enjoy and compare spoils. Our back deck housed a three-metre-long table where we divided up treats which had been offered in packages. It was a wonderful evening and I met many friendly neighbours.

My consulting work had been running smoothly for around a decade, but I had never been in a position to grow the business beyond a handful of clients, myself and a part-time PA. I simply wasn't able to take the financial risks involved in growing a business. I was satisfied enough in work, but relatively lonely experiencing few professional challenges. In September 2014, a former colleague approached me and asked whether I would consider coming to work with him. It was tempting, as the idea of having colleagues was very attractive. The invitation was to start a Queensland and Pacific Island Region for his business which was owned privately with two other directors. The goal was to grow that business, in the region, to a self-sustaining entity. At the time, they had one client in PNG and no clients in Queensland nor the rest of the region that it was proposed, I would cover. They had one Queensland based consultant whom I liked but rarely saw. Negotiations ensued and I subsequently let go of my other clients to embark on a journey to grow someone else's IT business as General Manager (GM)

Queensland and Pacific islands. This turned out to be a grand and eventually, extremely hurtful journey.

Once I signed up to sub-contract my business, I was full of ambition and hope. I was very much looking forward to growing a family of clients, colleagues and prospective clients. The first office in the region was my home office. It was a separate building to the Hilliup Street house, yet it was on the same property. The office overlooked our swimming pool. We lived not far from a golf course, and during sunset-thankfulness time, the sounds of bird-life dominated. The office became known as the business' *'Cabana Office'* and once we grew to a team of five, I set about finding rental premises in Toowong. Over the Christmas holidays of 2014/2015, I trudged through many empty offices in Toowong with three children in tow. Eventually, I found a place which was nice enough and not too swish, as a second office for our growing region. Until I left that job in in February 2017, I loved my work. Together, we grew a team of extremely competent consultants whilst maintaining a flat structure and a respect-centred culture where each member of the team acknowledged that we needed one another. In our team, one plus one, far outweighed two and there was no room for oversized egos, which were not uncommon in the IT industry. With my colleagues' support, I attracted many tier one clients and a good smattering of tier two clients. I had enormous respect for the clients that I account managed and I was very passionate about my work, always ensuring our team delivered value with integrity. I genuinely and personally cared for and advocated on behalf of those who worked in the region that I managed.

For the first time in nearly a decade, I was paid a regular income. I had previously worked for clients who gave me regular work, but the contracts came and went, as is typical of the work I had previously chosen. Most work involves pros and cons. In this new role, I lost some flexibility, worked many, many hours longer than I was used to, and I earned less money while enjoying income security and colleagues. Outside of family, all my energy was focused on the new GM role. I worked very hard, and the business, in the region for which I was responsible, grew astonishingly well under my management.

With a predictable income and associated sacrifices, Christmas of 2014 was the first Christmas in five years where I wasn't struggling to make ends meet. The divorce was done and dusted – no more legal fees which had nearly crippled me. The downside of December 2014 was that the kids were at an age where a $2 Christmas present could be distinguished from a $20 or $200 present. I had to say goodbye to the days of two-dollar shop Christmas gifts. My daughters continually informed me that there were things 'everyone else' had which they did not. These statements contributed to in-grained mother guilt. In my youth, I complained in a similar manner to my parents. In the 1980s, all the other kids had Nike's, while my three siblings and I wore Dunlop Volleys. Despite understanding that my children's declarations of relative poverty were inaccurate, I succumbed. I purchased for them as Christmas presents, many things everyone else apparently owned. We did have genuine first-world problems. Dare I admit to this? Our TV, for example, transmitted around 10 vertical black lines running through the screen. The children's sleepover friends were incredulous when watching this TV. *'How can you watch a TV that doesn't work?'* they would ask my kids. I had become accustomed to seeing only around 70% of the screen. The television was big enough and good enough for me. Apparently, though, it needed an upgrade. Hence, a new big screen TV was purchased and delivered Christmas Eve. Although, for five years, I had continued to pay for private music lessons, I had not been able to afford a piano. As such, the children had practised, post my separation and then divorce, on an old $150 keyboard. I valued the education of my children more than their things, so from my perspective, ongoing music tuition was more important than a piano. Music lessons would help with maths, learning other languages and enjoyment of multiple skills I never mastered. Team sport would build social skills and keep them fit. Scouts would assist to build social skills and foster resilience. Fortunately, the children enjoyed the extra-curricular activities they participated in; pleasure and education packaged together. Regardless of my education prioritisation, I was excited when I was able to have a new piano delivered that same Christmas Eve and my daughters squealed in delight. My kids knew how to use an xbox. Even Granny and Papa had purchased an xbox for their grandchildren. A new xbox was opened Christmas day. It was an expensive Christmas. It was exciting to be able to spoil the kids a little.

During the school holidays of 2014/2015, I purchased a Dreamworld (theme entertainment park) family membership. On our first visit, we remained together as a family unit, orienting ourselves and fitting in as many rides and animal exhibitions as possible. Subsequent visits saw the girls independent in getting themselves around with mobile phone communication keeping my motherly anxiety at bay. I trust most parents experience a certain degree of anxiety as our children grow wings. We visited Dreamworld around 15 times during our membership year, and for around 14 of those visits, my routine with Edison was predictable. My Dreamworld visits with Ed consisted of three main activities and we would fill the entire day with these. Once or twice, at the end of the day, I managed to coax Edison onto a ride with me, but our typical routine involved trains, crocodiles and food. The trains and crocodiles fascinated Edison. Eventually, we brought packed lunches so as to not leave trains nor crocodiles in order to eat. For Freya-Grace's 10th birthday, we managed an all you can eat Dreamworld restaurant lunch which Edison capitulated to, in the promise of more trains and crocodiles to come. Freya-Grace was delighted by her double-digit birthday party day, where we invited two of her friends. Now tall enough to experience all the rides, Freya-Grace was elated.

Early on, I unsuccessfully fought to expand Edison's Dreamworld repertoire, but I eventually accepted Ed's obsessions was an easier and more realistic journey. I reasoned that I was taking the kids on these outings for their pleasure and if Eddie was happy experiencing only trains and crocodiles, I had achieved one of my objectives. I spent many, many hours in Dreamworld watching typically developing families having a special day out. I don't like to admit it, but I did feel envy at times for those who could have a day off from autism and experience relatively stress-free family outings. My personal Dreamworld entertainment routine came to consist of reading whilst enjoying hanging out with Ed. Edison and I grew closer in our routine, most often in the comfortable silence of shared train and crocodile rapture. In Edison's final visits to Dreamworld, the months were cooler and we would sit on the concrete path in front of a glass wall for several hours, never seeing the hibernating reptiles move. Somehow, they still fascinated Edison.

Edison had always been terrified and in awe of crocodiles. One of his favourite books was Ronald Dahl's *'The Enormous Crocodile'*, which I likely can still recite verbatim. At one point, we had a figurine crocodile in our fish tank which would open and close its mouth as air filtered through the plastic tail into its three-centimetre-long terrifying jaws. Edison was so petrified of the plastic creature that he would not enter the playroom where the fish resided whilst the crocodile's pump was working. Eventually, the fish tank crocodile moved out. On one occasion at a visit to Australia Zoo, Edison became competition for the croc show as he screamed and carried on to get the hell away from the creatures he desperately wanted to see. The Australia Zoo staff ordered us to stay in our place as Edison's stress and hollering heightened. I ignored them. Things would only get worse if I didn't rescue Ed from being 50 metres away from safely contained crocodiles. As Ed and I escaped, I ordered the girls to stay put – I would find them at the end of the show and I reminded them, *"You know our stranger-danger rules."* My eldest, now in charge of her little sister was only aged 13, yet I had no choice but to desert them as Ed's distress became a potential threat, via distraction, to zoo staff conducting the crocodile show. I am not a crocodile psychologist, but I also didn't want Ed's behaviour to stress the crocodiles, the Australia Zoo audience, staff, nor my daughters. I didn't want the crocs to get stressed and hit out at their trainers. Again, my brain and animals... Even I don't understand my thinking. The big word for how I sometimes consider animals is anthropomorphism (loopy!). Edison and I made an escape with zoo staff chasing us. I maintain that I made a good judgement-call and that it was better and safer to remove a hysterical Edison than to follow the zoo's staff rules of staying put. When the staff caught up with us and observed Ed's state, they reluctantly seemed to agree.

Chapter 19
Which Secondary School?

As 2014 rolled into 2015, I became increasingly focused on Ed's high school options. I was excited and anxious when I contemplated my baby boy on the cusp of entering secondary school. Francesca was due to start high school in 2015, and Freya-Grace would join her in 2017. As Ed's primary school graduation loomed 18 months into our future, I pondered, *'Can I manage a full-time job supporting and parenting my kids if they attend three different schools?'* I had worked for a couple of decades to ensure I could perform as a competent mother and income earner, but my role in my children's impending adolescent education frightened me. I wasn't willing to outsource overseeing the potentially risky teenage years of their emotional and social development to others. Never-the-less, I began to accept the unwelcome possibility I might need some help. Mainstream with inclusion versus special education became a relentless internal debate. The notion of how I could cope with three different schools continued to play on my mind. I was often reminded, by those who cared, that in the context of my family unit; if Jillian doesn't cope, nobody copes. I had, for a long time, battled the effects of positive and negative aspects of my daughters sharing a school with their autistic brother. I also never lost sight of Ed's impact on his peers.

I have heard, since Ed's death, many stories from children and parents who benefited from knowing Eddie as a member of their mainstream school. Generous sharing of such stories was comforting. Post Ed's death, the encouragement from others provided me precious peace and confirmed that I had made a non-adversarial decision by placing Ed in a mainstream setting. Sharing primary school with their brother, the girls became independent and inclusive; they were kind and wonderful advocates for people from all walks of life. Edison, also, was demonstrating kindness and independence within his means. As Ed faced his challenges every day, he remained a salient source of inspiration and strength.

Noting how well the children were doing, I debated, '*Why rock the boat and swap to a special high school?*' Choosing a high school for Eddie was complicated. My social life was virtually non-existent and as such, I had little opportunity to banter with friends about my thoughts on Eddie's schooling options. I knew wallowing in self-sympathy regarding my relative loneliness might pave a road to depression and as such, I did my best to avoid it. I simply needed to endure the pressures associated with school selection falling square on my shoulders.

Moving onto high school changes up the social game for children to a whole new level. At least, it did in the 1980s for me. My childhood was sheltered. Outside of ABBA, we mostly listened to Christian music and most visitors to our home were either from the church or came to us through community endeavours the church supported. It wasn't until high school that I learnt that people who were not married could actually have sex. This basic fact taught to me by my peers shocked me. I was innocent, and my ignorance of worldly ways was not a safe grounding for high school entry. If early years of high school were tough on me, how much harder would it be for my children's generation? They belong to an era that participates in and succumbs to non-stop social media. Back in my day, innocence was associated with primary school years. Today's internet savvy children cannot possibly claim a sheltered childhood. Considering my children's adolescence, I anguished over their future and the likelihood of being exposed to a myriad of inappropriate or overwhelming information. My parenting style, which always centred on openness and respect, embraced a modern teenage world which was foreign to me.

Our sense of entitlement in Western society is sobering. For me, it is not comforting. The rudder guiding me when I researched which was the best high school for my kids begged questions such as, '*What is in my children's best interest, both individually and for us all, as a family? Will my decision potentially take them down a hurtful path in whatever direction I choose?*' Attempting to answer these questions, I was consumed with options, torn and confused. Yet somehow, I realised that I was right to be concerned and confounded. Inclusion, inclusion, inclusion… was fundamental to my parenting. Would Ed have a better life in a special, sheltered world with mainly special friends or would he be happier in the wider world where 'special' was a spice and not the norm? How could I choose the best educational setting for my daughters? Girls can be cruel… I didn't want my daughters to be teased for having a brother with autism. For years, the angst of the decision making of 'which school?' haunted me.

One of the reasons for selecting Jindalee State School for my children back in 2012 was that it was a feeder school for two high schools which catered for special needs children. I had thought Ed's two high school options would be the Special Unit, with maybe some mainstream inclusion, at the local Centenary State High School (CSH) and the other was Mount Ommaney Special School. It weighed heavy on my mind the potential consequences I was setting my soon to be adolescents up for. For around 18 months, I stepped up my due diligence with regards to secondary school options. I was familiar with the local high school, so it was logical, from my perspective, that my more active investigations start with the local special school. I managed to secure a meeting with the principal of the special school. The principal was warm, friendly and informative. I explained to the principal ways in which autism manifested in Eddie's life. We communicated over several weeks. After much consideration and history and file sharing between schools, it was determined that Edison wasn't special enough for the local special school. The Mount Ommaney Special school had recently begun taking on more able children in the younger grades, but I was advised that Edison would have no cohort who he could relate to should he attend the Mount Ommaney school. It was concluded that Edison was far too advanced for those around his age at this school, and he would find himself isolated. I was recommended to investigate the Inala Special School (just 12 kilometres up the road), recently renamed the Western Suburbs State Special School (WSSSS).

I mustered the strength to challenge my unethical bias against schools which only accepted special people and investigated this previously unforeseen option. Feeling apprehensive, I organised a visit for Eddie and I. When we arrived at WSSSS, Edison was truly delighted as he watched students pile off the (yes, yellow adorned) bus. His deep blue eyes glistened, reminding me briefly of the Moreton Island ocean that he relished. A pang flooded my heart as I remembered how I viewed 'those' kids when I was an ignorant high school teenager. My heart palpitated as I tried my best to hide my shame. At the same time, full of mixed emotions, I delighted in observing my boy's joy. I watched intently, noting the demeanour of the children and the general vibe of the scene. I was surprised to see how caring the students were towards one another and how happy they were to be at school. They lined up with little fuss, and Ed's new buddy coached him in the morning routine with some spoken language and quite a few non-verbal prompts. Edison was taken to his new temporary, trial classroom for the morning. He appeared relaxed and although he didn't exude the same electric excitement he displayed at JSS, I was pleased to see how well he integrated. For some time, I observed Ed in this special environment whilst sharing hushed anecdotal remarks with the deputy principal and my mother who had also accompanied us. Once Eddie was settled, he was left with his new class peers and I was given a personalised tour of the entire facility bar the very-special-needs-kids area. As that area was pointed out to me, I once again appreciated my most fortunate life.

I was impressed with the attention to individual needs and care which was shown to the high school students. They grew their own food which they learnt to cook, cooked and packaged commercial dog biscuits, they fabricated wooden equipment and reassembled donated computers. Life skills education included the three R's of Reading, wRiting and aRithmatic – all in the context of 'real life'. If only mainstream education was so tangible and life-skill focussed... During our tour, we encountered one of the senior girls who was celebrating her birthday. Her friends had baked a cake and they were ecstatic, awaiting the morning-tea break so that they could celebrate and share in the excitement of eating cake together. I was observing kids – special kids – with friends. A reciprocal, equal friendship for Edison was something my heart ached for, had fervently desired and chased for over a decade. I was teary and emotional encountering such warm friendships shared between these kids. I relished the birthday girl's encounter. I could not help but to imagine my son being so happy with friends. As we wandered back to Ed's music therapy lesson, now in a different room, I could not have felt more conflicted. Clearly, this school had it right when it came to the care and education of their students. I was warmed by the school's obvious love, care, empathy and insight. Before leaving, I was advised when and where the special bus could meet Edison and I was informed that myself or another authorised adult would have to accompany him or welcome him for each return journey. More money. More logistical issues. Even though my at-office work hours were flexible, at around only 25-30 hours a week, my total work hours, including nights, was closer to 60 hours a week. Whilst Ed was in primary school, I could manage successful and professional work without compromising typical motherhood and my *one of them* duties. But with three kids enrolled in three separate schools, and no practical adult or local family support, I predicted that something would break... As my mum, Ed and I drove Ed back to JSS, I reflected on the professionalism and the time that the Western Suburbs state school invested in helping me to make an informed decision regarding Edison's high school options. They truly cared; better, they understood.

Following the impressive visit with WSSSS, I shared what I had learnt with staff from Ed's SEU, Leigh and Alice in particular. Of course, I bombarded my almost daily sounding-board, my parents, with relevant mixed emotions and rational conflicts. The Western Suburbs school was a stand out for Ed but would, in peak hour traffic, require a minimum of two hours travel between drop off and getting to my at office work in the opposite direction towards the city. If I were to transport Ed to this school myself, this would necessitate that the girls fend for themselves with regards to school transport. Another option was to pay a carer to supervise Eddie travelling on the special school bus. The 'easy' option of using the special yellow bus would also interrupt the girls' school transport choices, as it was not an option for Ed to be picked up from home. I felt, *'dammed if I do, dammed if I don't...'* I felt sick. I wanted to be the only transporter and carer of my children and outsourcing parental responsibilities was never a comfortable option. The encouragement by many well-intended advisors to employ carers was unwelcome… I wanted to do well in my work and to support my kids. That whole work-life balance thing seemed a constant juggle. Seriously, it's likely unattainable for most, so why did I bother aiming for it? Something was going to have to give. Understandably, the staff at Ed's Special Unit were interested in the progress of my research and wanted to learn from it, not just because they genuinely cared about Edison, but because they had other parents asking the 'which high school' question for which SEU staff had no clear answers, direction or first-hand knowledge. They did not have the time nor funding to skim the top of the research I was conducting, especially given that most of the research had to be conducted within school hours. I decided that it would be remiss if I didn't go one-step further in investigating Ed's two options. I decided to invite the two teachers who were key to Edison's education to conduct a visit with me to WSSSS and the local CSH Special Unit. Arrangements were made. Alice, the head of the Special Unit at Ed's school was granted time to join me, but the person whose opinion I valued most in this regard, Leigh's, was denied. Alice and I set out on a day of visiting Ed's two options. We wanted to be at the school when the special bus arrived, as such, I made plans to drop my daughters at schools early. It was unimaginably difficult for me facing this school evaluation process, ruminating on whether I could manage three kids at three separate schools as a single parent with full-time work. Life was a juggle as it was. I did have to earn money. Did I have it in me to make my life even more complicated? Was I grown up enough (yet), to stick my kid on a special bus? Practical impossibilities overwhelmed me as I weighed up the various pros and cons of Ed's options and the prospective flow-on impacts for all of us. The visit to the Western Suburbs option played out as predicted with a slight angle on educating Alice more broadly. As Alice and I drove to the CSH Special Unit, we had much to discuss and high expectations of our next destination. Now this (Centenary) school is a respected school and at the time was under the leadership of a very talented principal. I was aware that he was liked by his students and respected in the community. He took time out of his office almost daily to walk the school grounds and chat with his students. Additionally, his pedagogy and teacher professional development approach was to be admired. Unfortunately, the audience we were given at the Centenary Special Unit was less than average (maybe it was a busy day). The facilities were good. I could see Edison could deal with and maybe even learn and be happy within this environment. It was certainly good enough. Could I predict Edison would flourish there as I knew he would in WSSSS? Not likely. A decision must be made. Crap. Hard. I pressed pause on my 'which school' decision making button.

Chapter 20
Idyllic Life Before Fire

Edison was a hugger, and as he matured, his hugs changed. One memorable afternoon, I returned home after a stressful workday and crossed paths with Edison in our hallway. As Edison approached me in the hallway, he reached out and predictably, he hugged me. This was not a typical Eddie hug though. Ed truly embraced me. Notably, we made eye contact as he supported me, wrapping me in strong arms, while offering a pat, pat, pat on my back. I guess in sensing my vulnerable emotional state, he wanted to comfort me. I was overcome with love. At once, I noted Ed's emotional maturity and I sensed for the first time, a fear of my boy becoming independent of me. This hint of Eddie's developing independence, which together we had worked so fiercely towards, was as terrifying as it was uplifting. By 11 years and 48 weeks of age, Edison's Adam's apple had emerged. He was well and truly progressing in the journey of puberty. Outwardly, it was obvious Edison was entering manhood. This hug though revealed something which no one could physically observe; it revealed his theory of mind was also maturing. Mothers are never ready to lose their baby boys to adulthood, regardless of how hard we work on preparing them for it. I was bursting with pride in Ed's comforting love for me in that bonding moment. I think previously, he offered simple love when embracing someone, but on this day the depth of his actions seemed not just loving but empathetic. No matter what the experts at times espouse, my son often demonstrated that he was capable of a myriad of deep and appropriate emotion. Although, I didn't deliberately seek Edison's comfort, those few minutes with Ed felt like a banner was being passed. Our hugs were no longer a one-way street. Nursing this memory today, I believe Edison met, with his loving gesture, a comfort which was a need I was not yet aware that I possessed. Perhaps this need for comfort existed somewhere within me, waiting to be born to a special hug. Parents who lose children often romanticise memories... In my mind's eye, this memory is not an idealistic reminiscence.

Friday, 12 June 2015

"Why are you all dressed up?" Freya-Grace asked as we warmed our hands on a cuppa.

"Today is my first Friday of paid work in over a decade." I was excited to be graduating from tuck-shop volunteering, classroom reading groups and madly working without pay on Fridays. The school never let me work with Edison in the tuck-shop anyway, which was the plan when I had volunteered. Year-six children were allowed to help in the tuck shop, and apparently Edison had enjoyed tuck-shop duty, but never with me. Our weekday routine unfolded predictably after cuppa-tea time and the children were dropped off safely to school. The peak hour traffic I encountered on the way to work didn't bother me. I was simply happy to be going to work.

I settled into an empty office, pleased that my colleagues were making money consulting on client sites. I was feeling grand that I was now a grown up enough parent to work fulltime when my phone rang at 9:24 am. One always answers when the school rings. *"Jillian, Edison has attacked Mr McKinnon and threatened Mrs Hackett. You need to come and get him and have a chat with us. This will mean an in-home, informal suspension."* I left the office and while driving to JSS, I found myself questioning what many years ago, used to freak Ed out to a point of overwhelming panic each time we passed a certain billboard on the way to transporting Francesca to Fame School. I pondered – as much as I *get* Ed, there is much of his behaviour which remains a mystery. I was hoping that when I arrived at school, I'd be able to shed some light on Edison's motivations which might have fed his morning's reported assaults. I had experienced worse car trips and worse alerts regarding Ed, and I was more thoughtful than stressed. I contemplated my son. Via some remote-control mindlessness mechanism, I found myself arriving at school. I mocked myself, *'I managed 24 minutes of an in office working Friday... good job. Only took a decade...'*

I parked my car and followed the all too familiar trek up to the Special Unit. Alice was the first to converse with me, *"We should move Edison to another room while we discuss what happened this morning."*

"No, we shouldn't, he understands what we are saying and he needs to be held responsible for his actions. What went on?" Always conscious of the fine line a mother treads as a supporter of the school and an advocate for her son, I remained calm and open, communicating my desire for Ed to be included and understood.

"Leigh picked Edison up from the office after you dropped him off and on the way to the Special Unit, Ed tackled Leigh to the ground and when they finally made it to the 'unit', he threatened Mrs Hackett."

"How?"

"He said 'I'm coming to get you'!"

"But Leigh and Kathy are his favourite teachers. Ed, what's your favourite movie at the moment?"

"Monsters Inc. Two," Edison grunted with his unique intonation while grinning from ear to ear.

"I'm coming to get you, is from Monsters Inc. He would have been teasing, not threatening but there's no excuse for tackling Leigh, and of course I'll support the school however I can." Edison's photographic memory and his tendency to act out scenes from movies had once again found him in strife. I wanted Ed to show remorse. When he knew he had done the wrong thing, he consistently expressed remorse. The lack of remorse Ed showed that morning indicated that he didn't understand he'd done anything wrong. His actions were often judged by others without consideration of the context of Eddie-style-play intentions. The assessment of his behaviour was most likely and understandably confirmed by Eddie expressing zero guilt.

"Why do you think he tackled Leigh?" asked Alice. Alice was intelligent and competent. She was well presented and wore the most glorious heels every day to school. I appreciated her questioning and her ongoing intention to understand Ed better.

"I'm guessing it was watching the State of Origin football as a family two days ago on Wednesday night. It's the only football we watch in our home. I figure without a dad, it's my responsibility to expose some football Australian culture to my kids, and three games of rugby league a year ticks that box. Maybe Edison saw that how men behave with each other when they are playing is to tackle each other. He was probably copying the footballers. A compliment really to Leigh – never the less, inappropriate."

"OK, that makes some sense... He can come to school Monday, but he needs to be removed for the rest of today." Alice was understanding, and the dialogue was a little longer and warmer than my recount purveys. There was an unspoken acknowledgment that the education system in which we operated, required at times, to turn a blind-eye to empathy for autistic behaviour. I was OK with Edison suffering consequences for his actions. It silently irked me though that little regard was paid to his intentions, most likely motivated by kindness and play.

There are school standards and societal standards. It was my job to teach these standards to Ed explicitly and implicitly and explain the countless consequences of unacceptable actions. This wasn't as simple as imparting community rules, norms and expectations, which most children learn (metaphorically) via osmosis. I accepted that Eddie needed more help than many other people to interpret and understand the implications of non-conformance with generally accepted social behaviour. A high priority for me in loving Ed was helping him to fit in while also supporting him to feel comfortable in his world. I was cognisant that as Eddie would become more independent; any failure in my teaching of societal nuances could have destructive consequences for my boy and perhaps for those with whom he interacted. Driving home from school that Friday, I considered the suspension an annoyance. Ed loved being on his trampoline and iPad all day whilst I performed the familiar work from home juggle. The suspension was only a punishment for me. I didn't look forward to managing Ed's confusion when, five hours later, we would be in the car to pick the girls up from school. Predictably, he didn't cope well seeing his sisters and peers in the school pick-up zone, and he likely did not understand why he wasn't with them. I don't live with regrets but more than once, I questioned the wisdom of my move to this state school whose SEU specialised in autism, and speech and language disorders. Many of the staff were fantastic. Most were dedicated, yet a basic understanding of how Edison's mind worked three years after our move, seemed elusive to many. I am sure many times Edison's behaviour was frustrating for the dedicated staff. Never the less, I was frustrated with the lack of insight into Ed's intentions… They were poorly funded perhaps. I do know that 100% of the staff put in more than the hours for which they were paid and (outside of one staff member) I only ever witnessed dedicated care.

Whilst watching Ed deliriously enjoying the trampoline during his suspension, I considered the courage it took for me over 12 months ago, to call the Inala based school (WSSSS). Shamefully, I had once harboured an in-built, bigoted and ignorant bias against this school. I reflected on the school and the school community's philosophy regarding education and the aspirations they held for their students and respective families. Essentially, the main goal for each child in their care, was to build the skills to live a meaningful, enjoyable, integrated and where possible, independent life.

The day of Edison's suspension, which essentially resulted from his autism, I ruminated again on Ed's high school options. I was again conflicted. I didn't have the appetite to continue to play expert for Ed's future specialist educators. I decided that no matter the emotional, financial or physical cost, I would enrol Edison in a high school that would delight him – a 100% special school. I envisaged that when people would ask me in the future what school my children attended, I would build the courage to admit with pride and confidence that one of my kids was too special for mainstream and he attended WSSSS. I'd learn to become a braver version of myself. My values have never discriminated against people of different abilities, social status, races, religions nor abilities, yet social judgment affected me. I repeated to myself, *'Just do it'*. Ed had his values right. He didn't give a rats about Nike nor any other brand. He wasn't bothered by people judging him. I was going to be as mature as my son. God, I hoped I could… I envisioned that somehow in 2016, I would learn to work, to feed, transport and love three kids in three different schools with three lots of multiple extra-curricular requirements, to ensure Edison and the girls would thrive in environments which enriched them. Mustering this strength, I telephoned the deputy of the Western Suburbs Special School and informed her that I wanted to formalise Edison's enrolment in her school for 2016. I was anxious and stressed about our future, yet I felt convicted that Ed deserved to be understood. It felt good to have finally made a decision.

Saturday, 13 June 2015

A chill was in the air as I pulled myself from slumber to face a Saturday of children's activities and what I considered, in my half-awake state, the doldrums of parenthood. The day began like all others with cuppa-tea time. Always, electronic devices were disallowed. Predictably, I had coffee, Francesca had tea, Edison had Milo with two marshmallows and Freya-Grace had hot chocolate. Cuppa-tea time banter had been enjoyed only one week earlier on the top deck of the villa discussing funerals – a conversation instigated by one of my daughters.

"Mum, when you die, what kind of funeral do you want to have?"

"I'd want lots and lots of flowers and colour, everyone wearing flowers and people singing my favourite old-fashioned hymns."

"How about if a child dies, Mum, what should their funeral look like?"

"Oh, everyone would have to wear black. It's truly a terrible thing for a child to die. No cause for celebration of a life. Only mourning of a life lost too early. Maybe because it's a child's funeral, there should be a splash of their favourite colour with the black."

The funeral centric conversation lingered into the mid-morning as we shared stories and thoughts while overlooking the beautiful Tangalooma beach on Moreton Island. Back on the mainland, cuppa-tea was faster paced. Basketball was looming…

"When's my game, Mama?"

"Your game is 10:50 and Freya-Grace's is 9:20 – then we'll pop home before I take you to Anniella's party and Freya-Grace to Charisma's party. Ed and I will do a grocery shop whilst you guys enjoy your friends."

Basketball was riveting, at least for me. I wondered why the parents who had their heads buried in their smart phones bothered to show. During basketball, Edison's head was most often buried in his iPad as he rocked to the beat of the latest Wiggles tune blaring through his headphones. I'd dragged him along to watch his sisters play basketball for many years, always bearing the burden of guilt resulting from the fact that he was not welcome to play. He often watched other kids playing and years ago, he used to try to join in. I couldn't explain to him in terms he could comprehend why he wasn't included. Inclusion is a personal passion of mine, but I couldn't change the Brisbane Basketball League. I must admit, I never tried. Soon, we were home, proud of two good wins. The girls were becoming quite talented players. Basketball had really helped their self-confidence. I could see it in their advocacy for all things right and always for their brother. Coach says, *"If you're not fouling, you're not playing."* Defence was toughening them up. Not that life had really given them any opportunity to be soft. Activity ensued; showering, sharing lunch, finalising a grocery list, wrapping presents and writing cards… Francesca was the first stop at her friend's 13th birthday, next was Freya-Grace's friend's party drop off.

Edison came in with me when I dropped off Freya-Grace. I'd never met Charisma's parents before and it I thought it was minimally polite to introduce myself and thank them for hosting my daughter. They looked like Ken and Barbie – an incredibly handsome couple. They were very friendly and welcoming. Eddie didn't understand he wasn't one of the invited party kids so I let him hang out a wee while, whilst I took in the magnificent view from Charisma's family's back deck. Edison was excited, beseeching me with his eyes for permission to eat the chips and lollies. He'd never been invited to a birthday party independently of the rest of his family. My heartstrings torn, I asked, *"Can Eddie have a couple of chips please?"* Thankfully, he was invited to take a few handfuls. This time, I didn't bother to explain his curious ways and we exited fairly swiftly.

I dragged Eddie away for a therapy grocery shop. I loved special chapters that I shared with Edison and me alone. Eddie had his own shopping list, every item written perfectly and spelt correctly with different coloured felt pens. I had my list, a scrawl in biro; items noted since our last grocery expedition occurring only days ago.

"How many apples, Ed?"

"Fifty." His cheeky grin stretched from ear to ear as the pools of blue in his eyes sparkled.

"How about seven? Come on, you count for me." Many people in our postcode of 4074 knew us directly or knew something of who we were. Years ago, when we first moved to 4074, I was excited at the proposition of relative anonymity. That's not how things turned out for us; and we have lived with that, in the knowledge that we are *one of them* and that our *themness* brings out both the best and worst in people. A few pleasant conversations with locals interrupted our shop as Edison perused the shelves for blue chips, marsh mellows, popcorn and vegemite; his staples. He hit a lady he didn't like.

"Sorry, Edison has autism. Edison, you know you can't just hit people. Apologise now."

"Sorry."

Ed took an instant liking to certain people, few others, he simply did not like. Auras maybe? I've never seen an aura but that doesn't mean they don't exist. We don't know what we don't know... Sally was on the checkout with her bump now more prominent – she had a couple of months to go, and she had previously shared that she was expecting a boy. I wondered whether as lovely as she always was to us – especially to Ed, whether she secretly hoped and prayed that her boy would come out 'normal'. I thought to myself, *'Thankfully, life's beaten me into learning that normal is overrated. Don't phase Sally and share your experience...'*

We had 25 minutes to kill before the first birthday party pick-up. Lee's Bakery was one of Edison's favourite hangouts. Together, we unpacked the groceries into the car before settling in to Lee's delights. I had a meat pie, which is rare as my rule was to only have meat pies when returning from Moreton Island on the ferry. Edison had a chocolate slice.

The smell of pizza wafted through the open doorway as we approached Charisma's house to pick up Freya-Grace. Potential disaster… Edison didn't eat pizza, he breathed it in. Most of his dining was conducted with fervent enthusiasm; pizza was certainly no exception. Time to explain autism, pizza, Edison… Thankfully, Charisma's parents were again kind, and somehow understanding even. They are part of the 4074 postcode, so probably they had advance warning, via the local grapevine, that Ed was sometimes a little odd. Perhaps in sharing local knowledge, the grapevine communication method is faster than the internet in my community. Assuming an inaccurate stereotype, I insinuated, *'Charisma's parents don't look like people who would understand special needs. They look – well – just right – like I thought I'd be when I first began the journey of marriage and children.'* They appeared like beautiful and well-adjusted people. I soon learned that they were. Edison was offered a party bag and three slices of pizza in a serviette. Through kindness, these people didn't know what potential drama they avoided, and I left extremely grateful.

Sunday, 14 June 2015

I have always been drawn to the skies in Australia. On this Sunday, we were gifted a brilliant, clear, crisp blue ceiling to our world. It was a wonderful day for entertaining. I built a blazing fire in our fireplace, burned incense and opened all our doors and windows to welcome the day. Rob and Katie and their kids arrived at noon. I watched them from the kitchen window as they strolled up the footpath which I had recently lined with colourful bulbs and Lagerstroemias (a flowering tree sometimes referred to as Pride of India). I was looking forward to future years when those beautiful deciduous trees would provide a colourful, arched, natural walkway for my friends and family to be welcomed by our little family. That day, the trees were naked sticks as it was the middle of a mild Brisbane Winter.

Katie was in check with her wicked sense of humour and was animated, explaining her new work to me while I cooked beef patties for our 'make your own burger' lunch. I had worked with

Rob (and sometimes Katie) on and off since 2005. They had become trusted friends; we'd also shared a couple of family holidays together. Their kids and the girls were playing, and Edison was in his bedroom. I excused myself a few times to encourage the so-called typically developing kids to include Edison. This attempt proved an impossible task, however, the children did try.

On the back deck, we had a three-metre-long, Indian rosewood table, lined either side by forms hand crafted by my father. This was a beautiful place to dine; half inside, half outside, inviting enjoyment of the beauty of our back garden. A pang of angst arose in my gut as I was last to the dining table, whilst serving up lunch sides, I noticed that the spot left for me, separated me from Edison. During meal times, Edison and I were tied at the hip. In fact, as often as possible, we stayed close-by one another, especially when other people were around. Months later, I looked through my parents' photographs and noticed that we were always next to one another. This bond, in part, stemmed from Eddie's need for touch which filled a void his lacking proprioception created. The desire to be physically close to Ed had become a need of my own too. I don't know why. Maybe it was just a bond of love between mother and son.

"Bring the burger to your mouth, Ed, not your mouth to the burger. No, no, not like that… Put your head up. Yes, that's right and now bring the burger up to your mouth."

Edison was hilarious as he then proceeded to skull his burger. I was reminded of my youth when a layback at a bar, was sadly not uncommon. Had I been sitting next to Eddie, my polite dining advice would have been provided non-verbally. Katie and Rob remarked at how well Edison was doing, how far his language had come along. Katie, in particular, noted how beautiful it was to see how eager Edison was to please me. I got seriously lucky when these three children were handpicked for me to raise – and for them to raise me.

Monday, 15 June 2017

It was two weeks until school holidays were to commence. Monday was busy with work, more groceries, piano lessons and the general buzz of family life. Cuppa-tea time that morning occurred in the lounge room. The fire in the fireplace from yesterday had expired, and so we rugged up under our cuddle blankets. I had coffee, Francesca had tea, Edison had Milo and two marshmallows, Freya-Grace had hot chocolate.

"Look, it's raining out the back."

"No, it's not."

"Yes, it is."

"Why don't one of you go outside and see if it is actually raining?" Slave puts down her hot chocolate and ventures outside. Freya-Grace is a most delightful child, always the first to offer help, encouragement and to be the fetcher. Slave explored...

"Oh, Mum! You need to see this, I've never seen a rainbow like it!"

"Well, if you're facing that way, we'd get a better view from the front deck. Let's grab our drinks and finish cuppa-tea time out the front."

The sun-shower had created the first and only complete double rainbow I have ever had the pleasure to view. Directly in front of our home was a mountain which was a nature reserve. The double rainbow arched over that mountain with our family and home at the dead centre viewing position.

"Wow, look what God has painted for us!" Sunsets and rainbows are gratefulness times for our family. Time to stop and smell the roses, so to speak, while sharing what we are thankful for. Today, from my perspective, rainbows are reserved for Edison memories only. When the children were young, they had a cooked breakfast every day. This routine disintegrated into fend for yourself breakfasts following cuppa tea with the remaining demand of zero electronic devices. Freya-Grace often helped with Edison's vegemite on toast and Ritalin. Edison took Ritalin for the school. He rarely had it on weekends or holidays. I always gave him a choice, when lack of Ritalin wouldn't offend people outside our trusted circle. Ritalin dulled him. The school liked this, Edison and I preferred him in his raw state. Off to school and work, we went.

I picked the kids up from school and moved through the, *'How was your day routine?'* I felt one of the most important parts of the children's day was allowing them to unload after school immediately when the good, bad and the ugly would simply spill out. After that, they generally retreated into their own versions of a man cave for a while. Francesca had enjoyed a great day at her new high school where she had chosen a bunch of fantastic, smart, self-motived and kind friends. It's still so good to see her interacting with this friendship group. I doubt any of those girls will go off the rails. She makes good choices. Freya-Grace had also had a positive day. I expected my usual response from Ed.

"Good."

"What was good about it?" I expected another 'good'.

"Everything was good, Mum." I was pleasantly surprised. His language really was coming along. I thought to myself, *'Maaaan, I love these kids...'* Home from school and with work and piano lessons over, we set out to eat the four beef patties and four buns left over from the previous day's lunch. Edison prepared his own, as did the girls then Edison prepared mine and ate that too. Edison consumed more food in a day than I do in a week. That was OK, I'm not a big eater and it was a night off from cooking. The post dinner routine began. Edison loved his showers and after 15 minutes, I checked to make sure he'd washed all the appropriate parts of himself and I assisted him to wash his hair. I recall, when Brisbane was in drought, receiving a 'please explain' query from the council as to why our water usage was so high. Back then, I explained to the council representative, the concepts of vestibular feedback and proprioception in the context of the needs of those with autism, and how water provided essential therapeutic support for my son. I didn't hear from the council about water usage again.

Thankfully, I had all the housework and washing under control as a result of weekend chores. As such, this Monday night was an easy night where we settled in and watched Master Chef on TV. There was no need for a fire that night, and so we decided to cosy up on the couch under our quilts and cuddle blankets. I attempted to draw Edison out of his bedroom to the lounge and our company, away from his iPad where he was madly typing memorised code. Three attempts were successful, for at least five minutes. Master Chef over, it was then time for our bedtime routine. A couple of years ago, my father purchased electronic toothbrushes for the kids because many years of teaching Edison to brush his teeth had largely been unsuccessful. The girls slept in rooms at the other end of the house to Edison and me. My daughters' doorways were opposite one another. I am so pleased to this day that they have each other. We have the occasional squabble in our home but the majority of the time, these two girls are tight friends. Freya-Grace's prayers and songs occurred first, then Francesca's.

I arrived to settle Edison and he was in party-mode. Edison generally fell asleep readily, in a heap or he partied for long periods before he could settle himself. Over the years, I have learnt that trying to calm party-mode can contribute to the opposite result of my settling objective. Ritalin didn't help his sleep and a dull school day left him with lots of energy to spare. The school had reported a good school day. Perhaps dull, perhaps simply calm – a positive for all involved except those involved with Edison's sleep. Eddie was in his element, lying in bed, calling out excitedly, "*Line-up, line-up! Keep your hands and your feet to yourself! Again, and again and again and again!*" Ed loved his Disney movies in which Disney promoted the line, '*Your family will love these movies again and again and again.*' At around 9:15 pm, after around 20 minutes of lying in bed, listening to Eddie party, I gave up and called my mum.

"Hi, Mum, I know it's late, but Edison is in party mode and I won't go to sleep until I know he's safe and sound. You guys up? You generally go to bed late."

"Yes, Jillian, we are up, what kind of day have you had?" Mum and I are were on the phone for approximately 40 minutes. We discussed the double rainbow, Eddie's improving skills and communication, Dad's health and inspiration for Edison's quilt, which was my mother's next project. We finished our call at around 10:40 pm. I checked on now sleeping Eddie who was cuddling his iPad and then I went back to my bed to enjoy a peaceful sleep in the knowledge that our little family was safe and settled.

Chapter 21
Fire

11:30 pm, 15 June 2015

WEEHA   WEEHA   WEEHA   WEEHA   WEEHA   WEEHA
WEEHA   WEEHA   WEEHA   WEEHA   WEEHA   WEEHA
WEEHA   WEEHA   WEEHA   WEEHA   WEEHA   WEEHA
WEEHA   WEEHA   WEEHA   WEEHA   WEEHA   WEEHA
WEEHA WEEHA WEEHA

"Rubbish faulty fire alarms," I say aloud to myself, remembering last weekend at our villa when the kitchen smoke alarm went off twice with the teeniest bit of encouragement from my delicious stir-fry cooking. I rise from my bed and head towards the only smoke alarm I can hear in my home. The blaring alarm is placed in the hallway between our kitchen and open family room, where we do most of our living. As I head down the hallway, I am alert to look for signs of smoke or fire. I am not panicked. I am not ambivalent. I am responding to an annoying noise and my intellect is intact enough to check for signs of fire. There are no signs of fire inside nor outside and the working alarm between my bedroom and Eddie's is not sounding. As I glimpse through to the back yard, revealed by the glass walls of my lounge and bedroom, all appears a normal cold June night, except the alarm.

Ten paces in, I'm at the alarm... I observe fire consuming our cuddle blankets in the family room to my right. This room is between where Edison and I sleep and where my daughters sleep. Abruptly, I switch gears – it's a primitive mechanism – my amygdala and hypothalamus engage a sense of survival and protection of my wee tribe takes over. Immediately, I am all adrenalin and focus. I take in and assess the situation in the one second I have. In high alert mode, I instantly recognise that I need to get to my daughters first as there is no sign of an inferno inside or out, nor at the end of the house where Eddie and I sleep.

I scream my daughters' names, *"Francesca, Freya-Grace – girls!"*

"We're here, Mum."

I see two girls who elicit such pride from me even in that brief moment. They got themselves this far – now it's only me and the fire between their exit. Their beautiful faces are light by the glow of the ensuing threat. They are tucked into the corner of the kitchen; the blanket burning fire not one metre from where they cower threatens. I am fleetingly pleased they have partially followed our fire evacuation plan.

"Stay low and when I scream at you, come to the front door and run!" I exclaim.

As I run the three or so metres to the front door, I am aware danger is escalating. I clamour to open the front door lock and I twist it with my right hand. Whilst then turning the door knob with my left hand, pain surges through my body as my flesh rips off my palm onto the burning, hot brass.

"Come now – UP, run!" I scream.

As I watch my daughters escape from what was our home and is now *the* fire, they hesitate to leave their brother and me. The safety of my children is my only goal – I yell another order. *"Off the property now, just run!"*

"But why haven't you saved Eddie?"

"Off! Now!"

Not a second passes before I turn to save my beautiful boy, intending of course to run back into the entrance and towards his bedroom. What I don't realise is that by feeding a smouldering fire oxygen, in the middle of winter in a fully closed-up home, I had nourished an inferno.

Immediately upon facing the entrance of my then home, I am literally blown back by the ferocity of the fire and heat. Suffering severe burns now to my face, I run across the front deck to Edison's bedroom window, literally screaming, *"Ed! Edison, Eddie!"* I look around for something to throw through his window so that I can break it and drag him out. Nothing. '*I'll use my body.'* I can't even make it now to within even two metres of the front of my home and my hysteria builds as the furnace builds.

"Edison, Edison – get my boy – get my boy." It's literally a blood-curdling scream. Neighbours suddenly appear.

"Where is he?"

"In his bedroom."

Alarmed at my stupidity, most likely, *"Where's Ed's bedroom?"* my neighbour asks. He is also a father and no doubt has pending fears for his own family. I don't recognise this fact. I am in one world only – a world where I have been torn from my son. Pointing to a wood reinforced window I say, *"There, that one the first to the right."* Then screaming to no one and everyone I shriek, *"Get my boy! Get my boy!"*

"Is there something we can break the window with?"

People are touching me kindly, patting me and asking me to calm down and come with them... Something like that... I don't want to be touched. I don't want to be managed. Why the hell would I calm down?

My son is in my burning home and I can't get to him.

Raised voices. Rain begins trickling down, the activity around heightens as I focus on one thing only – *get my boy*. Ironically, it rains in the cold of winter while my son burns... I have no recollection of the time it takes for emergency crews to arrive. It seems, immediately after the exchange with my brave neighbours, which was not a conversation – it was survival yelling... I vaguely sense a conversation ensuing between fire officers and my neighbours. Periods of no memory at all follow. Shock does incredible things to one's functioning. I am being commanded off my property by fire officers. I don't cooperate. I won't leave my boy. Eventually, I find myself capitulating to the requests from various emergency services personnel. There's some equivocal, rational process pulling me away (along with a stranger's force), so that they can get Edison out without me in their way.

As I plod the path from the front of our home to our bricked front fence with its iron gates; a path ruminated by blossoming bulbs, various annuals and Lagerstroemias which I have planted only months earlier, my attention shifts. My house is blazing behind me. I am consumed with empathy for my son now that the job of saving him is out of my hands. *'Where is Edison at right now?'* I have no idea whether he is asleep, dead, unconscious, or burnt like a well-done steak... My stomach folds, yet I feel he is with me. I talk with Edison as I move along my then forever home's entrance path. We are not talking with one another out loud, but I have a knowing that we are connected. I tell my baby boy that he might have to make a hard decision soon. I hope he gets to make a decision and that the decision is not made for him. It goes something like this…

"My boy, my beautiful blue-eyed boy. You may have to make a decision soon. The girls and I would love you to stay with us. We love you so much Mr Magoo, and our life is so much richer with you in it. I'd love you to choose to come back to us. But this is your life, Ed. This is your decision. I think the alternative to coming back would be pretty appealing. Love, pure love and no more suffering. Can you see a light, Ed? If you can, that's a beautiful thing and I want you to know as much as it breaks me into tiny bits and pieces to think of you not with me, I can heal knowing if you choose God, pure light and love. This is your decision, Edison, your life; you are the owner of your life. You have my blessing and my love. I hope to see you soon. I love you."

Later, I was media informed that my house was consumed in four and a half minutes. I know the Fire Station is 2-3 minutes from my former home. The pondering of the timing and actions of emergency services occurred retrospectively, not on the night of *the fire*. That night lasted around a year in my time-space continuum.

The prime viewing point for the show, it seems, was from my opposite neighbour's front yard. I also happened to be close socially with these people and as such, their driveway became the gallery where many gathered for the viewing. It was the place to which I was ushered by strangers. My daughters had previously been shepherded to this area and I noticed that they had people around them and did not appear hysterical (as I had been earlier). I don't know if my faculties were wired soundly at the time to make logical decisions. For some reason, I decide to not connect with the girls just yet. They knew where I was, they were safe and my single and all-consuming focus is Edison.

As I crouch, knees embraced by limp arms in the newly falling rain, I am numb. I have no news of Edison as yet and I shutout anyone who wants to speak with me, outside of basic politeness. I see fireworks. They display the remnants of my home, my garden, my art, my life. The flames are reaching at least 30 metres into the black sky and deafening explosions occur to remind me that this is real.

Eventually, I am clawed from my perching, foetal position to speak with authorities. I have enough composure within me to recognise the messenger's facial expression as one not bearing good news. He informs me that my son has been removed from the house. I have nothing more in me but to utter, *"More?"*

"He's alive, Jillian." He takes in my relief. My slackened body prises itself a little straighter.

"He's not stable, Jillian. The paramedics are working on him – we will keep you informed."

I beg to be beside my boy. *"I won't interrupt. I won't interfere. I promise I'll just stand by and watch."* I need to be close to him more than I have ever needed anything.

"Jillian, the paramedics are doing their best and you will not be allowed to be near Edison."

"I can stand back – I can be metres away."

"No, Jillian, the best thing you can do for Edison right now is to let the paramedics do their work."

Defeated, I draw deep into myself as my neighbours erect a tarpaulin to protect us from the rain and wrap blankets around us. Some onlookers, I remember vaguely, as being annoying whilst they tried to penetrate my much needed personal, mental and emotional space. I was in one place, grasping onto the hope that my son did have a choice and he therefore, must live. Within several minutes, hundreds of people and many emergency vehicles flood our cul-de-sac. I know this because I saw it later, on the news.

The paramedics worked on Edison for 45 minutes. During this 45 minutes, I am urged several times to enter an ambulance and I am repeatedly asked for permission to have my daughters taken in an ambulance to hospital. I refuse. I will not be separated from my daughters and I will not leave my son. I also know the girls are physically fine. I harboured two out of three of the children to safety in the seconds I had, without a blemish. I know this. Outside of fighting the brave and commendable emergency services personnel, I remember little of what happened around me in these 45 minutes. I do remember not knowing what to pray and praying anyway.

My son has already spent most of his 11 years conquering the challenges of autism. If he was physically disabled as a result of the fire or if his photographic memory had been affected – how to pray? As a Christian, death is not to me a bad thing. It is a sad thing, but the event (circumstances and causes aside) of death isn't innately bad. We will all die. Death is natural. In this time, nothing is less natural than the threat of losing my son.

All I wanted was for my live healthy little man to be in my arms. My life, my work, my friends, my former marriage and subsequent divorce had all been sculptured around giving three children the best life experiences I could provide. With autism, Edison came consequently with more constraints than 'typically developing children.' He was not the centre of our lives and he was no more loved than my daughters. However, as special needs dictate, the relationship between Edison and I was stronger than steel. There is a sentence in the bible, "Jesus wept." In that forty-five minutes, Jillian quietly wept.

Of course, my phone was burning along with all I owned. As such, I don't know how my parents were contacted. Only two hours earlier, I had finished a long and lovely call with my mum, most of the conversation focused on Ed and the girls, their piano lessons that afternoon, our gift of a double rainbow that very morning and so forth. We discussed the quilt Mum was dreaming up for Ed, how wonderful Ed was today when I picked him up from school – and how important it was that Mum keep me awake and alert until I knew Edison was settled safely.

I am not aware, but my precious son, my most valuable teacher – is pronounced dead.

I am standing near the ambulance. I cannot fully describe this scene, but I will proffer the anecdotes which I do accurately remember. It's a paramedic this time, not a police officer nor a fire officer who is burdened with the role of messenger. *"Jillian, I am sorry. Edison has died of smoke inhalation. Paramedics worked for 45 minutes and did all they could. The fireys worked tirelessly in getting Eddie out. They managed to break the window and take him from his bed. I am so sorry. You and your daughters now really need to get to the hospital. Would you like anyone to go with you?"*

Composed, *"I need to see him, I need to say goodbye to my son."*

"No, Jillian, you are to get into the ambulance now."
"I won't leave here until I see my son. I will see him."

A scene inside a scene commences. There are police, paramedics, fire fighters all cajoling me into cooperation, into changing my fiercely determined mind to move the way 'that's right'. I stand my ground. There may even be family and friends trying to turn me. I am only aware of the fight I must win. That fight is with the present authorities. They are kind and warm. They are not hostile, but all I feel is hostility. I was informed that my home had become a crime scene and I cannot enter the crime scene. I argue; I am calm. I am steadfast in my insistent request. Eventually, they capitulate, perhaps because my burns require urgent treatment. I am eventually instructed that I will be taken to my son's body for a time specified (which I can't remember because I didn't intend to follow their rules). Another condition is that I am accompanied by a trusted person and a bunch of authorities. I later found out that one of my supervisors or supporters, along with the officials, was my sister, Kylie.

I slowly plod towards Edison's still, now empty body. His piercing blue eyes are shut to the night sky with rain pattering over our world. I lie beside him on the soaking-wet grass. I think illogically about all that water poured out to save my home and Edison's life, in vain. I touch his face. He looks angelic. I am relieved he's not all charred. He is leathery. He's not obviously burnt. (Well, I find out later that he was, yet I saw only a cherub). Perhaps I am not burnt either. I am not aware of my own physical state. I kiss Edison's face. His flesh does not soften to the impact of my kiss. Lying beside Edison now, I talk with him aloud. I feel his spirit might be still hanging around. I tell him what joy he has brought to my life. What a gift and blessing it has been to be his mother. I tell him that he has taught me more than my university degrees or anything else in life. I thank him. I share with him how precious he is to his sisters and me. I tell him that he's going to a better place, a place where he can have as many marshmallows as he wants. I tell him that I love him, and I will miss him every second of the rest of my life.

I am once again ushered towards the patiently waiting ambulance paramedics. I am not fully cooperative yet. I must be the one to tell my daughters that our beloved Edison is dead, and we must all stay together. We cannot be separated. I am informed that my injuries are too great to have my daughters in an ambulance with me. I must be taken first and treated enroute. My daughters will follow and will be delivered to the same hospital as me, in an ambulance together shortly after my arrival. I understand. I ignore this. Again, the authorities allow me a grace, to speak with my daughters before entering the ambulance. I usher Francesca and Freya-Grace away from the lights, TV crews, neighbours, officials and curious onlookers. How can so many people and vehicles fit into a small cul-de-sac? We sit at the top of the street in the gutter, rain falling lightly on my family of now three.

"Beautiful girls. I am so sorry. Eddie didn't make it. He's with his Creator now. He didn't burn to death. It might have been that he wasn't even aware. I've been with him and he looks peaceful. They did everything they could. I love you both so much. I'm proud of you and we will be strong together in this." I then pray with my daughters. This prayer is from the heart, perhaps centred on hope, peace and comfort. I do not remember what I prayed.

I see my girls safely into their ambulance before I finally offer myself up to the paramedics. I was told later, that upon hospital arrival, I was fierce in my fight to not be separated from my daughters. My daughters required no treatment, yet in my opinion they required a couch they could sleep on, close to me. We were accommodated together with two recliner chairs placed in my room for the girls. I vaguely remember getting out of bed several times that night to close the door for privacy, and each time being reprimanded and told I was not allowed to do that. What was their problem? I have learned that I wasn't very cooperative when I arrived – in particular when I was encouraged out of the ambulance into a wheelchair. I am told, I uttered, *"I have legs. I can walk. I have a dead son. I'm not a cripple."* I learned later that my parents arrived at the hospital in the middle of the night. I do not remember this either.

I never view Edison's body at the morgue later. Thankfully, my sister is there for me, to do this. I have already said my goodbye. At around 6:00 am, I came to. I think hospital staff must have drugged me as I don't think I awoke. The girls were there beside me and I could see they were worried. I had no idea that my face was covered in blisters and my clawed hand displayed a lot of open flesh. We talk, and they see I am OK. I learn we have been checked for smoke inhalation and none of us show any signs of it.

There are other people in the room. I don't remember them all. Eventually, the room is pretty full. I ask why Mum and Dad didn't come to see me and I am informed they have been here since they journeyed the two hours from their home to the hospital in the dark of the night, and had only 15 minutes ago left, to rest themselves. Apparently, I had been conversing with my parents for hours. My angel ambulance chaser, Lisa is here. Lisa was the first to arrive on the scene to offer practical and emotional support the year before, when my daughter was hit by a car in front of Edison, Francesca and I. With Freya-Grace unconscious, it was my job back then, to ask others to control traffic and wait for paramedics, ensuring that nobody moved Freya-Grace. I was the protector of Freya-Grace's spine back then. Somehow, Lisa materialised as our protector in that hospital.

Many confronting events unfolded in that hospital room. It was tough having to explain to the police that our custody orders meant that the children's father could not communicate with his kids, be present within their school grounds, nor attend their extra-curricular activities. My ex-husband's new wife had called the hospital several times that morning with a request to unite our living children with their father on the day of Eddie's death. That was a bizarre proposition from my perspective. I needed to explain to social workers, psychologists, hospital staff and police that after around six years of zero contact, this was not the time to force 'dad' onto our daughters. My copies of Family Court Orders were clearly burnt. I had no ready paper-based evidence to prove that my decision, to not reunite my living children with their father on this day, was backed by law. Somehow, outside of my character, I suggested that if anyone was to be complicit in breaking court orders, there would be consequences. My ex-husband's wife clearly had good intentions. I didn't want to shutdown her well-intended request with a non-response. I don't harbour hate and I always am ready to build bridges. Especially, I don't want to incite adversity with a woman who loves my children's father and by all means appears a very decent human being. Today is not the day though, to introduce my daughters to their step-mum for the first time and reintroduce them to their father. I had a heart for the pain my ex and his wife would be feeling and upon request, my cousin, Shelly returned their telephone call. I'm sure Shelly provided empathy, an ear and understanding. Another drama unfolding within a drama mollified.

Understandably, hours of police interviews were conducted in the hospital that morning. I insisted that a trusted family member be present to accompany my daughters during their individual police interviews. This request was ignored by the police officers. I later was informed that they broke child-protection law in disregarding my request to have my daughters have a trusted adult accompany them for comfort and support. The police demanded that we give up the only items we now owned, which were the clothes we were wearing. Even our underwear became forensic evidence for the crime scene. There was a flurry of activity to find us warm clothes, underwear and shoes. Somehow, we were redressed in items borrowed from those around us. During this first police interview, I was naïve and honest, and likely I was in shock. They reported later that I wreaked of alcohol (I had consumed two glasses of wine the night before) but they neglected to test my alcohol blood level. My fragmented memory of this incident, informs me that this first interview wasn't unpleasant, and I was cooperative. Sadly, further police interviews were less innocuous. My hospital police interview was the first of around 30 hours of police interrogation. Formal interviews amounted to around 50 hours including, insurance and fire department questioning. Those approximate 50 hours excludes hundreds of hours of informal communications with other officials and the media. The police were not that nasty at first. My dealing with the police in the past, having birthed a runaway son, were numerous and very positive. After my house burnt down and my son died, I learned that when on the suspect side, positive police interactions are not the norm.

There were many encouraging events which occurred in that hospital room. I was taking business cards and phone numbers on scraps of paper and pointing to my bedside table, declaring, *"This is my purse, my handbag now, just throw everything there."* Observing this, my cousin, Shelly emptied the contents of the nicest handbag I've owned to date, onto her lap and announced, *"No, this is your handbag, Jilly."* As I thanked Shelly for her generosity, I complimented her on her earrings. She promptly ripped those earrings out of her lobes and announced that they were now my property. I decided to never complement Shelly again on her clothes or accessories. She was extremely generous, but she did deserve to be clothed and adorned with pretty accessories and maintain ownership of her things... My eldest daughter's former teacher, Selina, being alerted to our situation via the morning television news, arrived with pencils and art gear for the girls. I don't remember seeing Selina. Perhaps using Selina's gifts, my then 10-year-old daughter drew. That morning Freya-Grace presented me with a picture she'd made during our hospital sojourn. This drawing, which is now plastered to my home-office white-board, continues to stir my heart. Freya-Grace's picture depicts a rainbow held up by clouds with two angels above welcoming her brother to greet God who is dressed as an artist under the ceiling of the rainbow. We had fostered a habit of sharing what we are grateful for at sunset or when a rainbow appeared. We would often declare during gratefulness moments, *"Look at what God painted for us!"* In Freya-Grace's picture, she's deciphering that God has painted a special rainbow to welcome Edison into his heavenly presence. Her insight today strikes me.

With promises of a 'responsible person' around me 24x7 and daily visits to treat my burns, the girls and I were eventually released into the care of others. I guess I was on suicide watch. Many people mourned my son's death. News of his death was all over the TV and newspapers. The day Eddie was born, Brisbane's River Fire festival and fireworks, in my mind, marked his welcome into the wold. The fireworks of my home burning saw this same city which I love, mourning the loss of a very special person. The ensuing hours and days after leaving hospital, were full of police interviews, media, sleeplessness and pain.

Chapter 22
Burying a Son

Outpatient hospital visits and regular GP consultation occurred for weeks following my discharge from hospital. I urged myself forward in the hope that life, or a semblance of life, would tick on. Where to live as a now homeless family, was my first big decision. We had strangers, friends whom I trusted, as well as relatives offer for us to stay in their homes. It was overwhelming, and I am sure I was still suffering from shock whilst trying to choose where next. When I piece together the events of those early post-fire days, I realise that I felt safety and a complete respect for my privacy pervading from Lisa. I really didn't know her well back then. Maybe there was some safety in being with people who didn't know us so well... I don't remember travelling a logical nor rational path to reach a conclusion when deciding to stay with Lisa and her husband, Brent. I did take into consideration that Lisa's home was close to my children's school and locating ourselves close to my daughters' friends was a priority. In the main though, unlike my usual modus operandi, I went with what felt right.

I had no comprehensive reasoning and no justification for my choice. Homeless and sonless, I set up a nest in someone else's home. One of Lisa's children gave up her bedroom for Francesca and Freya-Grace and I bunkered down in their spare bedroom. Lisa's husband, Brent, proved to be an amazing, relaxed and welcoming host. Lisa and Brent's lives continued with cub scouts and netball and their family's various extra-curricular activities while the aftermath of the fire, swarmed as a whirlwind around us all. Their home entrance became a revolving door for the next few weeks. Much of this time is also a blur to me, but I recollect thinking that it seemed there was nothing that could push these caring and generous people to a brink. I'd encountered my brink many times before.

Lisa protected us as well as she could, early on keeping our location a secret from the community at large. Perhaps the 4074 postcode grapevine knew Lisa had been with us in hospital or maybe residents had witnessed police vehicles in her driveway. In my thinking, other than these suppositions, there was no obvious reason for Lisa to be targeted with questioning as to our whereabouts. I overheard a revolving door of, *'Do you know where Jillian and the girls are? Do you know if there's anything they need?'* questions. Lisa never lied, but somehow, she managed to keep us under the radar for a few days. Unfortunately, as much as those close to us tried, no one could keep the police at bay. I had never met police like this before, particularly the female in charge of the investigation. The police were relentless in their interviewing, never informing me of my rights, and I was in no state to question their objectives or motives. I simply knew that I never, ever wanted what had happed to our family to happen to another family. The police did not let up with their questioning. Even when I had gone days without a decent sleep, daily I cooperated with the police, in the hope that I was proactively, in some way assisting other families. The police line of questioning proffered no boundaries. I was asked about my friendships, past relationships and present sex life… I was questioned when I last had a sexual relationship and who might want to hurt our family. I was asked in 50 different ways about my sexuality and it was clear that the female police officer did not believe me when I told her how long my sexual drought had been. It was incredibly stressful and intrusive, and I was always questioned alone.

Meanwhile, I was organising a funeral for my son. My mind was overridden with decisions I had to make… *'Would he be buried or burnt? What kind of coffin would he have? Which cemetery would I prefer? What songs would be sung? Which bible verses would be read? Who would play what role? Should pall bearers always be men?'* Some questions were easier than others to resolve. During the barrage of decision-making, I knew some things for certain. For example, I didn't want to identify my son's corpse. As previously mentioned, my sister, Kylie kindly stood up and offered to do that for me. I have never asked her about that event. I don't think I've even thanked her – I guess I don't want to know about her experience in that moment. Too raw… Of course, all Edison's clothes had been burnt along with the rest of his belongings and it was logical (to others with their faculties at hand) that he not be buried in charred pyjamas. *"What would you like Edison buried in?"*

"Does it make a difference if there's an open coffin?"
"There will be no open coffin, this is a child's funeral and children will be attending. We need to make this as easy for Ed's peers as possible whilst respecting and honouring Edison and celebrating the short time we had with him." In some matters, I was certain and decisions came easily.
"What should he wear?"

Red and then green were his favourite colours and it was the middle of winter, as such I didn't want Eddie to be cold, as well as in the dark. He didn't like shoes, but I didn't want his feet to be cold so he needed socks. Kylie gently listened as I rabbled off non-sunscald talk of what my son's body should wear, his spirit long departed. I never saw Edison after the night of the fire, but I am certain Kylie did a beautiful job in attiring departed Edison.

By Wednesday afternoon, I worked up the courage to visit the remains of our cherished home. Surprisingly to me, I was not allowed to set a foot on my property, but I could visit neighbours and view our ruins through burnt holes in wooden fences. The cul-de-sac remained full of media, and I mean full. The police did their best at outnumbering the media whilst protecting the crime scene. Of course, the insurance investigators were plying for a spot also. No one other than authorised government personnel were allowed on the crime scene. In fact, the police officer in charge lied to me to coerce me into yet another interview weeks later, telling me that the crime scene would not be released until I gave yet another filmed interview. I was threatened by her lie, which I swallowed hook, line and sinker. Living with little privacy and zero stability, I was desperate for personal space and a glimpse of a future. If they didn't release the crime scene, I couldn't practically move forward.

My sister, Kylie had met a man called Louie Namoski the day before I first saw the ruins of our home. She and several of my friends had met many people asking for interviews and offering exclusive deals, requesting my contact details. I had no email access, no phone nor home, yet somehow these people presumed I was readily contactable *and* willing to be contacted. This Louie guy though, Kylie suggested, seemed the real deal. It seemed he simply, genuinely wanted to help. He is the founder of the Logan Housefire Support Network. Unbeknown to me, his charity had supported many victims of house fires. Relying on Kylie's advice, I agreed to speak with and then meet Louie. I had seen what was left of my house on television and in newspapers, but I really wasn't prepared for what I was faced with in 'real life.' Once news was out regarding where the girls and I were residing, Lisa and Brent's home overflowed with flowers. I should have expected some flowers at our burnt property, yet I was moved and my heart-warmed when upon arriving at our ruins, I observed the front of our home littered with more bouquets and cards from well-wishers. I asked those with me, to please collect all the cards but we couldn't possibly gather all the flowers. My daughters did not accompany me. It would have been healing for the girls to see the outpouring of love first-hand, but I needed to protect them from the media. They were not kept completely in the dark as they were able to observe 'the make-shift memorial' growing at the property, on the news, via Brent and Lisa's TV, each night.

Before meeting Louie, I spoke with him on someone's phone. Louie taught me about photoelectric versus ionisation smoke alarms and I was saddened to learn that, had I installed photoelectric alarms in my home, my son would likely be alive. I backed this information up later with my own research. With the message of the importance of the right fire alarms as my main objective, I agreed to be interviewed at my former neighbour's home by select journalists recommended by Louie. If only one life could be saved… On the day of my first post-fire media interview, exiting someone's car and walking towards a former neighbour's home, I was told to be careful what I said. *"The microphones of those guys 50 metres away will be able to pick up every word you utter."* I had agreed with Louie to an unpaid interview with the two top 6:30 pm current affair style TV shows. There were reasonable conditions. They could cut the footage as they liked but I was to give one interview only. They would have to pre-agree to the questions they would ask of me and the duration of the interview was to be ten minutes at most. I was not pre-informed of the questions to be asked. Perhaps that helped with the authenticity of the 'story'. Before the interview, I walked with Louie, peeking through burnt fence holes trying to glimpse anything I used to own. The TV interviewers and crews were very decent and the minor event of being televised was harmless to me, and hopefully helpful to someone.

The time leading up to Eddie's funeral transformed Lisa and Brent's home. There were constant knocks on their front door. I don't know how they managed all the activity. *"What can we do?"*

"How can we help?"
"What do they need?"
"What do they eat?"

Clothes were pouring in, and our hosts' playroom became storage. I had never seen so many clothes. Today, around 90% of my clothes remain 'fire clothes', as I like to call them. My previously desired anonymity was now a complete failure. I am still not keen on popping out locally for a shop. When I do, I am almost always recognised and often approached by people I do not know. We had mums from JSS and CSH schools writing initials on clothes which would fit a size 8-10 45-year-old, a small size 8 ladies 10-year-old and a size 12 for a 13-year-old. The instructions I provided to generous helpers were likely as jumbled as my mind. Without these initials scribed on the tags of our donated clothing, we would not have known one person's clothing or underwear from another's. My daughters and I provided no input into which items we would each receive. It was relieving to have friends and strangers making such decisions for us. People were very generous. Three years on, I still find certain things in our home when I ask my daughters whether we own them. Beach towels are a common item to question as we have a swimming pool and many, many kids come and go. I never know what's been left by other children and what is ours.

I was in sporadic contact with various staff members of both the schools leading up to the funeral. Clearly, the fire and

Edison's passing had an impact on the local community. It seemed everyone had a story which related to Edison. I would overhear parents for months to come, talking in grocery queues of how their children were afraid to go to sleep 'after that dreadful Westlake fire'. Strangers who approached with eyes tearing up had positive intentions but it was not always easy to deal with their emotions.

In the main, the event brought out the best in an already tight-knit community. I was informed that most of the kids in the primary school and almost all the staff had requested special leave to attend Edison's funeral. I planned the funeral for the last day of school before the June/July school holidays, so as to minimise impact to the schools, Edison's peers and their families. I was informed that we were to expect several thousand in attendance, and so I organised with the church I had chosen for Ed's funeral, to provide spill-out audio-visual areas. I had been raised attending Kenmore Baptist church and although I was no longer a regular church attender, there was a homeliness to the church of my childhood. I had also taken the children there a few times in 2015, and so several people in the congregation were familiar with our family. The staff at Kenmore Baptist were very accommodating and worked with the funeral director and myself ironing out many organisational details. The wonderful principal who supported us through Freya-Grace's car accident had been moved on and a new principal was in place. I telephoned the new JSS principal early in the week of Edison's funeral to inform her that arrangements had been made to accommodate around 2000 attendees. I asked that if there was a notice to go home to families, our family would welcome all those wishing to attend. Instead, the principal, without my prior knowledge, and certainly not with my sanction, sent home a note to the families of over 1000 children that the church could only accommodate 500 people. She instructed her school community that those who did not personally know Edison or who did not have a child in year 6 were not welcome. Those who were to attend were ordered to be dressed in JSS formal school uniform. Few of Ed's teachers were granted leave. What kind of a principal turns a child's funeral into a public relations stunt for her school? I was righteous to be angry about her obtrusive betrayal. Such justified anger was easier to manage than facing the death of my son.

When it came to the decision of where Edison would be buried, I had a very clear preference. My grand plan of married happily ever after with one-of-us kids hadn't worked out. Most of my fix-it and less grandiose plans hadn't fallen the way I had imagined either… but if Ed could be buried where I had envisioned him growing up, it would be a comfort. Brookfield boasted a beautiful cemetery and it was very difficult to get into. I was told that people were literally dying to get in there. I was encouraged to consider the Centenary cemetery. At the time, I felt I had no roots in the Centenary suburbs. It was a place I landed based on decisions regarding my children's education. I was living in housewife burbs with no husband. The people were lovely, but it was not my 'fit', it was not my stomping-ground and perhaps also was not my future territory, especially now that Edison was gone. Louie Namoski from the Logan Housefire Support Network made a few phone calls for me and within days, I was pleasantly surprised to learn that an anonymous, yet well-known businessman and politician had donated a plot in the Brookfield cemetery for my boy. I was extremely touched by this stranger's kindness. At times, I have wanted to scream to the media that his anonymous kindness was a ripple in an ocean of his unpublicised generosity. When it comes to politics, the public have an appetite for bad news stories. I counselled myself to protect this man's requested anonymity, even though he could have done with a bit of positive publicity.

My parents and my sister, Kylie, were an enormous help in bringing the funeral together. In fact, they did most of the work outside of the significant decision-making, which they respectfully left to the girls and me, as appropriate. My sister, Fiona was working in Brisbane for a new and short assignment at the time and visited, supporting us when she could. Fiona and I think differently and as such, she offered pearls of wisdom which I would otherwise have not considered. My brother and his wife made the trek from Harvey Bay more than once during those two weeks. It was good to have family around. We were well cared for.

My friend, Sally, from the villa next door on Moreton Island had a sleepover at Lisa and Brent's the first Saturday after the fire. She was such down to earth and easy to take company. Being with Sally was like pulling on an old favourite cuddle jumper, something which I no longer owned but which I could figuratively enjoy. Sally's sleepover at Brent and Lisa's was the first night in weeks, where I slept for a decent period. I am reminded of a Dinah Maria Mulock Craik's quote which was displayed on a brass plate on my childhood toilet wall...

"Oh, the comfort, the inexpressible comfort of feeling safe with a person; having neither to weigh thoughts nor measure words, but to pour them all out, just as they are, chaff and grain together, knowing that a faithful hand will take and sift them, keep what is worth keeping, and then, with a breath of kindness, blow the rest away."

I have memorised this prose since childhood and quite unbelievably, an exact replica of these words, printed onto a brass plate turned up after the fire, from an unknown person as a donation. The new plaque now hangs on my children's toilet wall. My daughters have now also memorised this prose.

My father was extremely articulate and intelligent. Before Google, if a question was raised in my childhood home, the answer was often, *'Go and ask your father'*. In my home today, I say the same thing, and my daughters know 'father' equates to Google. It's a quirky in-family joke. Dad offered to draft Edison's eulogy with my input and edits. I implicitly trusted him and knew no one could deliver, on this occasion, better than Dad. The first draft of the eulogy was very political in my opinion. I guess my father and mother had been on the end of thousands of teary (and a handful of joyous) phone calls from me, exuding the trials and tribulations involved in raising Edison. Living a relatively tumultuous life, I probably didn't call my parents to tell them good news as often as I would call to ask advice or to borrow a shoulder on which to cry. Raising Edison, within my values and worldview, caused more fights, politics and miscarriages of justice than any parent should suffer. This is a characteristic I am sure I share with most other parents of non-typically developing children. Each parent who fights the good fight and wins, makes the journey easier for the next. There were many who came before us and many who will come after.

Dad and I crafted his wise words into the eulogy he delivered Friday, the 26th of June, 2015. He spoke eloquently and clearly.

The feedback I received was overwhelmingly positive. Many people commented also on how well Dad looked. It was fairly common knowledge that my father was a very sick man. People found this hard to believe as he never complained, he carried himself well and he always held himself up with a positive and authentic spirit. My father, around six months before his own death, delivered Edison's eulogy. It went as follows.

Edison's Eulogy
Spoken and Authored by Alan Maxwell Ginn

Today, I hardly know where to start – things are all back to front. I am one of Edison's grandfathers, and grandsons are not supposed to pass away before their grandfathers, are they?

I am going to speak to you about Edison, of course; now Edison was quite disabled by his autism, but there was so much more to Edison than his autism – it is **most important** that we understand that while the 'A' word was a limitation for him, it did **not** define who Edison was.

I am also going to speak to you about his mother, Jillian, my daughter and what I consider to be her heroism in battling all the odds over the years to give her son something of a chance in life, despite his problems. It is not practically possible to talk about Eddie without speaking of his mother. Make no mistake about it – it has cost her dearly in money, marriage, friendships, emotion and trauma and none of that is about to stop just yet.

Edison was born on August 30, 2003. There was nothing unusual about him or his birth, except that he was the apple of his parents' eyes. His parents wanted him to have a significant name as they rightfully thought it important for their son, and they came up with the name Edison. We all know Edison as the inventor of the electric light bulb in 1879, but he was a remarkable man who achieved far more than that in his lifetime.

Edison's second name was Maxwell and is far more prosaic in origin; it is my second name and comes from Father, but I was and am proud to have been so included in such illustrious company.

For the first year, Edison reached all the usual milestones of early childhood development as any doting parent could possibly hope for without any hiccups at all. Friends of mine have since told me of this happy talking child with his peers who were their grandchildren at Upper Brookfield.

Then suddenly, everything started to go haywire and the Edison we knew disappeared, but the new one remained largely hidden; that was a terrifying story for his parents. Jill eventually obtained a diagnosis of autism with some special variation. Now, I had no knowledge of such things and as Robyn and I were rapidly educated, we realised that we probably knew of such a child in our school days 60 years ago, even though the label did not exist then and we had not come across it since.

Medical science and paediatric specialists have done an enormous amount of research in recent times to get to the bottom of this almost epidemic – many theories are advanced, but so far there is no universally accepted explanation of what is happening or really how autism can be successfully treated.

Jillian's life and Edison's life since that day almost ten years ago amounted to one continuous battle to draw Edison out of that world, and at the same time, to obtain such assistance as our society was willing to provide for Edison and other children with the same problem. Now, we are not going to have a public policy discussion here today about the Eddies of this world, but I despair at the lack of insight, even willingness of our so-called leaders to really embrace our disabled people of all descriptions – they love a good PR story, but they are not really coughing up the dollars necessary to really make a substantial difference to the thousands of severely damaged families and individuals. I'll say no more!

And the 'good news' stories on TV do not really add much either; they are either too shallowly focused to be useful or so determinedly positive as to be laughable.

Jillian has from the start of Eddie's autism determined that he is to be included in every aspect of the family's life, no matter how inconvenient that may be at any given time. **'Inclusion'** was the watchword. As grandparents, we could weep to wonder what was going on in his poor tortured brain – there was no sense to it, and we were only visitors. It was obvious that others thought that he was a spoilt brat with an over-protective mother, but there was literally no communication from him except extreme unhappiness in a tiny child. Apart from the head banging, for example, he reacted violently to fluorescent lighting (think about shopping centres) and the distant noises of trains and on and on it went.

After a couple of years, he learned his numbers and letters and before he was five, he would type perfectly on his computer, 'Edison Hellmuth is going to bed', show it to you and go to bed, but not a sound! Early on, there were endless sessions with speech therapists to attempt to help him to speak; there were many other costly and very specialised programmes to assist, some gave marginal benefit, but none were revolutionary and they all cost lots of dollars.

At the same time, Jillian had two other children to raise and to earn a living to help keep the family's financial world going around.

Edison was educated at two schools, the first at a private school at Wooloowin – it started well, but after a change of leadership, it became less than satisfactory and Jill's changed circumstances forced her to look elsewhere. She finished up at the Jindalee State School after considering many options, and the family moved to the school's catchment to be eligible for Edison's enrolment there.

It was a good move in many ways, but it does seem that we cannot hope that any school can really meet the needs of a child such as Edison. It seems that the bureaucratic policy settings imposed on schools by the Education Department constrains school leadership so much as to be plain silly at times from an outsider's viewpoint. Yet the teachers and leadership involved with Eddie embarked on learning curves and have been supportive as far as they are able to be. I have no doubt that they have all learned many things through Edison that they have never even thought of previously.

In this context, I want to make special mention of Mr Leigh McKinnon, Edison's Case Manager at the Special Ed Unit of the school. Leigh, I do not mean to embarrass you, but it is obvious that you loved that boy and went far beyond your work responsibilities in caring for him and thinking about his development; you made his school life generally so much better for him in so many ways and it is greatly appreciated, I can tell you. Thank you, Leigh, you are a very special man.

Now, there are a lot of young people here today who knew Edison at school, some of you perhaps better than others. You have known and accepted Eddie with all his unusual ways – I want to say that is major credit to you, and as you grow up, us oldies look to you to carry those attitudes into your adult life – it will make an enormous amount of difference to the sort of society that we become and that you become leaders in.

Less seriously, I want you to know a few of the little things to remember Eddie by.

★ Eddie loved his food and he looked forward to pizza – meat lovers was his favourite. So, we would have a family discussion about what the order should be and I would go out for the three pizzas. Now, Eddie thought that the meat lovers was his alone and he had trouble with the notion that it should be shared around, so he would try to eat it as fast as he could to get it all – can you imagine it? So, I had to teach him, "No, Eddie, eat it slowly" as he chewed. Well, that didn't work very well either, so I made him put the slice down after each bite and I would repeat, "Eat it slowly" after every mouthful as he chewed some more as fast as he could. We will never forget his 'eat it slowly', even if it was never quite observed as we had hoped.

★ Now, Jill wanted to teach him how to stack the dishwasher… She explained that things had to go in upside down to properly clean them – he got that in the end, but the next day when everything was unpacked into the drawers, all the items (dinner plates and saucepans), were stacked upside down – perfectly logical where he came from.

★ Personal ownership labels placed on the back of DVD's do not belong; they make the case less than perfect, so they all have to come off. So, if you loaned the family a DVD, it often took quite a while to get it back. This was not helped by the fact that he also had his own way of filing them that no one else really understood; his mind was such a puzzle to the rest of us.

★ He had photographic memory and loved typing up the credits of every DVD and movie that he ever saw into his iPad with a little piccy to go with it. There were thousands of them.

★ One day when he was on school holidays with us, we saw a lot of stuff on his computer that made no sense to us. I forwarded it to a friend, and his IT specialist son said that it was programming language that he had somehow got a hold of and was playing with his own script. We have no idea where that came from.

★ From the time he could crawl, he loved trains of every description and the house was always full of them. Even when he visited us in Toowoomba, the train box would come out and we would have his trains from one end of the house to the other.

★ He loved to play with paper money, and it was rather disconcerting for Jill to find him fluttering $50 notes out on to the footpath from the high windows at the front of the house, so she then had to get the play stuff and be really careful to hide her purse.

★ On one occasion about five years ago, Robyn and I were caring for the children overnight and in the morning there was no Eddie to be found anywhere; he had run away, it seemed. Robyn scouted the neighbourhood in the car and I called the police. He turned up in a McDonald's (he loved his McDonald's) in the city, barefoot at a railway station in his pyjamas after a ride on this wonderful train. Then he was brought home in marked police car – what a perfect day!

★ He had always had a bit of difficulty sorting relationships outside his immediate family. Now, his granny is top of the heap, but I have a little less status, so I became Granny-Papa and had to learn to respond accordingly.

★ On the other hand, every older male person in the shopping complex would get an 'Alan' hands up and the older ladies got a 'Robyn' hands up.

★ I cannot forget to tell you of the hours Edison spent on the trampoline; the continuous jumping seemed to give him some small respite as well as working some energy off. In the end, I bought one as well and he seemed to love it hidden down in the back of the garden.

★ Every morning, there was toast and vegemite with marshmallows, on the verandah in warm weather, inside when it was cold – the routine had to be.

★ I could go on and on, so this is the last one; Edison knew the name of every child in his school, what class they belonged to and who their class teacher was; for him this was no big deal in such a large school, it was just the way things were.

Now, I did say at the beginning that I would like to say some things about Edison's mother, Jillian, so I trust that you will be patient with me just a little longer. You have no doubt noticed that we are in a church today, not merely a large auditorium. This is the place where my family worshipped for many years until we all went various ways. Many things have changed since then, but Jill has maintained her Christian faith in great adversity and has endeavoured to raise her children in the same way; it has not been easy, churches by and large still do not 'get' autism either, it gets in the way in all sorts of situations, but perhaps one day that may change.

I have been blessed to be the father of four children, three daughters and a son, and Jill is the third daughter. Other members of the family have had their difficulties over the years, but Jill is the only one who has been drawn into a lifestyle maelstrom such as she has endured over such a long period.

When Jill was little girl, I made her a doll's house and we called it 'Sunshine' because she was always so happy, and her mother and I figured that her personality would make her willing to share it with her sisters. This is not a criticism of anyone of course, but it does seem that some of us have that happy ability to be able to share more readily, and she was one of those.

Since then it has been Jillian's lifestyle to share everything about herself and her possessions, good and bad all her life. Some have benefitted greatly from that and she is philosophical about that too, but it has caused continuous hurt and frustration when our society has failed to reciprocate and to include her son at basic levels.

One of her most precious dreams for Edison was that he would be invited to a birthday party or to a sleepover by one of his school peers. Do you know that it never happened, not even once? Think on that for a moment. He was harmless, even innocuous, never caused trouble, but people were uncertain because they had not troubled themselves to know him and so were not prepared to take the 'risk' on him. So sad, really.

One of my own friends from my teenage years is a man of Jewish descent and we have maintained our friendship for more than 55 years. Now, I make no bones about my own Christian heritage and how in many ways it grew out of the Jewish heritage, though many Christians today don't want to talk about that.

In ancient times, a boy was regarded as becoming a man on his 12th birthday. In the last few days, Robyn and I have been going through photos of Eddie for today's service and we have been singularly struck by the changes in Edison's physical structure in the last couple of months, even his facial structure has changed greatly as he has started the move from boyhood to manhood. That means that if you remember his birthday, 30th August, he was too early for spring, he was in too much of a hurry, and he did not quite make his 12th birthday. But it does mean that his mother had him for all of his 'traditional' childhood and the memory of her 'beautiful boy' will be with her for always as he spends his eternity with his Creator.

Arriving at Ed's funeral in the sea of faces, I saw high school friends, friends of my parents, many, many children, people from the various schools we'd attended, work colleagues and standing out amongst them to me was the warmth of Dr Geoff. How generous he was to give up his practise for the morning to attend Edison's funeral. The faces of everyone seemed a glow of care. I recited to myself, '*I am safe. I can get through this day*'. We sang Amazing Grace, one of my life-long favourites, and a favourite of Edison's also. I tried to keep my tears from becoming convulsive crying.

The congregation watched a slideshow of Edison memories to the tune of Keith Green's 'Oh Lord You're Beautiful'. When Edison was in bed at night and I was allowed to choose my own music, this song was my go-to. Both Francesca and Freya-Grace bravely shared briefly. During Francesca's speech, she offered, *"I don't feel as if I've lost a brother, I feel as if a part of me is absent."* Francesca reminded us the extent of Edison's love and reach, *"His family will miss him, his friends will miss him, his teachers will miss him, even the lady at Coles he high fived will miss him."* Freya-Grace described a day at the shops when a person we did not know returned Edison's wave with a warm hug, *"It was the best day of my life."* Ten-year-old Freya-Grace described her brother as, '*the most loving boy*'. I think on this for a moment. Edison's emotions were pure and he was incapable of manipulation – what you saw was what you got. For my 10-year-old daughter, a simple act of return kindness from a stranger towards her brother marked 'the happiest day' in her life. Of our family values being independence, encouragement, inclusion, co-operation, respect and kindness; surely kindness must be the easiest to give. Kindness can come in the glimmer of an eye, a warm meal, a heartfelt thank you, a compliment, a listening ear… Kindness from a stranger to a boy who spent so much of his life pouring out love moved my daughter. At age ten, she was able to use kindness as a lesson to all who were there to mourn and celebrate her brother.

The congregation sang:

You are my Sunshine, my only Sunshine. You make me happy when skies are grey. You'll never know, dear Eddie, how much I love you. So, please don't take my sunshine away.

This was the song I sang for Edison as I put him to bed each night. I will never sing this to him again but singing it, I felt hundreds of hearts carrying me as they sang for my boy. I did end up choosing only males as Edison's pallbearers. They were my broken, physically weak and ill father, friends Rob Cheesman and Brian Stenzel, two of Edison's cousins, Brydehn Hellmuth and Rory Black and Edison's uncle, my brother, Bruce Ginn. They carried the undersized coffin on their shoulders out of the church. A heavy burden to carry. Watching this, I wondered how I could stand and take one step.

Edison's favourite food was popcorn, closely followed by pizza. For cuppa-tea time though, his treat was always two marshmallows. After the service, the congregation was offered marshmallows to share whilst they awaited the departure of the hearse. Francesca and Freya-Grace found the minutes outside the church extremely stressful. I had told them that media coverage inside the church would be controlled and that only four television cameras would be allowed. (Louie protected us and organised so many things for us, many of which I am probably ignorant of). I had explained days earlier to my daughters that the funeral would be a public event and not a closed one, as such, we couldn't control which media could and couldn't be outside the church. I had not fully prepared them though for what they faced. It was surprising and over-whelming for me, and clearly more difficult for my children. The media was wonderful during the months following Edison's death; that doesn't mean it was easy for the girls to handle public attention as they prepared themselves to bury their brother. We stayed as long as we could to have the church emptied, and hundreds of coloured balloons released into the sky while many mourners put up a little prayer or memory – or hope for the future, in their private balloon release. I then, as quickly as I could, I ushered Francesca and Freya-Grace into a waiting limousine to follow their brother's coffin to his burial site.

I invited immediate family and select close friends to join us at the burial. There were only about 25 of us in number. Included with this intimate group were Edison's two favourite JSS staff members, Mrs Hackett and Mr McKinnon. I was honoured that they attended. I was reminded that only two weeks ago to the day, Edison was suspended by school management for inappropriately (autistically) showing his care for these two beautiful people. Mrs Hacket and Mr McKinnon made Edison's school life rich and rewarding and went beyond any school staff members' dictum in the care they provided for Ed.

Earlier that day around dawn, I had held myself together having woken teary and relegating myself to the bottom of Brent and Lisa's garden. I felt the day hadn't really started when I chose to sit in the winter sun's warmth, praying that the day would end quickly. Time cannot be measured in minutes…

After the funeral, we waited a while for all to arrive at the burial site and I was mesmerised by rain falling all about us – 360 degrees, whilst our little plot of the cemetery remained dry. Edison loved the rain, he'd have to dance, he'd have to swim if it was raining. Waiting by my son's grave, I remembered that when authorities told me my son had been pulled from our fire alive, the previously spattering rain started falling heavily.

Non-indigenous Australians do not have long-held Australian traditions and customs. Our longest traditions are young. We can pick dates for example, 1901, when Australia became an independent nation, or 1770, when the British claimed eastern Australia. Whatever date we choose, our non-indigenous traditions are less than 250 years old. I am not sure we mourn or celebrate as well as we could. I know I do not do justice in marking events or times of cultural or life-transforming significance with the ceremony they deserve. On this day though, I wailed like a Greek woman (bred from thousands of years of culture). I could not control my emotions, and I will not cry like that over the loss of my son again. It wasn't until Edison's coffin was being lowered into the ground that I fell into the dirt and broke. I shattered. I simply could not remain standing nor control myself. After a while, with my brother gently easing me to my feet, I gathered remnant pieces of myself together into something resembling Jillian. After a while, encouraged by my parents and daughters, I headed back to the limousine to attend Edison's wake, hosted at a golf club.

Edison was a big fan of golf. When we first moved to Hilliup Street, I inquired after children's golf lessons for him. The local club was McCleod Country Golf Club and they offered Saturday morning children's lessons, which in the case of Edison, I would also have to attend. I wanted to attend with him, remembering that before children, I had enjoyed the game of golf myself. I hadn't played since being pregnant with Francesca, but I enjoyed hitting the odd ball with Edison at home. Francesca and Freya-Grace played basketball on Saturday mornings, and because I couldn't be in two places at once, Edison never did start formal golf lessons. This did not thwart his golf tuition though. Edison would pour over internet lessons on his iPad or laptop for hours before venturing outdoors to improve his putt or his swing. It was fitting and inexplicable when McCleod Country Golf Club generously offered their facility, catering included, at no cost to us, for Edison's wake. The girls and I agreed to invite their closest circle of 10 or so friends to the wake and outside of that, we left it up to individuals to choose whether they would attend, with a couple of exceptions. One invited guest was a year six boy who Mr McKinnon had told me, always looked out for Eddie. The other notable exception was a child in Edison's class named Maddie. Maddie was a kind child and Edison was very fond of her. I was fortunate enough to meet Maddie for the first time the Thursday before Edison died. We came across Maddie at the local Food Works where my eldest daughter later worked part-time. All three kids sang out a '*hello*' to Maddie as I clamoured to introduce myself. I told Maddie how thankful I was for her kindness to Edison and how much he valued her companionship. I shared with her that for years, we had rarely shared a meal or cuppa-tea time without Maddie being mentioned. She was tickled. Thankfully, her mother and Maddie attended the wake and I was able to express how pleased I was that Edison had children as kind as Maddie in his life.

A few hours into the wake, the children were becoming restless and I was asked if I could request some music from our host, so that the kids could heat up the dance floor. A good friend, Judy, whom I knew from Moreton Island, took the children's entertainment request under her wing, and soon the children were playing on the practise green close by the deck of the Country Club House. It was surreal watching children play at my son's wake. Life goes on. Everything is futile. Not long after the children gathered on the green, rain began to fall, but only on them. We could see right across acreages of the golf course from our vantage point and the only place it was raining was on the children. My heart felt a little a flutter as I again remembered Ed's innate delight in rain.

As the crowds dissipated, friends gently guided us back to Lisa and Brent's house. Mum and Dad stayed at Lisa and Brent's awhile, but it had been a big day and it was clear that the thing we all needed most, was space. Together, we watched the top TV news stories. All four major stations led with Edison's funeral. It was surely my top story but a part of me questioned even then, why we are so insular in what we will accept in the developed, safe world, as news. So many children around the world die every day with no media attention… I was pleased that the media covered Ed's passing honourably, and I noted that the flowers were beautiful. My mind was a little all over the place.

Lisa was rightfully exhausted having held my family and her own together for two weeks whilst herding hundreds of well-wishers through her play room and home. Lisa went off to bed for a well-earned rest and Brent and I stayed up and chatted. I wanted to be alone but Brent wouldn't grant me such privacy (maybe suicide watch stuff again – maybe just care). Brent is the kind of man who is as easy to take as a second skin and I somehow accepted that I was better off with his company than I would have been without it. Clearly, it hadn't been a big drinking day. There are days such as Christmas, Easter and the funeral of one whom you love, which I put aside as days to always remain sober. Never the less, an hour or so into our conversation, I began to convulse and I vomited. I vomited like I have never before. It was like all the foul police interviews, sadness, not-yet-grief and immediate post-fire activity needed to come spilling out. In this, my body revolted. Brent gently washed my feet and caringly helped me make my way upstairs to his spare room which I shared with Freya-Grace. Brent is a beautiful man. When Lisa and Brent first came into our lives, we found ourselves two of the best people that the planet has to offer.

Chapter 23
Forging On

In my experience, it's not until after the wake that the permanency of death settles for those who have lost a loved one. My work choices, my friendship groups and all my spare time had been dominated, for around a decade, to ensuring I could give Edison the best childhood and subsequent adult life he was able to lead whilst doing my best in this recipe for the girls. My will had the girls sharing equally 25% of my assets, Edison having 25% in trust and another 25% was to be used as a slush fund for Edison as he grew old. For the slush fund to be accessed, two independent special needs third party organisations needed to deem, once every few years, that that Edison indeed required the slush fund to live well. I had planned meticulously for my son's content and safe adulthood. With Ed's death, everything that I had planned literally went up in smoke. I wasn't enjoying my road trip.

Eventually, I did manage to see our burnt home up close. When I finally was allowed on my property, I was surprised to find that the blackboard displaying our family values, my bible and silver cutlery, given to me as a wedding present (in a fire proof box) were the only things of any value in the house to survive.

Life had not allowed me to have self-care pass times nor interests for over a decade. Providing the groundwork for my children to live full and meaningful lives had been my singular motivation and this was all consuming. Along with Edison's preoccupation for film credits came an obsession with certain songs which marked a chapter of his life. Before his death, his favourite pop song was Katie Perry's 'Firework'. Edison and I would cook and dance and scream in the kitchen, 50 times over to Katie's song. Edison would never allow his chosen song to be played only once and on the odd occasion, when I attempted to play some music which I wanted to listen to, it was quickly shut down. Bonding was a prime objective and as such certain things like listening to music of my choice, had for many years fallen by the way side. In the month leading up to Edison's death, his favourite children's song was the theme song to the movie 'Charlotte's Web' which was 'Zuckerman's Famous Pig'. If we heard it once, we heard it one thousand times. The luxury of now having choice in many areas, such as listening to my preferred music, remains for me, very difficult to grasp. It didn't occur to me for a while that I had been denied listening to my favoured music for a very long time. Now that Eddie was dead, I had unfamiliar freedoms regarding such basic choices, including what I could eat. I wasn't ready for such freedoms. I didn't know how to look after myself. I had lost those skills in looking after others. With regards to music, post-fire, there were no devices to listen with, and no music (in those days CD's) remaining in my possession, in any case. This allowed me to remain encased in the now comfortable prison of lack-of-music-listening independence. There were so many tiny, yet extraordinarily confronting new experiences and liberties post-fire life presented to me. Eddie had dictated what we would eat for dinner every night. This helped me when I was compliant, as back then I had a motivated student to teach cooking skills. I could say good night to the girls and not have to wait to hear excited cheerful screams from my boy becoming subdued as Ed settled... The fact that most of my choices were no longer dictated by Eddie's needs, in an odd way felt a new imprisonment.

Although, work slowly took its toll in the 18 months following Edison's death, it provided a welcome and practical distraction. People I worked with were supportive in the early days following the fire. There was absolutely no pressure to return to work early and although I was not an employee, I was invited to invoice as usual. The directors of the business I worked with were generous with their time, care and money. Several of their staff flew from Sydney or Melbourne for Edison's funeral and wake. The director who brought me on-board and his wife were two of those people. His wife was a doctor and a quilter. My mother, an accomplished and internationally recognised quilter had something in common with her, and I am pleased they met. My father and the director who had invited me to work with him, had little in common apart from possessing brilliant minds and caring about me. They were two of the smartest men I knew, and at Edison's wake, to my delight, they spent several hours talking one on one. I was devoutly loyal to my work and I was privileged to experience the support of many colleagues. Additionally, workplace affiliates, customers and partners such as Microsoft, City Beach and Data#3 were inspiring and humbling in their care. I was back working from the rental house fairly soon after Edison's funeral.

The police were relentless but finally abated when one of Sally's barrister friends stepped in. Sally proved to be helpful in providing her input into my rights with regards to the police. She is a barrister, but not a criminal barrister, yet with her education she knew more than a little about the law. Sally called the police one morning after I hadn't had a day without being harassed (bar the funeral) and asked if they could grant me a day off from interviews because I was exhausted and really needed to rest. They agreed to Sally's request and subsequently, I was left alone at Lisa and Brent's for the first time in what felt like forever. About 15 minutes after their home was vacated, I answered a knock on the door. It was the police again on the Sunday that they had promised Sally that they would not bother me. At that time, the crime scene had still not been released and I was told that without further police interviews, it would not be released. The consequences of this for me included holding up demolition, insurance and anything that could resemble the practicalities of moving forward and finding a temporary home (outside of Lisa and Brent's) for my shrinking family. I really wanted to be cooperative and I certainly did not want to be perceived as thwarting the police officers' cause. The police officer in-charge though, was different to the police I had dealt with in other matters during my life. She wasn't on the same team as me. I was a slow learner and her probable intentions eventually had to be spelled out to me from a third party. That morning, I was taken to the district's police headquarters, I was not offered advice that I could/should consult a solicitor. I was not informed of my options nor my rights as a gruelling, videoed interview commenced.

Unbeknown to me, during this interview, Lisa returned home to find me missing. At the time, I was not aware that I was under adult supervision suicide watch. I had been encouraged by friends to stay put and have time out. They wanted to give me space, trusting in the policewoman's promise to Sally, to give me a day off. My car was with Volvo being re-keyed (the keys burnt), as such I really didn't have many places to escape to other than Lisa and Brent's backyard or spare bedroom. Finding me missing with no car to drive was a little alarming for my 'carers'. I attempted to consult my formerly rational mind to return my wits when making the decision of whether to again cooperate with police that morning, after being informed by friends of the policewoman's promise to give me space for one day. I failed. Stupidly, I ignored friends' and informal legal advice and went with the police. Upon returning home and discovering that I was missing, Lisa telephoned Sally to tell her that she suspected that I was with the police again. Meanwhile, I was well into cooperating with yet another interrogation. Unwisely, I didn't answer Sally's phone calls made to my newly borrowed mobile during the interview because I really just wanted the whole thing to be over. The misleading promises of no more interviews and the immanent release of the crime scene was extremely attractive to me. I also had no idea of how deeply Lisa and Sally were in 'protection of Jillian cahoots'.

About 45 minutes into the interrogation, when questions were raised yet again about my (non-existent) sex life, I became defensive and asked why we had to cover this irrelevant subject again. At around that time, the interview was paused when I was alerted that a gentleman had repeatedly called the landline of the police station which I had been transported to. I was asked by the police officers whether I knew the man who was telephoning and whether I'd like to speak with him. I did not know the man and I said that I'd like to take his call. Soon I learned, this man was one of Sally's friends, who was also a barrister. No doubt, the local police officers recognised the man's name because he was a successful Brisbane based criminal barrister, whom it seemed I might just need. Perhaps that is why they thwarted his Sunday morning's efforts to contact and protect me pro-bono. We spoke briefly on the police landline, and then upon his advice, I excused myself to speak outside on the borrowed mobile phone. The barrister informed me that I was being interviewed under the suspicion of the murder of my son. I hadn't, in my wildest imaginings thought that this was a possibility, let alone my current reality. I was provided sound advice which I heeded. The interview was then formally halted at my request and the investigating officers were sent notice to only contact me via my new barrister. I do wonder how the daily work grind was for the male police officer who partnered the not-so-kind, bullying female. He seemed a really decent guy. Often, we have no idea of the constraints others operate within. Who knows what motivated the female officer? Perhaps she really did think I had started the fire and intentionally left my beautiful boy to die. I guess, in a criminal detective role, police officers see much which the general public are protected from. No one can criticise the Queensland Police Department from not keeping us safe. If my situation was stressful, it's highly likely that their typical workday is tougher. Three years on there is still no closure and the threat of a Crown Coronary Inquest regarding my son's death is scary and real. I have nothing to be afraid of ethically and I have nothing to hide. I don't though want to attract public attention. It would be good to have this all behind me. It would be nice to have the clothes we were wearing the night of the fire returned to us… One day, when it's all over, we will be returned the clothes we wore the night Edison died. None of those clothes will fit us anymore but it will be comforting to see something we used to take as for-granted comfort.

During the funeral organisation fortnight, I rented a place sight unseen, from a person I knew through work. That was a foolish decision – both to rent sight unseen and to rent without a real estate agent. It was a terribly stressful place to live in. The house was a massive and heavily gardened property overlooking the river. I have no idea what that man was thinking when he offered to rent out such an enormous place to a family of now three with a small dog that could not be contained by the property's fences. He knew that whilst under investigation, the insurance company would pay the rent and as such, he would be financially secure with regards to this one of his many investment properties. I don't need to wonder about how he became extremely wealthy. Sadly, many people come to wealth by taking advantage of the demise of others. Only two of our pets died in the fire. Ironically, the dragon, Lilly, survived and the dog named after rising from the fire, Phoenix burnt. The rental was verbally described to me as a typical four-bedroom fenced Westlake property. Pets were OK and safe. The man who owned the property ended up cheating us out of bond to pay for repairs to faults which existed before we took possession. As a passionate nester, I have always despised renting. Not able to call the place in which I dwell home is something of an anathema to me. I recognise that this is a privileged point of view. Never the less, owning (or working to own) rather than renting, as a nester was something I had put decades of work into. Some landlords allow tenants to make their rental house, home. Most do not. In any case, my rental battle existed in the main, in my mind. Renting and losing independence in my abode left me fighting a battle which was an outward example of the non-acceptance of my new reality. Again, this wasn't my plan. I'd lost everything I owned (except Christmas stuff, an unreadable bible, a family values chalkboard, silver cutlery and my car). I had nothing to make a home with anyway – so why was I so uptight?

Week three after Edison's death, the rental was ready for us to move into. I brought my daughters together and explained to them that I couldn't promise beds, a TV, the internet and many other things, but I had managed to gather two mattresses and a couch. I was happy to sleep on the couch. I'd also been donated a toaster and a jug and some cups so we could have tea, coffee and toast. My car had been part of the crime scene for several weeks and was then was with Volvo for a week. Volvo recut the keys and a general service including replacing two new tyres which several police officers monitoring the crime scene, had encouraged me to replace. It was good to have a car back, and the hope of some housing independence and privacy. To my mind, what I was offering the girls was minimal. I hoped to give to them more in time, but a decision to set up as an independent family was based on what we faced – not what I hoped for. Did my daughters want to come glamping with Mum in the rental, or stay with Brent and Lisa for a little longer whilst I gathered a few other possessions? Together, we decided to glamp.

Somehow, news got around that we were moving on, on Friday in only two days' time and oh my, did the community rally together! An old school friend, Sonya, couldn't believe I was moving without a bed to sleep in and set about making it her mission to find me a bed and not just any bed, a new and comfortable bed. With Sonya's backing, a brand-new queen sized double ensemble arrived on the day we moved in donated by the local Forty Winks Jindalee store. By sundown on the Friday, we moved in and our glamping was indeed a more luxurious style of living than most people on the planet could hope for. I felt I was living someone else's life in a house in which I did not belong, yet we were doing OK. (So many don't even have safe, reliable shelter). In the end, we didn't keep much of the donated furniture – recycling it back to those in need.

There are certain donated items which we treasure today. The president of the McCleod Country Golf Club had not only organised to host Edison's wake at their facility, she had also brought her family together to discuss the future of their family heirloom piano. The family agreed that none of the grandchildren were likely to treasure the piano and her children did not want it. Their family heirloom was thus generously donated to us. (They could have sold it!) The piano is a beautifully crafted instrument which I never once, to this day, need to remind my daughters to play when enjoying their musical talents.

On the day of moving from Lisa and Brent's to the rental, TV crews were again in place covering our journey. They needed a good news story to bookend the tragedy. After this coverage was aired on TV, I was stopped in public by many people. Oddly, I was faced by many people unknown to me smiling and nodding their heads as they shared with me, "*It's great that you are now back on your feet and have everything you need.*" I didn't have a phone, a broom, saucepans and thousands of other things I had worked hard to acquire; I also didn't have a son. We were still reeling, and donated things, albeit greatly appreciated, didn't reverse our experience nor loss. I think the ignorance of the strangers who approached us made them feel good, which is understandable. It was uncomfortable for my daughters and me to comfort strangers in their false belief that everything had been fixed. I constantly counselled my daughters to note the positive intentions of those who reached out. The day we moved to the rental, I was questioned at a grocery store counter by a fellow shopper. As I placed eight pillows on the checkout conveyor belt bench, she innocuously stated, "*Wow, that looks like you're having a massive sleepover. Have fun!*" I told her that we needed pillows to sleep with after our house had burned down and I was purchasing basic supplies. "*Oh my god! That's you! You poor darling. We've prayed for you every day. I am so pleased you will have pillows.*" She was genuine and caring in her demeanour. We did our best to empathise with the distress others encountered arising from our situation. That was, in an odd way, somewhat healing.

As previously eluded to, it was ironic that Phoenix who was named after a creature which arises from fire perished while the dragon survived. After the fire, whilst renting on the river (a never changing pool of brown flowing water), our dog, Lilly, proved a huge challenge. She ran away almost daily, never becoming road-kill, mostly to my disappointment at the time. I did try to rehouse her, but only begrudgingly as after-all, she was one of the two pets which managed to survive the fire. Could I take that from my children when no other things they truly cared about had been salvaged? Within the first week of renting, I received a call from a local dog groomer.

"*I think I have your dog.*"

"*Well, I've lost my dog, so this is good. Sorry, we've recently been displaced, and I haven't had a chance yet to update her tag with my rental address. How did you find us?*"

"*Well, Jillian, after your fire, a member of the community asked me to groom Lilly and today she ran to us wearing the pink winter warmer jacket that we donated to her. She was instantly recognisable as yours.*" This was a bit of a God moment for me. Lilly didn't know this neighbourhood and she ran straight to her generous one time only groomers five blocks away who had my name in their memories – or perhaps found my new contact details now known to the media. Lilly caused me immeasurable stress, but somehow, there was comfort in her survival skills coming to the forefront.

In that same impractical rental, Lilly contracted an eye disease. For weeks, I was providing drops on a schedule of every two, three or four hours. The eye drops had been created from her blood cells, allowing me to treat her with her very own phagocytes. This was not inexpensive. After around a month of phagocyte treatment, I attended a Microsoft work conference for five days and my parents were kind enough to watch the girls and our shrunken zoo for me. They did an excellent job with the girls and one of the pets, however, the phagocyte drops were left for 'someone else' to administer. Eventually, upon returning from the conference, Lilly was back at the vet overnight as her eye disease had returned with vengeance. *"We can transfer Lilly to the Eight Mile Plains veterinary eye specialist clinic..."* We talked through options, expense, infection risks etcetera. '*Take her eye out*', was my decision. All in all, Lilly ended up in the veterinary clinic for one week. The result: one eye removed under general anaesthetic, two ticks acquired from the clinic and finally, managing to survive a case of blood excretions from her nose; plus of course a frightening invoice. Lilly became a pretty nice dog, having learnt that the threat of removing her other eye may be pending. She enjoyed the company of Milo, our relatively new RSPCA adoptee. Milo is white with dark brown patches on his head and so was named after Eddie's favourite drink. As I write, our pets are now becoming fewer. Lilly, along with our two cats, died in the last couple of months. Freya-Grace was the person emotionally strong enough to dispose of Lilly's stiff body. I was too physically wobbly to be of any practical help. For farming kids, the death of animals is often a way of life. It is not so for my children and I consider Freya-Grace dealing with Lilly's body with admiration. Too much death for my children... I am harsh, that along with sadness pertaining to the loss of loved pets, I consider the deaths my children have faced is a first world problem. None of the three of us know the suffering of others living in less fortunate circumstances. We were born lucky in peaceful Australia.

I was eventually allowed to visit my former home a few times before it was demolished. Officially, I wasn't permitted to touch any of the structures remaining as it was unsafe. There was little structure left in any case. My bedroom had no floor or exterior walls left intact... 'The worst house fire in the history of Australia,' the media reported. I know others have suffered worse fates. Demolisher workers and I spent an hour or so searching for treasure such as the girls' charm bracelets and came up with zip. It was confronting. Edison's bedroom was the least damaged room in the house. There were closed draws which had not been exposed to oxygen, therefore, nor fire. I could have opened those draws to retrieve some of Edison's treasures. In his big draw lay all his Toy Story friends. There were several hundreds of dollars' worth of Toy Story friends there, with no Ed to befriend them. Edison used to enjoy acting out scenes from movies. He would rip all the DVD's off the shelf in a dramatic show, mimicking Michael Wazowski from Monsters Inc. and he would often throw Buzz Lightyear, Woody, Jessie, Rex, Ham, Mr Potato Head and friends into a garbage bag and take them out to the 'trash'. We lost more than one Toy Story character with Ed assigning them to garbish while I constantly replaced or rescued them. If rescued in time, before the bins were emptied on the street, Edison would delight in observing how his friends had come to life and returned to his bedroom from the garbage. Searching through the ashes of my home, I asked myself, '*Do I want Ed's stuff? Do I want his Toy Story friends*?' I wasn't able, at the time to process decisions of this magnitude. Eventually, Ed's stuff was demolished along with the rest of our home and the Toy Story draw remained unopened.

The insurance company staff were generally decent to deal with. They needed to conduct their own due diligence and use their own investigators and forensic experts. I found myself answering the same questions many times which were asked by the police, the fire brigade and insurance company representatives. The man overseeing my insurance claim was particularly respectful as was the contracted, prime investigative insurance officer, who flew up from Sydney to interview me for a full day. Reluctant to provide a full pay-out unless necessary, the plight to claim insurance was my new nighttime, full-time job. I was reminded of late nights of divorce and child custody affidavit upon affidavit authoring. The media who were still milling around from time to time, offered to publish stories on my insurance plight, and exhausted with fighting I mentioned the media offer to the insurance company. I didn't want to threaten them but I wanted to move forward and they were the main thing holding us back. It was when I brought a friend of mine David in, who was a solicitor, that the pay-out eventually occurred. All it took was several hundred calls from me, around 50 other forms of documentation, hours and hours of interviews, a bit of media support and one phone call from a solicitor. Easy. We received a pay-out for around 50% of what we used to own and 100% of what we had paid insurance for. A good day.

Meanwhile, I needed to sell a block of land in the middle of suburbia where a boy had died. Years ago, I had met Peter Chew, a local real estate agent. When I first looked into real estate in the 4074 postcode, Peter proved professional in his approach. I observed, as a prospective buyer, that he was protective of his vendor and he very clearly represented her, as opposed to 'the deal'. When faced with selling a charred and empty block of land, I remembered Peter. I needed someone ethical on my side whom I could trust, and who wouldn't hide the truth of the history of the block (if that could be possible), from potential buyers. In a postcode where vacant blocks were as rare as hen's teeth, I required an astute agent who could cut a fair deal for all involved. Peter was appointed, and with his support, a potentially stressful process unfolded smoothly. The community and Kenmore Baptist pulled together and conducted a working bee with Freya-Grace and I to clean the block up post-demolition. Organised by Peter, the local newspaper published the sale of the land in a cover story. The land sold with four written offers within three weeks. Today, it is subdivided and hosts two modern, attractive homes. With very few hiccups, Peter closed a fair deal, providing a stage from which my family could launch our 'which-home-next?' future.

The fire occurred on a Monday night. Edison died at around 12:30 am on the Tuesday. I do not know the exact time that my son was pronounced dead. A few months went by before the government posted me his death certificate in an unmarked envelope. It floored me when I opened the envelope. The government should surely have massive red letters on these envelopes cautioning:

> *'Open with Care.'*
> *'Open whilst seated.'*
> *'Open with the support of others around you.'*

I didn't know how to handle myself holding a pretty piece of officially stamped paper, a credential of sorts, declaring (as I comprehended it), *'Your son didn't finish primary school but he made it to death'*. Very macabre, but what was I to think? I trashed the certificate which reminded me of his burnt birth certificate and took no notice of when the coroner declared the time of Edison's death. There were times during this transition which I couldn't possibly be prepared for.

Eventually, we purchased a new home and it was time to buy a house-full of furniture to fit it out. I liked old things but I also wanted to purchase all we needed in one day. I couldn't replace a lifetime of collectables readily, but I could efficiently furnish a home. In a former work role, I had been the account manager for Harvey Norman Big Buys. The gentleman who ran that enterprise, Kaine, offered all Harvey Norman products to our family at staff prices. This was very kind and generous of Kaine and the local Oxley franchisees. I ensured the girls were busily occupied with friends for the day as I set out to shop for stuff to turn a house into an almost home. It was a very confronting day. I shopped non-stop from 9:00 am – 5:00 pm and ended up with a household of attractive, quality furniture, most delivered a couple of months later. Shopping isn't my favourite pastime at the best of times. I did not relish replacing old treasure with new things… Prior to my fill-an-entire-home shopping expedition, Mum offered me a gallery of quilts to select from to decorate our new house. Thankfully, quilt selection preceded furniture selection. I had my priorities right. The new furniture and accessories matched the quilts (mostly hung as art on new walls). Over the following 18 months, I visited enough junk shops to make our home a little less 'display-like', and it's now slowly warming from a house into a home. My mother's quilts adorn our walls as the centrepiece of all our living areas. I lost well over one hundred thousand dollars' worth of art in the fire for which I was not insured, and to have Mum's world-class quilts hanging in our new nest, was a huge comfort. I continued to search for old stuff. In one junk shop, I purchased a Pinocchio puppet. I remembered my ex-husband joking, when Ed was only around three-years-old, that one day he would grow up to be a 'real boy'. Edison was always a real boy and he grew into a beautiful young adolescent man. No one was pulling his strings anymore, and I didn't want anyone pulling mine. The girls hate that puppet that hangs in the room where my eldest watches horror movies. I don't understand why toys become scary in horror movies, but Pinocchio is not going anywhere. I purchased that puppet in the knowledge that no matter what anyone said, my Ed was a real boy.

Christmas 2015 was on the horizon and the local councillor's office staff contacted us, to inform us that they had been raising money in conjunction with retailers from the Mount Ommaney shopping centre for our family. Many of the shops donated gifts to put towards hampers which had been raffled. They invited us to come down to the local ward office and receive the donations. We were floored and grateful that five months after the fire, the community hadn't forgotten us. My daughters and I made our way down to collect the gifts a few days later. We arrived to find that each and every person who had won a raffled hamper had all donated the contents of the hampers to our family and there was a money tin for us too. I began to tell the girls to get a Kmart trolley as that would be the only way were going to get all the goodies into the car. Francesca instead asked me, *"Mum, do we need all this stuff"*

"Well, we could use it," I replied. As I spoke, 13-year-old Francesca looked to a sign beside the counter on the wall above a large empty box labelled, 'Gifts for the Homeless'. I knew that the things donated could be useful for all three of us. I was also aware my financial situation was less comfortable than before the fire. I suggested that Freya-Grace would need to agree to Francesca's idea of passing forward our gifts. At age ten, I expected Freya-Grace to ask for at least one shiny new thing – we could rewrap the cellophane. *"No, Mum, we have a home now, so this stuff should go to people who don't."* Without any hesitation and zero prompting from me, the girls placed all the baskets of goodies into the 'Gifts for the Homeless' box. We were not entirely altruistic. We took the cash box and counted its contents as soon as we arrived home. Nearly $300. I didn't want to spend this generous gift on more stuff, even though there were still heaps of items we hadn't replaced. I wanted to give the girls an experience to remember. Things can burn and rot and get broken, yet if we are fortunate, good memories last. I wanted to mark my appreciation of the community's generosity and draw a memorable (and symbolic) line in the ground post-fire. Francesca's favourite musical at the time was *Les Misérables*, and it happened to be showing early in 2016. I topped up the funds a little and purchased tickets to *Les Misérables*. We had a

wonderful day. I noticed that my children were around half the age of the next eldest person in the audience. *'What a bunch of odd bods we are,'* I thought to myself.

Christmas day 2015 approached rapidly. This was my first Christmas in eleven years without Edison. I did not know yet that it would be the last Christmas with my father. My sister, Kylie was planning to be in Japan for Christmas and my other siblings had elsewhere plans. I didn't like the idea of our little family, along with my parents having Christmas alone, in a new house with all new furniture. My daughters weren't keen to go away for Christmas and besides, we had a new RSPCA rescue puppy to take care of. I called a few aunts and cousins to organise Christmas plans, but most people's celebration day was already organised. In the end, when I was able to contact my cousin, Shelly, she kindly offered for us to come to her home. She couldn't change her plans and come to our place because some of her guests were old and transport and other logistics had long ago been sorted out. I was very happy to agree to share Christmas lunch with Shelly and her family. I asked if I could drive right up to the entrance of her home so that Dad only had a few flights of stairs to traverse. Shelly agreed to this.

Planning for Christmas, I asked Francesca and Freya-Grace what they wanted. *"An X-Box"*

"You got one of those last year!" I joked. We had a laugh every so often about our misfortunes. Australians and the Irish are known to be able laugh at ourselves. This is mock humour and in its own way, is a bonding aspect of culture. Our Christmas decorations were stored in the garage, the only part of our home which didn't burn down. I have always been a bit of a Christmas freak. There are many who could compete with me on this and win. We don't do thousands of lights on the outside of our home. We do celebrate by placing some exterior decorations, but where Christmas happens for us, is inside the home. We began to unpack our first without-Eddie Christmas. It was exciting to see old things. A cross stitch enclosed in a bamboo wreath, which a parent made for me when I taught year one, once upon a time, read *'Merry Christmas, Miss Ginn, from Trent'*. I've always valued things that arouse sentimental memories. We had an enormous tree to decorate, and that year the girls agreed on whose turn it was to put the star on the top! Boxes and boxes of

reindeers, angels, Santas and nativity sets were opened and found new places in a new house... A place I refuse to ever call a forever home. My home planning decades had been an abysmal failure, so this place is home for now – just a part of my road trip. It came time to hang the stockings. We no longer had a fireplace to hang Santa sacks over, and so we found a new home for the stockings in the lounge. Edison's stocking came out of packing boxes along with our other stockings, including Granny and Papa's. We stopped decorating and discussed... I shared that I didn't want to have only five stockings hanging. I reasoned that it would just feel wrong to have Ed's stocking in a box. He wouldn't be with us of course. He was long gone. He would, though, always be in our memories. We all agreed that Ed's stocking would be included with ours, and six stockings hung in the window frames of our new lounge room.

Our first Christmas morning in the new house resembled most others. I awoke, and my first thoughts were of Edison not being with us. Quickly, I forced myself to change my focus. I lectured myself, *'Christmas is for the living and you have two beautiful daughters out there who deserve, more than ever, a happy Christmas.'* We had a lovely time opening our gifts and I was pleasantly surprised that with the grief and loss of Edison so obvious and palatable, we managed to experience peace, joy and love. My parents arrived mid-morning and received their traditional gifts, plus a few surprises. Always mint leaves (lollies) for Dad and clinkers (also lollies) for Mum. Dad spent most of his time on an old two-seater couch that we have kept from fire donations. The couch is situated in the main living area where family traffic and most of our living occurs near the kitchen. Dad found it difficult and painful to move, as such, frequently we came to him. Today, the couch is looking old and is torn in one place. It's fondly referred to as 'Papa's couch' and although it is further worn in 2018, it has not been replaced. It's soothing to have something old around. Mid-morning, we left for Shelly's. Her husband, Darren, and her adult children received us warmly. It was heartening to spend time with extended family at Christmas. As promised, the car park requiring the least number of stairs to enter the home was left free for us. Eddie would have said, *'Very kind, Shelly, very kind'*. When Dad arrived, he sat with the other oldies and he was full of smiles. If my father had the health or energy for a smile, he offered it. He always had the energy for a twinkle in his eye, especially reserved for my mother. Oh, how he adored her. The other oldies were in their 80s and 90s. Dad was 73 and thankfully, his mind remained alert until his last days. His body though, was punishing. Outside of the fact that Dad never went grey, he really looked a part of the peer group he sat with that Christmas day, most of them 10 to 20 years older than he.

Shelly's home is like mine used to be, bursting with treasure. I emotionally valued so many sentimental things. Humorously, Dad would refer to my sentimental ways as 'semi-mental'. An example of one of these items was my grade one school port with its 1970s stickers intact, which I had filled with a brick to act as the front doorstop of our last home. Shelly's place brimmed with 'primary school port' equivalents. I was so happy to see her in such a beautiful environment, filled with her own creations and memory-evoking knick-knacks. I wasn't envious of Shelly with all that treasure. I don't know how to describe how I used to feel being in a real home with all my material memories intact. I think the word would be 'satisfied'. It was Christmas though, and I managed to overcome my semi mentalism and make sure the happiness of the celebration won over my hidden sadness on that day.

Dad's health did not pick up after Christmas. Mum had lived with a seriously ill man for decades and it was always difficult to know when to press the alarm bell. During the three weeks following Christmas, for Dad to move from the couch to the toilet, became a momentous effort. He had finished his 120th chemotherapy treatment in December 2015, less than a month ago and had been told by his oncologist that this latest bout of chemo had likely bought him another two to three years of life. Dad was a fighter. The pain and suffering I saw him endure to hopefully gain more time, is something most of us are too mentally weak to bear. Those of us who are strong enough to endure that kind of torture often don't have the love for life, or an overriding motivation to keep living which my father fostered all the days of his life. Dad had developed chronic asthma in his early 20s and went on to develop a bunch of associated health issues, many which were due to asthma related medication such as extremely high, ongoing doses of cortisone. Some adverse effects he suffered included osteoporosis, mid-section bloating, severe heartburn, several allergies and high blood pressure. In 2002, at the time that I was in the Mater Mother's Private hospital giving birth to Francesca, Dad was in Saint Andrew's hospital having a cancerous tumour removed from his neck. The surgeon told my mother that the tumour was the size of his fist. During this surgery, my father had rods placed in his neck to keep it upright. Ironically, after this, neither of my parents could move their heads left or right, nor could they nod. Dad visited Francesca and I in hospital during his recovery and before returning to Saint Andrew's. It was an emotional visit and I can't imagine the effort it took for Dad to temporarily leave hospital care to visit us. Before the fire, I had a favourite framed photo of Francesca, Dad and I bundled into a hospital chair. The photograph was of newborn Francesca (mostly bald), my wonderful father (eyes glistening and scalp mostly bald from chemo) and me. It portrayed a bucket full of hopes, dreams and plans. My father's life was not an easy one. I am sure there were many hopes, dreams and plans that were replaced by his road trip. Still, he managed to exude, all his life, wisdom, love and kindness.

In 2002, Dad had been diagnosed with multiple myeloma and we were informed that the longest a person had lived, post a diagnosis of multiple myeloma, was 10 years. He therefore, was provided a prognosis of somewhere between a few months and 10 years to live. Dad's will to live, his fighting spirit, his love for my mother, perhaps some luck and an ocean-full of prayers, saw him live 14 years post-diagnosis. He kept abreast of modern medical breakthroughs and it was likely beneficial that the relationship he had with his oncologist was consultative and mutually respectful. Never in my father's life had he consumed too much alcohol and he had never smoked a cigarette, he ate well and he was as mobile as much as his body would allow. I am certain that his healthy lifestyle choices contributed to his relative longevity. It was January of 2016 that my father made his final exit from his home. Mum and Dad's 50th wedding anniversary was coming up and all the children and grandchildren had committed to celebrating this landmark event on the 12th of February, 2016. Dad had asked me to organise, as a surprise for Mum, a small wedding cake for us to share at the wedding anniversary celebration lunch. My sister-in-law, Varee, had an aunty in Toowoomba who made wedding cakes, and together we set about organising a mini-replica of Mum and Dad's original wedding cake. Right up until his dying day, my father put my mother as his first priority.

Up until one week before Dad died, he held onto the hope that he would return to his wife and their home. Dad was transported via ambulance from Toowoomba to the Wesley hospital in Brisbane where he had stents put in his heart alongside a few other procedures. We were living on hope. My daughters and I visited Dad in hospital Australia Day. Both the girls treasured alone time with their Papa that day. When we gathered together by Dad's bedside, Francesca and Freya-Grace, who both sing beautifully, sang for their Papa. It was particularly moving to listen to Freya-Grace's solo of the New Zealand national anthem sang in an indigenous dialect. The New Zealand anthem is very uplifting, and Dad murmured as best as he could, *"I hear angels."* Thursday the 28th of January after dropping my daughters off at school, while pulling into the Wesley hospital car park, Dad's specialist called Mum on her mobile. Dad's oncologist wanted Mum to see him before she went to her husband. I parked the car and let Mum traverse this part of her journey alone, as was her wish. The doctor had visited Dad earlier that morning to share with him news of his most recent blood counts. Not knowing this, I went to Dad's room and met a frightened man in deep despair. He looked up at me with tears welling in his eyes, pointing his index finger to his forehead he shared, *"Well, Jill, they've just given me the bullet between my eyes."* I held him, and we wept together. He remarked to me, *"It's such a surprise."* Now, this was faith. Dad had worn decades of sickness, medical drugs and treatments, more near-death experiences than I could count and here he was at 73, in shock, despair and surprise that his blood counts read 'death' as his only next move.

Following this, Mum had hoped to have Dad in palliative care at home, but his downward spiral moved fast. Dad was moved again, this time to Saint Vincent's hospital in Toowoomba, and shortly after to a beautiful facility dedicated to palliative care. I drove one of Dad's younger brother's children, Ashleigh and Helen up to Toowoomba on the 3rd of February.

They had lost their own father during their university years. The return trip with my cousins had been brought forward a few days, as I didn't think Dad would make it to the weekend. In the early hours of the 5th of February, 2016, my father passed to be with his Creator.

There was another funeral to organise, and again Kylie stood up as a key helper. She pulled together the slides and assisted Mum in putting urgent affairs in order. The funeral was long and there was more than one Baptist preacher invited to share a few words. I have met many Baptist preachers in my life. Not many can count 'a few' as well as the Catholics can. Most of the preachers spent around 20-30 minutes sharing their *few* words. There were just so many words to share in honouring Dad's life... I was privileged to speak at Dad's funeral. I spoke of his gift of the book, 'The Road Less Travelled' and the inscription he shared with me, explaining the importance of nurturing relationships. I also shared how my father described happiness to me when I was in my 30s. In my relative youth, I had asked Dad for advice regarding the concept of 'leading a happy life'. He thought for a while before he responded, *"Happiness is like a deer in the forest. If you stomp through your forest, crunching on leaves, heaving heavy breaths, breaking twigs and upsetting order, in pursuit of the happiness deer, you are very likely to chase the deer away. However, if you sit in a comfortable place in your forest and enjoy the smells and sounds, the life abounding around you, the deer is likely to creep up and find you."* I also quoted a saying of my father's, *"Intelligent people make complex things simple... Simple people make simple things complex."* My father was a wise and much loved man. As Dad's funeral was held on Mum and Dad's 50th wedding anniversary, the wedding cake that we had organised was cut and shared at his wake. People celebrated and mourned an honourable life.

Today, my mother remains a pillar of strength. I cannot fathom what it would be like to experience a marriage such as hers, and have it torn from you. Dad made his children promise to look after Mum. I've done a great job of this at times, but I've also put up my drowning hand for her help. We are there to catch one another's fall.

2016 was JSS's 50th year anniversary and Freya-Grace's last year in primary school. It was also my first JSS fete since the school community had sung 'Happy Birthday' to Edison around a year ago. I knew I must attend the fete for Freya-Grace, but being in public receiving sympathetic eye contact, was the last thing I wanted. With the 50-year celebration looming, I alerted the school that our Jindalee Coles shopping friend, Graham Nimmo was likely the longest serving, living teacher from JSS. If my memory serves me correctly, he started teaching at the school in 1968, two years after the school had opened and he continued his entire teaching career with JSS. Thankfully, the school acknowledged Graham's historical contribution to JSS on the day. I tried unsuccessfully to seek out Graham during the fete, hoping to follow-up on my efforts to make the day special and memorable for him. I was unsuccessful because I didn't try as hard as I should have. Observing crowds of kids, now in high school who had once been Edison's peers overwhelmed me with emotion. It was all I could do to make it through to watching Freya-Grace's class, choir and orchestra performances before I grabbed some other parents and asked them to, "*Please watch out for Francesca and Freya-Grace and bring them home safely.*" I had to go. I managed meagre smiles to meet the myriad of sympathetic faces aimed my way, as I made my way as quickly as possible to my car. I was a mess of tears as soon as I was out of sight of the school community. I think that day was the first really big sobbing, alone cry I experienced since I buried my son. Some days, it's very difficult to operate, celebrate and move on whilst harbouring a broken heart. Once home in self-soothing mode, I reminded myself, '*You can't lose what you never had. This is your only reality and you never lost the future Ed of 12+; you need to focus on the years you had – and the years ahead of you...*'

Chapter 24
Reality Bites

Around nine months after Edison's death, I was invited to share an interview with Steve Austin on ABC's local 612 radio station. Today, I remain an avid listener of the station. I agreed to the interview. The theme for the time slot was 'My Family Story'. The 20-minute interview barely scratched the surface of *my* story. However, there was overwhelming feedback from empowered listeners sharing that the interview encouraged resilience. I was shocked, during the live interview, when Steve commented to me that nine months, was 'early days'. Nine months without my son felt like forever. A few years on, I now know that Steve was correct. There were other interviews... I don't know if I could repeat such conversations today in the same manner that I did back then. I've had time to think and time to contemplate. I have post-trauma-matured thoughts and less words than I used to have. My outlook is no longer viewed through hope-rimmed-rose-coloured glasses as it used to be, but I'm working on that. Grounding stuff...

August 2016, the girls and I flew up to Cairns for Haley and Brydehn's wedding. My daughters were junior bridesmaids, and the wedding took place in the stunning location of Port Douglas. Jan picked us up and although we hadn't seen the children's paternal grandmother for many years, we gelled quickly. Jan is easy to take. There are never any games with Jan. She is kind and was clearly happy to see her grandchildren. Leaving Cairns airport, Jan drove us the 45-minute journey from Cairns to Port Douglas. Haley was a stunning bride, and I was elated that my daughters were sharing this special day with their cousin and included in the bridal party. The reception was a hoot... So much so that I considered moving to North Queensland. At the wedding, I was the only one in my family not related to this lot by blood. Yet somehow, I related to them instantly and with warmth. It felt as though regardless of not sharing genetic matter, we shared valued family history. The feeling was cosy. I'll treasure that comfort forever. Francesca and Freya-Grace's Aunty Debbie (Brydehn's mum and the girls' father's, youngest sister), was so much fun to be around. With her husband, Mark, they were raising caring kids and demonstrating responsible ways to celebrate and live. We took barefoot photos and I felt right at home. I met relatives I never knew existed and a very special memory was planted.

When we returned to Cairns, we made a trip on the Sky Rail to explore the Kuranda markets. I felt an emptiness without Ed, but I was determined to cultivate new memories for my daughters. Travelling around one hundred meters above lush rainforest, I hesitantly remarked, *"Eddie would be freaking out on this Sky Rail, and at the same time he would've been elated and busting with excitement."* Sometimes, it's confronting and confusing to know when to share feelings and memories with others who also miss a person now deceased. As my daughters shared their own memories of their times with Ed, most likely motivated by my courageous sharing, I felt that with baby steps, we were moving forward. The next day, we visited Green Island and enjoyed some of what The Great Barrier Reef has to offer. In sharing and enjoying our first family holiday without Edison, I harboured guilt, but it had to happen. We shared another break at the villa not long after. During this stay, I came to the realisation that I would have to sell the property for much less than the figure I purchased it for. I couldn't afford this, yet my connection to the property was now diluted and so I swallowed my reality. The villa made no sense without Edison. Today, still unsold, I dread the job of cleaning out his swimsuits, trains, toys, books and puzzles contained in our lockable storage. Some people lose children and have everything to clean away. I was saved that job. Small mercies.

After Edison died, I let nothing slide apart from self-care. I worked as hard as I ever had. I parented with my best foot forward, holding more sleepovers and parties than ever. I replaced, I replaced, and I replaced burnt stuff. I burnt myself out. In late 2016, I hosted a party for around 100 guests hiring a caterer. I wanted to celebrate Christmas, to draw another metaphorical line in the sand of post-fire craziness, and to thank people who had supported us. I was hoping the party would set the scene for a new *normal* for our family in 2017. Having a community to thank for support, I met many people for the first time that night. During the organisation of this party, there was an inkling growing in me that I couldn't keep up the pace I was living. I needed something to let up, but I didn't pause whislt my stress levels rose. To come down at night, I'd sometimes enjoy too many chardonnays and that would help me sleep without fire dreams, nightmares nor a brain overloaded by contemplating work-related stresses of tomorrow. Using wine (or any alcohol), as a sleep aid is a slippery slope. Alcohol does not assist in restorative sleep. I knew I needed healthy sleep, but my mind was too chaotic, managing what was on my plate along with the work hours I was holding down (often well past midnight), to meet our basic needs. My drinking buddy (chardonnay) didn't interfere with my work. I was earning as much as I ever had, my clients were well served, my team was motivated, and my colleagues continued to work well together. My buddy didn't interfere with parenting duties either. I was a sober taxi driver – to basketball, acting classes, training of all sorts, choir, school, orchestra, Francesca's part-time job and more. The children were fed, the bills were paid, and cuppa-tea time was never compromised. We remained a home always open to teens for sleepovers and I held myself responsibly together whenever required. In all this, I found little joy. I was simply pushing myself too hard. I felt like a rat on a wheel, madly running myself in circles, and into the ground. I never gave myself the chance to mourn. But I was coping well enough and doing it all.

At a time when my work situation provided necessary distraction from grief, feeding some form of sustenance of meaning and purpose, an event occurred which knocked me off my feet. A young, unqualified, ignorant colleague reported to one of the directors of the company I represented that I was suicidal. I have never been suicidal; she was wrong. In risk mitigation mode, based on no facts and involving no consultation nor due diligence with other directors, unnecessary measures were enforced. From work's perspective, it is likely that based on ridiculous conclusions, they had to do something and needed it to be on record, that they had done something to fix my falsely concluded state. The suicide-risk conclusion was prompted by my request for practical support in work. I was struggling – working unreasonable hours and playing too many roles. In my cry for help, I was dishonourably treated and humiliated. I shared, *"If I was going to kill myself, I would already be dead!"* My protests reiterating that I was only seeking support and the resolution of many unfulfilled promises fell on deaf ears. I was offered paid time to seek help yet the help I needed was only grounded in alleviating my ridiculously demanding work demands. This predicament resulted in finding myself in a position where I had to choose between two exclusive options; retaining dignity with honesty – or retain my work and continue to earn money with zero dignity. I decided to resign and go the dignity and honesty route.

The one director whom had encouraged me to be a colleague made the 'you need time out and suicide help decision' cited in writing that while working, I may have been drinking at times. He was right. Working at 2:00 am to make him lots and lots of money, I sometimes consumed a few drinks. He also cited I had been aggressive. Twice in the previous 12 months, I had been assertive when treated poorly. This direcor who swore on the phone to me almost daily somehow found a female's assertiveness a means for a dismissal warning. The other Australian director and international directors were not consulted with regards to this warning (at this point I had a global title) – one powerful man against one vulnerable female became my professional predicament. The months after this betrayal left me wondering whether I had it in me to return to the industry which I had successfully operated in for a couple of decades. I truly cared about and respected the director who betrayed me. Where next?

Earning no money and as the sole provider of my living children, I sat with myself and a new plan beckoned. In resigning from work, my 200 km/h operating speed was forced down to 60 km/h; a speed which was not comfortable for me. I began to feel things I hadn't before. I felt an intensity of anger I never wish to revisit regarding how two of my trusted work colleagues had treated me. I knew that accepting facts did not equate to condoning actions. I berated myself with circular thoughts. *'Accepting a past that was never in your control is only going to hurt you… But this is your past and you need to dilute anger and foster acceptance… Arrgh'* I still find acceptance of things, which are out of my control, very difficult. It's not that I'm a control freak, I'm more of a justice freak and a lack of justice is a thing I find very difficult to stomach. Resigning from my work marked the epicentre of my suffering. Constantly, I challenged my identity; *'Who am I now as a non-worker, non-ASD mum, non-owner of my life's treasures?'* I had held my family and my work together through so many difficulties. To lose face and an income, based on some young person irresponsibly setting off a panic button, was the primary catalyst to the demise of my day-to-day coping. I have not returned to the IT industry full-time since that event, which I think is a sad thing.

In my seething, accepting and not working days of early 2017, I considered when I had been most satisfied in my work. I saw a pattern of a stressed and unhappy Jillian when those who paid me, treated me as though my prime motivation was money. I noted that when I was solving difficult people and organisational design or change problems, my creativity and intellect was at its peak. These were the projects and roles where I was most satisfied. I remained keenly interested in business and assisting organisations and the people within them to be more effective and efficient. When I flourished and enjoyed my work the most, it was people and creative problem solving within the context of business that drove me. I had set out 12 years ago beginning my small business with a passion of care and business improvement. Eventually, I concluded that it was high-time, I returned to what motivated me, no matter the cost. Lack of sleep and what was later diagnosed as PTSD (Post Traumatic Stress Disorder) got in the way of such ideals.

Regardless of my motivations, I found myself in a rut, with children to care for and no income. I feared returning to the industry I had worked in for decades after being so badly mistreated. No matter what I tried, I couldn't climb out of my newfound world alone. Initially, I checked myself into an ex-boyfriend's mother's place. I needed timeout. I had a wonderful few days with my ex-boyfriend's mum and her partner in Mount Tambourine. Disappointingly, at the time, I did not manage to solve all the complexities I was facing during three-days off, of enduring real life. Driving back from this retreat, I was alerted by an emergency services siren. All my fright or flight jumpy responses were awakened. Certain stimuli including a siren, one of my daughters un-expectantly saying hello, a broken plate, or a person telephoning me when I don't recognise the number, produced responses I didn't like, and I couldn't control. I don't fully understand why certain things trigger me. I don't understand why I need to always know where emergency exits are. I don't understand why I always need to sit in a corner with no one able to see me from the back. Clearly, a siren makes psychological sense as a trigger, but a 'no caller ID' makes no logical sense. It seems that my parasympathetic nervous system does not work on logic. I doubt that a life of retreats will fix this. Hearing the siren on my journey home from my ex-boyfriend's mum's place, pulling my car over and stopping to breathe slowly, helped a little. The emergency vehicle with its siren blaring passed me by. As I completed my drive home, my stomach folded with major butterfly effects feeding a chasm of questions which most often led to, '*Who have I become?*'

Life was to serve me another lesson... Unusually, my natural, flowing mobility progressively declined from the time of Edison's death. I lost much of my balance and over time, I began to exhibit a jerky gait. I reminded myself that when I came to within an arm's-reach of Edison, on the night of his death, I fell to the ground; literally, I fell in a heap. I recalled witnessing Edison's coffin being lowered into damp earth whilst I collapsed, weeping, wailing at the foot of my boy's grave. Maybe my balance and physical constraints had their origins in these experiences? I questioned, '*Maybe I just didn't have it in me to literally keep walking forward?*'

'*Psychological babble,*' I told myself. Initially, my unsteadiness was noticed only by those closest to me and individuals who worked in rehabilitation or medical domains. It wasn't until my work failed me in December of 2016 that my jerky, unstable gait declined to a point as to hinder my motivation to spend time with friends, attend social events or participate in public activities. My gradual, physical demise contributed to an avoidance of anything outside of my home. I became very adept at online shopping. Purchasing groceries and other necessities; pretty much anything the girls or I needed, could be procured from the comfort of home. I was extremely self-conscious of my odd and unsteady walking, which for some unknown reason, presented far worse in public than in the privacy of my home. The major effect of the demise of this lack of balance trajectory though, was a physical inability to show love; the most healing feature of a fulfilling life. Eventually, I was diagnosed with Functional Movement Disorder (FMD) and I struggle to walk to this day.

During a quest for answers to solve why I couldn't walk unaided, I sought the counsel of a psychologist. I pondered whether I had a form of PTSD based Conversion Disorder. Hysteria! Of course, any psychologist worth their salt will not diagnose Conversion Disorder (or any other disorder) without a second opinion and full due diligence. I was encouraged to completely rule out an organic cause. The psychologist I chose was Tina, and she was a specialist in EMDR (Eye Movement Desensitisation and Reprocessing) which was a therapy aimed, in part, to assist those living with PTSD. I conducted research on Tina prior to selecting her. She was a lifelong learner and as it turned out, an excellent therapist. I began seeing Tina in early 2017 when I had not yet accepted PTSD as a diagnosis. From my sessions with Tina, I hoped for assistance and insight into improving my gait and for EMDR therapy to reduce my fire and terror nightmares. During this time, my seeking mind toiled and grasped around half answers which I didn't accept. I became more familiar with Dr Google than any sane person should be. With no clear answers from the internet, I eventually arrived at a surrender, of sorts… Who was I to ignore professional advice? I began to accept PTSD as a part of my unsteady gait, diagnostic conundrum.

I tried a few creative approaches in dealing with my grief and learning to accept my not yet defined, new identity. There are parts of who we used to be that external events will not change. I was no longer the parent of an ASD kid, I was now the mother of a dead kid. I had been stripped bare from my profession, my stuff, my son and many pillars of my identity. Yet I remained a heart-on-my-sleeve girl, but with my former career abandoned and no objects to remind me of who I was, I struggled with many internal conflicts. These conflicts were a gift. Many of us are not confronted with an almost naked questioning of who we are.

Life provided some stable comforts. A constant in our life, was that Freya-Grace would never sit in Edison's seat in our car. Once upon a time, his seat was on the back left side. This arrangement allowed me to supervise him via my rear-view mirror, as Eddie threw school hats, money and all manner of things, out the passenger window. Watching things fall and flutter was very attractive to Ed. I liked that Freya-Grace, for years, wouldn't sit in Ed's seat but I am pleased she moved forward. I wanted to encourage her healing... I took Freya-Grace to Toowoomba for 'The Carnival of Flowers' whilst 15-year-old Francesca was in China as an ambassador for Education Queensland. My mum had an open home as a part of the carnival and I thought it would be rewarding to help Mum on the day. Freya-Grace always helped me with my mobility and so it was possible to book a three-day adventure. I secured lavish, homestead style, private accommodation where Freya-Grace and I would have our own fireplace for a few nights. I was surprised at Freya-Grace's response to our holiday accommodation open fireplace. Two years after Eddie's death, Freya-Grace regressed that night, revealing her understandable fear of fire. I had expected it might be a bit scary for her, hence wanting her to be exposed to a fireplace in a safe environment. I didn't expect genuine fear though. My creative approach to deal with the collective effects of our fire, one issue at a time, proved useful. Perhaps surreptitiously, I employed a little CBT (Cognitive Behaviour Therapy) in my motions to encourage us forward. By night two, Freya-Grace and I were nestled together with a Netflix movie, snacking on delicious treats, basking in the warmth our very own, comforting fire.

On the one-year anniversary of Edison's death, I decided to hold a cemetery tree planting ceremony at dawn with close friends and family. This felt like a good idea at the time. It was somewhat therapeutic going to the nursery with my daughters to buy a Tropical Birch. I wanted to plant a deciduous tree that would shed a palette of autumn coloured leaves over Eddie's grave. We have deciduous trees in Brisbane, but not many that show off autumn colours. Jacarandas, for example, are green, sticks or purple. I sought the Brisbane City Council's permission to plant a tree in their cemetery. With reasonable restrictions, the council OK'd my request. I asked the council to inform the gardeners who tended to the cemetery grounds to not kill the plant in winter when it would resemble a stick. The day before the anniversary of Edison's death, I realised that I was not holding a dawn hole-digging ceremony and I therefore needed a pre-dug hole. After dropping my daughters at school, I set off for the cemetery with a mattock, water crystals and a shovel in tow. Oh my! The ground was as hard as rock. I spent over an hour digging a pitiful hole while in my peripheral vision, I caught glimpses of retirees from the local old people's home, walking to morning coffee on pensioners day. I wanted to yell to a couple of the 80 and 90-year-old men, *"Please help me."* Surely, they could do a better job than my pathetic efforts were producing? In my attempt to bury pain with loved others and celebrate memories of a hopeful future, I was alone. As I dug and fought, paradoxically, the rain began to pour over Eddie's grave and I. More than once, with exhaustion, I was forced to collapse at the end of my son's grave. Several times, I gathered strength to make the tree planting hole just that bit bigger. I wanted the tree to thrive. People were bringing things to hang on the tree at dawn the next day... The girls and I had purchased items we intended to hang from the tree or put at the base of the symbolic Tropical Birch. Attempting to dig a hole, I knew Edison was not there, but I had a laugh with him anyway at the notion of his mother, eyes filled with tears, sweating in the middle of winter in the rain, fighting mud and rock. Fighting. I'm still fighting. I'm so tired. A new seed of acceptance and love was fed. The dawn ceremony the next day was silent, outside of my friend Rob asking if I'd like him to make the tree hole a little bigger. Gratefully, I accepted and we all, once the tree was planted, decorated it with items that reminded us of Eddie... A Thomas the Tank Engine train and track, a big red car and dream catchers were positioned...

As Easter 2017 approached, I planned to revisit Edison's grave on Good Friday. I don't visit Edison's grave often. To join me in my Good Friday vigil, I invited my mum, who was staying with us and I also invited my daughters. I made it known that I was committed to visiting Ed's grave and that it was up to each of them individually, if they want to join me. No strings attached... My mother and daughters decided to join me Easter morning and I planned to take them to a local café for breakfast after. In 2016, I had ordered, with my mother's blessing, a plaque for Dad to have laid at Edison's grave. Dad was cremated and so there was nowhere specific for Mum to go to have silent moments of remembering. The plaque, authored by my Mum, read:

Alan Maxwell Ginn
Husband of Robyn Hope Ginn
Grandfather of Edison Hellmuth
Forever with Jesus
1942-2016
God's grace sufficient

That day visiting Ed's grave was the first time Mum had seen the plaque placed on Ed's tombstone in honour of her husband. It was emotional for Mum and me, but the girls were not in the moment. I think they were there for the free breakfast. That was OK. Each to their own… We grieve differently. I was saddened though, on that morning, because someone had destroyed Edison's tree. The chimes and artwork which hung off it were gone, not even placed by his tombstone. The Tropical Birch had been a healthy green-leafed spring plant the last time I saw it driving by the cemetery when dropping one of my daughters off to music camp. Ed's tree didn't last a year. Not because it wasn't healthy, but because it was wiped out. It has been suggested to me many times to plant another… I don't know if I'm finally learning acceptance, surrender, or to be defeated. Either way, I have less fight in me than I used to have. I am sad that Ed's tree was killed. I am saddened enough that to this day, I have not returned to his grave.

Easter came and went, and I was not in a busy place. Having time on my hands was not my comfort zone. I had time to feel and I didn't like it. In part, in response to my failing attempts to adjust to not having fulfilling work and to my grief, I checked myself out for three weeks of belly button gazing, quiet, soul searching and sobriety. Whether I liked it or not, I figured that I needed to feel whatever it was that kept bubbling up from my broken heart. I was aware that since the fire, everything felt futile to me. Everything I had created, down to artwork, clothing, vege-patches and garden beds was burnt – gone. As Ed would have

261

said, *'Nothing. Not any more left.'* He used that phrase over popcorn, time with an iPad, my patience – all matter of things and as he spoke, his beautiful face would screw up so sadly. Edison had learnt to feel fully the feeling of *'Nothing, not any more left'*, long before I.

My belly button gazing stint was confronting. I received very little outside help from others during this so-called retreat time, but it was positive that the change of environment provided reprieve from parenting and provided me time to think. I had no issues with the sobriety aspect of my escape. Sobriety was simply a by-product of my self-imposed existential thought invoking experiment. Life slowed down even further during my retreat, and the reality of my son's passing loomed larger than it had since the first raw couple of weeks following his death. In my mind, futility abounded. As a philosophical creature, I felt very lost without the distraction of too much work, or much at all to achieve. Deep sadness and meaninglessness crept in. I was not depressed. I was sad.

If I was clinically depressed or clinically anxious, I would not have seen that as bad news per-se. I admire courageous men and women who have fought battles with anxiety and/or depression head on with grace, determination and resilience. Many live with life-long chronic conditions, while others suffer episodes of mental (ill) health only when spurred on by specific events. Worthy of admiration in conquering or living with their struggles and bravely sharing their coping mechanisms and stories are several well-known individuals. Some that come to mind include Sarah Wilson, Grant Thorpe, Bruce Springsteen, Adele, Ellen Degeneres, J.K. Rowling and Anthony Field (the blue Wiggle). Incidentally, Anthony was central in my landscape of insomniac attempts to sleep, during my early parenting Wiggles era; thank you, Anthony, you had quite the calming effect on me. Listening to and reading the stories of such brave survivors encouraged me in my own bizarre and not always so stable mental, physical and emotional health journey. The sharing of an honest story is generous and always has the potential to assist in the healing of others.

During my three weeks' time away, I remembered the Bible passage of Ecclesiastes 1: 1-18 chosen for Edison's funeral and graciously read by Dr Geoff Catton. Dr Geoff offered an introduction to the reading, providing context. He shared some memories of treating my son, and a former patient of his *"Baton down the hatches! Edison is coming!"* As I listened to Dr Catton speak during my son's funeral, I engaged in self-talk... *'What was left?'*

> *'Did I want to create a new vege-patch from scratch?'*
> *'Not really.'*
> *'Was there any sense in creating art work?'*
> *'Not really.'*
> *'Did I want to go shopping, to Buddahfest, to the markets or on a picnic?'*
> *'Not really.'*
> *'Is there a reason to anything?'*
> *'Probably not.'*
> *'I want my boy back.'*
> *'Not possible. Pick yourself up.'*

Again, I was not depressed, yet I remained sad and deeply in tune with how futile the world felt to me. I was experiencing a rational response to lost hopes and dreams. I looked up the Bible verse my father had recommended for Edison's funeral which can be summarised as 'Everything is Futile'.

Ecclesiastes is a heavy book. Many of us lead heavy lives, in particular, if we take them seriously. Ecclesiastes encourages us to be satisfied by the good things, to live and to invest in life. The passage read at Ed's funeral concludes with a prophecy that God will bring every act into judgment. Tough stuff. I don't believe in good and bad people. I certainly know that I can be both good and bad and a lot of rubbish in between. I've been given gifts, burdens and blessings. I've worked hard and tried my best, often facing failure. My big question remained, *'Where to from here?'* I needed to ponder being simply satisfied by the good things; satisfied with living and investing in life. I could not answer, *'What does that look like for Jillian Ginn?'* My naval gazing set me down a path of clear thinking, and (welcome or not) clear feeling.

As I struggled with my emotions and now in-my-face grief, my daughters remained virtually straight A's academically. Attending a large school, Francesca was year 10 student leader last year and Freya-Grace was selected for student leader also for year 8. Francesca also focused on the University of Queensland Young Achiever's scholarship she had secured. She became the 2018 Youth Parliament member for our electorate. Violin lessons, orchestra, choir, sleepovers and basketball etcetera continued... The wheels were spinning on the home front and everywhere I looked, my daughters were standout students and citizens – more importantly, they were demonstrating kindness within their community.

I progressed in dealing and acknowledging grief through meditation while imposing new and disciplined daily living routines. Mindfulness was suggested as a coping strategy which I researched and actively employed. I had ceased my few weeks of psychological therapy. My mind was very full yet this mindfulness stuff didn't work for me. Instead, I found that mindlessness was quite useful. My brain was like a highway which I tried to settle into a suburban street with self-invented mindlessness exercises. A big part of my mindlessness strategy was to listen to music or the radio and practise an acceptance of my inability to manage my now. Some would argue my tactic was indeed a form of mindfulness. Mindfulness focusses on now. My now, was just too hard to focus on when I couldn't shower safely with my mobility issues. I downloaded some useful hypnosis relaxation apps.

I continued to chase my tail in my attempts find a clear path forward – a new plan. I reluctantly accepted my bourgeoning road trip, yet still, I sought realistic goals, a map, a destination and an understanding of where to best direct my energy next. A book of encouragement was born. I may not have been able to walk independently, but I could provide love and encouragement via a keyboard. I will do my best with what I have been given in life in the hope I can walk again properly while actively and abundantly sharing care and love. FMD has become another hit to my ability to cope. It's not fun to be unable to walk independently. Importantly though, I'll thrive forward in the knowledge that this wonderful rich life that we all have the honour of experiencing, brings with it responsibilities, rights, sorrow, joy and love. I have been advised it is possible for me to recover from FMD. There is a beacon of hope signalling the beginning of a new plan to work through the road trip of life.

Inspired by Edison's spirit of strength and resolve, and with my daughters, Francesca Hope and Freya-Grace as motivation, I know I have the hope to move forward and I trust I can do this with spiritual and (eventually) physical grace.

Chapter 25
To Infinity and Beyond

(Inspired, of course, by Edison's love of all things including Toy Story)

Edison is not lost. Edison taught me how to receive pure love. Edison taught me joy. Edison taught me what it looks like to live authentically. Edison taught me strength. Edison taught me humour. We grasp at these things. Eddie mastered them.

Thankfully, our lives are fuller, more joyous and more meaningful – having learned from Edison's fortunate life. *'Boom, boom, boom – you made them go ah, ah ahhha...'* just like a firework. Eddie certainly was a pivotal aspect of my family becoming *one of them.* Our *themness* provides meaning and teaches us many life lessons whilst providing meaning to our lives. Our *themness* makes us all, *us.* Memories of how Edison faced his daily trials continue to help me to Plan*2b*Real.

I didn't want to speak at Edison's funeral. I knew it would be televised and I wasn't there to give a performance. Instead, on my behalf, my mother read an ode I'd written to Eddie...

Jillian's Ode to Edison

Mr Magoo, I miss you
Memories of trampoline jumping, screaming, life itself...
"I love you, Mummy – I'm good – you good?"
"Line up! Keep your hands and your feet to yourself!"

I have been blessed to be the only parent left standing on the beach as you splash and delight in the ocean, in heavy rain.

You did learn to share – beautifully – yourself – your life – your popcorn – in unison, we would say, "Nice sharing, Eddie, very kind."
"Nothing, not any more left."
"Maybe next time."
"Have to put it on the list."
"Have to buy some."

You were named after light –
How insightful – love is light.

"Again and again and again and again and again…" We will enjoy you as our family favourite blue-eyed boy.

Eddie spaghetti
As part of our nightly prayers conclude… "May your angels spread their wings around, Eddie…"

Edison painted a double rainbow May 2015. He was awarded a prize.

God painted a double rainbow 15 June 2015. That night, He took my son into his loving arms to be with Him in heaven.

2019, is now my turn to paint my next chapter – planning to be real and true to myself along a road trip which I intend to experience from a position of love.

Ecclesiastes 3:1 reads *There is an occasion for everything, and a time for every activity under heaven…'*

Thank you, Edison Maxwell Hellmuth, my teacher, my son.

Short Synopsis

In 2006, Jillian Ginn's only son was diagnosed as acutely autistic. With her marriage in tatters, in 2009 Jillian instigated what turned out to be an expensive and abrasive divorce. In 2014, her youngest daughter was hit by a car and suffered from a brain injury. In 2015, her home was burnt to the ground and her beloved son died of smoke inhalation. In 2018, Jillian was diagnosed with a disability which inhibits her ability to walk independently. This is a must read memoir; a collection of stories inspired by the author's resilient, loving son. The strong message conveyed throughout focuses on learning to live with acceptance whilst fostering personal peace by giving with love, even when one's life plans fail, and trauma un-expectantly revisits.

CPSIA information can be obtained
at www.ICGtesting.com
Printed in the USA
LVHW081218281019
635540LV00007B/208/P

9 781528 946001